THE WAR ON PAPER

Published by IWM, Lambeth Road, London SE1 6HZ
iwm.org.uk

ISBN 978-1-912423-00-2

A catalogue record for this book is available from the
British Library.
Printed and bound by Gomer Press Limited
Colour reproduction by DL Imaging

Every effort has been made to contact all copyright
holders. The publishers will be glad to make good
in future editions any error or omissions brought to
their attention.

10 9 8 7 6 5 4 3 2 1

THE WAR ON PAPER

20 Documents
That Defined the
Second World War

ANTHONY RICHARDS

Contents

Introduction

History is largely told through documents. For thousands of years people have recorded key events in their lives by using the medium of the written record, sometimes in order to preserve collective history, while at other times to ensure that individual experiences are not forgotten. We see this process of recording history as particularly notable during eras and events which encourage the most extreme responses. This invariably means war and conflict, and as such the Second World War remains one of the most important events in recent times to generate a massive body of documentary evidence, both official and personal in nature.

This book tells the story of the Second World War through twenty key documents. Each document made a difference, however great or small, to the course of the war and thus can be seen to be influencing history rather than being purely responsive. In some cases, for example as with military orders or political agreements, their effect is wide-reaching and obvious. In other cases, the document is representative of a larger theme (such as rationing, for instance) which impacted on many different lives during the conflict. In addition, particular documents are featured which had an enormous consequence on a more personal level – such as with the immigration papers allowing Jewish children to enter Britain as part of the *Kindertransport* scheme.

The other link shared by the documents featured here is that they are all preserved in the archives of the Imperial War Museum (IWM). Since its formation in 1917, the museum has sought to preserve and make available for public study original documents of this nature which help people to understand the experience of war. IWM's Second World War papers remain one of the finest such archival collections of its kind in the world, and some of the most iconic and memorable wartime records in its care are reproduced in this book.

It has been my privilege to have worked with the IWM documents collection for over two decades, and in that time it has never ceased to impress and at times surprise me with its depth of coverage and insight into how the war was fought and experienced. The story behind the creation of certain documents proves fascinating, and I hope that you will find the examples included here to be both interesting and thought-provoking, as they portray the events of the war in a most immediate, direct way.

Anthony Richards
Head of Documents and Sound
IWM (Imperial War Museums)

5th June, 1943.

ONLY

TUG

TUG   TUG

SALTASH   HALCYON   SKIPJACK   GREENELL   DUNDALK

LA PANNE

NOTE (1) INSHORE EAC
18 MOTORBOATS
(11) SIX
TO EACH
S SH

FM/75
76

D3e 52

Captain (Acting Major) wit

e purpose of
n no way co
permission t
fficer of th
formed).

to this indivi
after an aircr
.A. Madrid. All
in your case by
gu to your chief
stion* with a req
should be stopped.

equently it became
nder his pseudonym o
List of Casualties
that has given rise t
5920 dated 2nd June,
ho has referred the R/S
e to "Major Martin" was:
ived. May particulars b

should be most grateful if
there is no need to make an
s "officer's" death must no

view of the very great need
work that this individual was
roy this letter.

(   ) C.A.

43.

CHAPTER ONE

The Era of Appeasement
The Anglo-German Declaration

30 September 1938

While a major European conflict in the 1930s was predicted by many, substantial efforts were made by successive governments to avoid such a war. We therefore remember the period as an era of Appeasement. While the fascist regimes controlling Germany and Italy challenged the European balance of power by asserting themselves in ever greater ways, other countries' governments sought to avoid war with Hitler and Mussolini by offering them a string of political and material concessions.

The greatest challenges to this policy of appeasement arose in 1938, beginning with the *Anschluss* of 12 March which saw the annexation of Austria to become part of Nazi Germany. This act was in direct violation of several key diplomatic agreements, including most notably the Treaty of Versailles, intended to curb German expansionism following their defeat in the First World War. Yet the response of other European nations to the *Anschluss* was extraordinarily restrained. None of them wanted another war on the scale of the 1914-1918 conflict, and any military response to the fascist threat was therefore deemed unnecessarily harsh while the possibility of diplomacy remained.

Following his successful move to incorporate Austria, Hitler's attention was directed towards a potential annexation of Czechoslovakia, which contained in its Sudetenland border regions a largely German-speaking population. The Sudeten German Party led by Konrad Henlein was directed by Hitler to cause agitation within Czechoslovakia in order to prepare for a secret German invasion, scheduled to begin no later than 1 October 1938. Relations between the Czech and German governments began to deteriorate and it was therefore in response to these rising political tensions that the British Prime Minister, Neville Chamberlain, flew to meet Hitler in September to seek a peaceful resolution to the crisis.

The result of their discussions was the Munich Agreement, named after the city where the negotiations took place and signed in the early hours of 30 September 1938. Bearing the signatures of Chamberlain, Hitler, Mussolini and the French Prime Minister Édouard Daladier, the Agreement permitted the German Army to occupy the Sudetenland regions of Czechoslovakia, while proposing that an international commission would resolve the question of other disputed Czech territories.

Signed by British Prime Minister Neville Chamberlain and German Chancellor Adolf Hitler, the Anglo-German Declaration was symbolic of both countries' desire not to go to war, 30 September 1938.

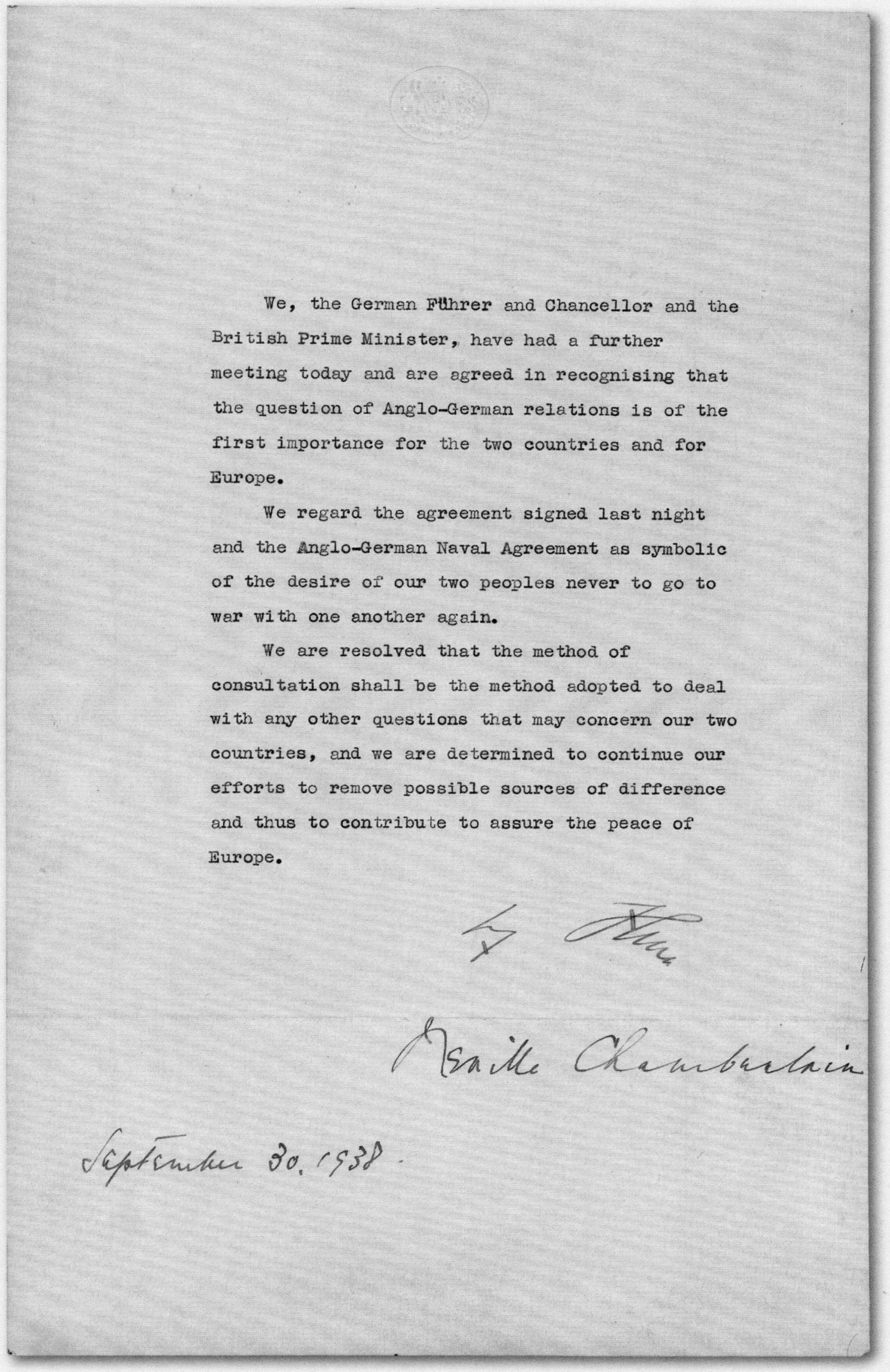

We, the German Führer and Chancellor and the British Prime Minister, have had a further meeting today and are agreed in recognising that the question of Anglo-German relations is of the first importance for the two countries and for Europe.

We regard the agreement signed last night and the Anglo-German Naval Agreement as symbolic of the desire of our two peoples never to go to war with one another again.

We are resolved that the method of consultation shall be the method adopted to deal with any other questions that may concern our two countries, and we are determined to continue our efforts to remove possible sources of difference and thus to contribute to assure the peace of Europe.

[signature]

Neville Chamberlain

September 30. 1938.

Buoyed by the positive outcome of his discussions with Hitler over the Sudetenland, Chamberlain sought an additional benefit to take away from their meeting. This was an opportunity to placate the British people back home and waylay their fears of another war with Germany:

> I asked Hitler about 1 in the morning, while we were waiting for the draftsmen, whether he would care to see me for another talk. He jumped at the idea, and asked me to come to his private flat, in a tenement house where the other floors are occupied by ordinary citizens. I had a very friendly and pleasant talk, on Spain (where he too said he had never had any territorial ambitions), economic relations with S.E. Europe, and disarmament. I did not mention colonies, nor did he. At the end I pulled out the declaration, which I had prepared beforehand, and asked if he would sign it. As the interpreter translated the words into German, Hitler frequently ejaculated 'ja, ja', and at the end he said 'yes, I will certainly sign it; when shall we do it?' I said 'now', and we went at once to the writing-table, and put our signatures to the two copies which I had brought with me.

The resulting document was the Anglo-German Declaration, a signed agreement 'symbolic of the desire of our two peoples never to go to war with one another again.' While many have since regarded the Declaration as an empty promise of little value, this opinion is largely influenced by the benefit of hindsight. While signing such an agreement meant very little to Hitler, it meant the world to Chamberlain, who had obtained exactly what he had wanted: an understanding between Britain and Germany which would form the basis for future peace. In 1938 such a policy of appeasement was, on the whole, very popular. Nobody wanted another Great War.

The signatories to the Munich Agreement. Shown from left to right are the British Prime Minister, Neville Chamberlain; the French Prime Minister, Édouard Daladier; Germany's leader, Adolf Hitler; the Italian leader Benito Mussolini; and the Italian Foreign Minister Count Galeazzo Ciano, 29 September 1938.

Ticket detail (upper portion):

NAME OF CARRIER OR CARRIERS / NOM DU OU DES TRANSPORTEURS: BRITISH AIRWAYS LTD No. BA/WS 18249

For Addresses see page 2.   Adresses en 2e page.

Passenger's Name / Nom du Voyageur: THE RT HON NEVILLE CHAMBERLAIN

From / De: LONDON   to / à: MUNICH   AND RETURN

FARE / PRIX: SPECIAL FLIGHT   R

Leaving on / Partant le: 29/9/38   at / à: 08.30   Time. Heure.

From / De l'Aéroport: HESTON   Airport   Via Line / Via Ligne / No(s)

For agreed stopping places see time-tables of Carriers concerned.
Pour les arrêts prévus voir les horaires des transporteurs respectifs.

RESERVED FOR CARRIER.   RESERVE AUX TRANSPORTEURS.

AGENT. AGENCE.
BRITISH AIRWAYS LTD
TERMINAL HOUSE
52, GROSVENOR GARDENS
LONDON S.W.1
28 SEP 1938

Place of Issue / Lieu d'émission:
Date of Issue / Date d'émission:

FOR CONDITIONS OF CARRIAGE : SEE BACK OF TICKET
CONDITIONS DE TRANSPORT : VOIR AU VERSO DE BILLET

Validity / Valable pour:
Date of Expiry / Date d'expiration:

For Aerodrome of departure.   Pour l'Aerodrome de depart.

This portion to be completed by the Carrier.
A remplir par le Transporteur.   7

Baggage check for ticket No. / Bulletin de bagage pour le billet passage No.: BA/WS 18249

Name of carrier or carriers / Nom du ou des transporteurs: BRITISH AIRWAYS LTD

For addresses see page 2.   Adresses en 2e page.

From / De: LONDON   to / à: MUNICH   AND RETURN

Weight of Baggage / Poids de Bagages: .... kg.
Free Allowance / Franchise: ... 15 kg.
Excess / Excédent: .... kg.
Rate per kg. / Tarif par kg.:
Total paid for Excess / Total payé pour l'excédent:

Number of Packages / Nombre de Colis

Place of Issue / Lieu d'émission: .... Date ....

FOR CONDITIONS OF CARRIAGE : SEE BACK OF TICKET
CONDITIONS DE TRANSPORT : VOIR AU VERSO DE BILLET

Transkrit
PATENT FANFOLD

MR CHAMBERLAIN'S
TICKET TO MUNICH
29/9/38

The defining moment distinguishing Chamberlain's perceived success was when he returned from Munich, stepping off his aeroplane to address the crowds at Heston Aerodrome. To thunderous cheers, he held aloft a copy of the Declaration:

This morning I had another talk with the German Chancellor, Herr Hitler. And here is the paper which bears his name on it, as well as mine. (Cheers from the crowd) Some of you have perhaps already heard what it contains. But I would just like to read it to you.

"We, the German Führer and Chancellor and the British Prime Minister, have had a further meeting today and are agreed in recognising that the question of Anglo-German relations is of the first importance for the two countries and for Europe.

We regard the agreement signed last night and the Anglo-German Naval Agreement as symbolic of the desire of our two peoples never to go to war with one another again.

We are resolved that the method of consultation shall be the method adopted to deal with any other questions that may concern our two countries, and we are determined to continue our efforts to remove possible sources of difference and thus to contribute to assure the peace of Europe.

After reading from the piece of paper, Chamberlain lifted it high to show to those assembled. It was this triumphant image which appeared on newspaper front pages the next day, and which was to be broadcast in newsreels around the world. No other image is so redolent of the British policy of appeasement.

Even the descriptions of the papers give no idea of the scenes in the streets as I drove from Heston to the Palace. They were lined from one end to the other with people of every class, shouting themselves hoarse, leaping on the running board, banging on the windows, and thrusting their hands into the car to be shaken. The scenes culminated in Downing St, when I spoke to the multitudes below from the same window, I believe, as that from which Dizzy [Disraeli] announced peace with honour 60 years ago.

Chamberlain and his piece of paper would guarantee, as he declared to the crowd amassed below him outside 10 Downing Street, 'Peace for our time'.

We now know, however, that any peace was to be short-lived. In the words of the Foreign Office diplomat Sir Stephen Gaselee, writing in January 1940, the Anglo-German Declaration 'seemed of the highest significance then, but I am afraid that its implications are now ironical.' The following year, on 15 March 1939, Germany began a full invasion of Czechoslovakia and the country soon became a Protectorate of the Third Reich. This paved the way for further German territorial expansion, resulting in the invasion of Poland on 1 September, barely a week after the signing of the Nazi-Soviet Pact which effectively shared large swathes of territory in Eastern Europe between Germany and Soviet Russia. Hitler had broken his promise, and the stage was set for war.

< Shown here is the counterfoil part of the British Airways Limited three part ticket, issued for Prime Minister Neville Chamberlain's flight to Munich on 29 September 1938, where he met with Adolf Hitler.

German-speaking women welcome German troops into the Sudetenland following Germany's occupation of the territory, which began on 1 October 1938. The remaining parts of Czechoslovakia would be invaded in March 1939, with parts of the country being annexed and the remainder becoming a Protectorate of the Third Reich.

Neville Chamberlain holds aloft the Anglo-German Declaration to the cheering crowd that greeted him on his arrival at Heston Airport, 30 September 1938.

CHAPTER TWO

The Rise of Nazi Antisemitism
Kindertransport Identity Papers

February 1939

The rise to power of Adolf Hitler's Nazi Party in Germany during the 1930s was marked by a proliferation of antisemitic policies based on ideas of racial superiority. The concept of *Volksgemeinschaft*, a united community fighting for the national good, singled out certain peoples who did not fit in. These *Gemeinschaftsfremde* ('Community Aliens') were considered to oppose the national interest and as such should be treated as criminals. Among this group were Jews, Gypsies, homosexuals and others considered to be harmful to the community.

Hitler declared a national boycott of all Jewish businesses on 1 April 1933 while various new legislation, most notably the Nuremberg Laws introduced in September 1935, effectively legalised widespread antisemitism within Germany. Marriage between Germans and Jews was forbidden, severe employment restrictions were put into force and Jewish citizens were routinely harassed and subjected to violent attacks.

These new laws had a crippling economic and social impact on Jews living in Germany. One such family were the Braunschweigers, living in Honsbach, a town situated near to Cologne in the north-west of the country. As the youngest daughter Nora recalled:

I had a fantastic life until I was seven years old. It was a happy and wonderful time in my life. Unfortunately it was not to last longer.

My family had lived in the village of Honsbach since at least the 1700s, as the local records show. In the 1930s there were six Jewish families, all relatives. They were well regarded by the rest of the villagers. My father, Josef Braunschweiger, owned a materials business. He made a good living. Our house had the only flushing lavatory and bathroom, and my father even had a car, all of which was unusual at that time. We had a happy family life. But soon it was all to change.

Unlike the people of Honsbach who were very friendly towards us (they were mainly Roman Catholic while the rest were Lutherans) the neighbouring villagers were rather nasty. In 1937 they came to our village to disrupt it. As they were singing songs full of hatred against us and making attacks, my father was yelling back at them from the balcony. He was detained by the

Sent to Britain as part of the *Kindertransport* scheme at the beginning of 1939, sisters Nora and Inge Braunschweiger had to apply for a plethora of identity documents to authorise their journey. Shown here is Inge's passport, issued in 1938.

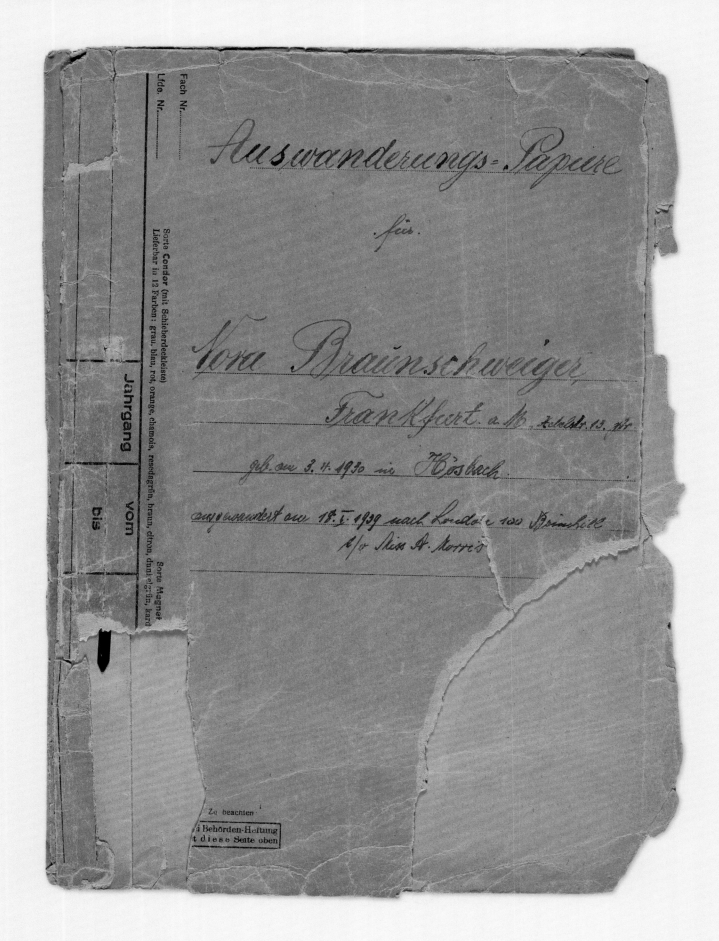

police and taken away and only returned home after some weeks.

My father was forbidden to work and was even forced to sell his business along with our two houses, the cattle shed and two or three pieces of land he owned, for next to nothing. By late 1937 we had no choice but to move to Frankfurt. We all lived together in a flat. My father was unemployed. All Jews were forbidden to work. Eventually he found a small job moving furniture.

The violence and prejudice shown against the Jewish community in Germany came to a head on the night of 9–10 November 1938, when a widespread pogrom against Jewish homes, businesses and synagogues was implemented by both German militia and civilians. The debris left after this widespread looting and smashing of shop windows led to the event being remembered as *Kristallnacht* ('The Night of Broken Glass'). Such violence had now escalated to the point where families began to look for ways to remove their children from the constant threat.

In Britain, the concerted efforts of a number of British, Jewish and Quaker groups, together with overwhelming public support in the wake of *Kristallnacht*, led the government to loosen restrictions on the temporary immigration of Jewish children from Germany. The children, unaccompanied by their parents and ranging

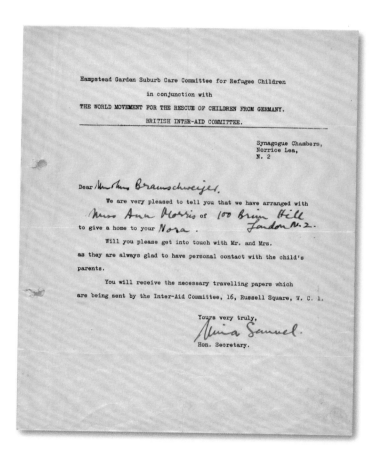

⟨ Nora's father carefully preserved all of the paperwork concerning his daughters' journey to England in this folder.

∧ Nora's parents received this letter, informing them of the family who would be providing a foster home for their daughter. While such arrangements were intended to be short-term ones, many Jewish children would find that their move to England became a permanent one.

∧ Among the essential paperwork required for *Kindertransport* children was this vaccination certificate.

Aufstellung
=====================================

des Reisegepäcks für Kind Nora Braunschweiger, Frankfurt a.M.Hebelstr.13pt

mit Kinder-Verschickung nach England

1 Schulranzen mit Inhalt
1 Turnanzug, 1 Paar Turnschuhe, 1 Trainingsanzug
4 Paar Schuhe, 1 Paar Gummiüberschuhe
1 Paar warme Hausschuhe
2 Mäntel, 1 Regen-Cape
2 Mützen, 2 Pullover, 1 Strick-Kostümchen
4 Winterkleider, 5 Sommerkleider, 4 Waschkleider
4 Blousen, 2 Röckchen, 8 Schürzen, 9 Hosen
4 Unterröcke, 1o Leibchen, 6 Garnituren
12 Hemdchen, 8 Schlafanzüge, 6 Nachthemden
12 Paar Strümpfe, 1o Paar Socken,
3o Taschentücher mit Behälter
  Bademantel, 1 Trikot,
2 Paar Handschuhe, 2 Handtaschen, 1 Schirm
1 Koffer
1 Beutel mit Toiletten-Gegenständen
1 Kissen, 2 Shawls
1 kleines Pelzchen
diverse Kleinigkeiten(Nähzeug, Schuhputzzeug, Schuhriemen, Ball, Puppe und
                      Spielsachen)
1 Armband-Uhr, 1 Kette mit Anhänger, 1 Ring (einfach)
1 kleines Köfferchen mit Reiseproviant.

Photograph of Nora Braunschweiger and her family, dating from shortly before Nora and her sister travelled to England as part of the *Kindertransport* scheme.

This detailed list of the contents of Nora's suitcase had to be presented to the German authorities before her embarkation to England. The entries underlined in red indicate possessions which were left behind in fear that they might have been confiscated – a wristwatch, a pendant and a ring. The document records that Nora's possessions were inspected on 17 January 1939 at Frankfurt prior to her embarkation.

from infants up to children of 17 years old, would be looked after in foster homes provided by volunteers. The scheme began in December 1938 and continued until just before the outbreak of war in September 1939, with some 10,000 Jewish children transported to the United Kingdom under the auspices of 'The Movement for the Care of Children from Germany'. With the situation for Jews within Germany worsening as the war progressed, the vast majority of these *Kindertransport* ('Children's Transport') children would never see their parents again.

The documents shown here relate to eight-year-old Nora Braunschweiger, who was sent with her older sister Inge to live in Britain. These records were typical of those accompanying each child refugee – a list of clothes and belongings they were allowed to take with them, family photographs, identity cards, a vaccine certificate and confirmation from their foster family:

By the time I was eight, my parents had to send us both, my sister and I, to unknown people in England in order to save our lives. My mother was one of four sisters. My father one of four, three brothers and one sister. One brother died in World War One, another left to [go to] Brazil. He was going to arrange for us to emigrate there, and that was the reason I agreed to leave my parents. We were supposed to reunite in Brazil in a couple of months. Unfortunately he died suddenly and therefore the rest of the family remained trapped in Germany.

I remember leaving three months after Kristallnacht. I was eight. I remember the station but not the goodbyes. I remember as the train stopped in Holland we were given some food and a strange drink. It was tea with milk! In the overnight boat trip to Harwich we slept in bunk beds. We were given cardboard containers in case of sickness. I remember being worried of having my jewellery stolen, so I decided to hide it between two of the cardboard containers. The next morning after I left the boat, I suddenly realised that I had forgotten it. Luckily I was taken back and found them where I left them.

After the war, as with so many of their fellow *Kindertransport* refugees, Nora and her sister would find themselves the sole survivors from their family.

My parents remained in Frankfurt at least until April 1941. Later they were deported to Terezin concentration camp. Once they saw a soldier, not Gestapo, who was a man from our village. My mother immediately removed her valueless necklace and gave it to him, asking him to hand it to her daughters. He took it. He went for leave and when he came back to the camp my parents were gone. They eventually ended up in a concentration camp in Minsk. My mother was found dead in the pharmacy, it seems she took an overdose. My father was probably killed in the extermination camp. All the family was murdered by the Nazis, from both sides, with the exception of one cousin.

A Berlin synagogue lies in ruins following the Nazi-instigated *Kristallnacht*, a pogrom against Jews in Germany and Austria, which occurred on the night of 9–10 November 1938.

The reverse of Inge Braunschweiger's German passport bears a slightly faded red 'J' stamp (on the left), indicating that she was Jewish. Inge was only 11 years old when she arrived in Britain at Harwich. The passport bears the Harwich port authority's stamp and attached consular permit, allowing Inge into the United Kingdom as part of the *Kindertransport* scheme.

Zur Auswanderung nach England.

Der Polizei-Präsident.

(Ausstellende Behörde)

Frankfurt (Main). , den 7. DEZ. 1938 193

17.12.38

Kinderausweis Nr. 10075138

(Nur gültig bis zur Vollendung
des fünfzehnten Lebensjahrs)

Familienname: Braunschweiger

Rufname: Inge

Geboren am 17. 2. 27

Staatsangehörigkeit: DEUTSCHES REICH

Wohnsitz (dauernder Aufenthalt): Frankfurt (Main).

Gebühr —,50 RM.

Geb.-Buch Nr. 2878/38

des ___ Pol. Rev.

A 56 (6. 32) Reichsdruckerei, Berlin

(24) 7 65

CHAPTER THREE

The Nazi Invasion of Poland
Führer Directive No. 1
31 August 1939

Hitler's *Lebensraum* idea of reconstituting ethnic German-speaking territories as part of the Third Reich meant that the western regions of Poland were regarded as appropriate targets for Nazi annexation. Since coming to power in 1933, Hitler had worked towards this aim through aggressive negotiation and by exploiting political unrest caused by German nationalists within Poland. These increasing demands and threats from Germany led to Poland forming a military alliance with Britain and France on 31 March 1939, which was intended to assure protection for the country in the event of a German invasion.

Tension mounted and on 28 April, Hitler withdrew from the German-Polish Non-Aggression Pact and the London Naval Treaty. The latter had placed restrictions on Germany building a substantial naval fleet, and their unilateral rejection of this agreement signalled Hitler's clear aggressive intentions for the future. Then, on 23 August, the Nazi-Soviet Pact was announced which indicated that any German attack on Poland would be unopposed by the Soviet Union. Poland was now effectively surrounded by enemies, and it was clear to all that military action was imminent.

On 31 August 1939, Hitler issued his Directive Number 1 for the Conduct of the War, signed in his own hand and containing the official order for the invasion of Poland. Eight copies of this important document were issued, with Copy Number Two shown here being issued to the Naval High Command. As well as ordering the start of the invasion, it outlined the defensive and offensive measures to be taken by the German armed forces, with particular reference to neutral countries, in the event of France and England declaring war. The release of the Directive would, effectively, kick-start the Second World War:

1. Since the situation on Germany's Eastern frontier has become intolerable and all political possibilities of peaceful settlement have been exhausted, I have decided upon a solution by force.

2. The attack on Poland will be undertaken in accordance with the preparations made for 'Case White', with such variations as may be necessitated by the build-up of the Army which is now virtually complete. The allocation of tanks and the purpose of the operation remain unchanged.

This and the following images in this chapter show pages from Führer Directive Number 1 for the Conduct of the War, ordering the Nazi invasion of Poland, 31 August 1939. This particular copy of the document, numbered 2, was issued to the Naval High Command (OKM).

Der Oberste Befehlshaber der Wehrmacht   Berlin, den 31. 8 39.
OKW/WFA Nr. 170 /39 g.K.Chefs. L I

8 Ausfertigungen
2. Ausfertigung.

Weisung Nr. 1
für die Kriegführung.

1.) Nachdem alle politischen Möglichkeiten erschöpft sind, um
    auf friedlichem Wege eine für Deutschland unerträgliche La-
    ge an seiner Ostgrenze zu beseitigen, habe ich mich zur
    gewaltsamen Lösung entschlossen.

2.) Der Angriff gegen Polen ist nach den für Fall Weiss getrof-
    fenen Vorbereitungen zu führen mit den Abänderungen, die
    sich beim Heer durch den inzwischen fast vollendeten Auf-
    marsch ergeben.
        Aufgabenverteilung und Operationsziel bleiben unver-
    ändert.
        Angriffstag:.1.9.39..
        Angriffszeit ....
        Diese Zeit gilt auch für die Unternehmungen Gdingen -
    Danziger Bucht und Brücke Dirschau.

3.) Jm Westen kommt es darauf an, die Verantwortung für die Er-
    öffnung von Feindseligkeiten eindeutig England und Frank-
    reich zu überlassen. Geringfügigen Grenzverletzungen ist
    zunächst rein örtlich entgegen zu treten.
        Die von uns Holland, Belgien, Luxemburg und der
    Schweiz zugesicherte Neutralität ist peinlich zu achten.

- 2 -

C-126 c

Die deutsche Westgrenze ist <u>zu Lande</u> an keiner Stelle
ohne meine ausdrückliche Genehmigung zu überschreiten.

<u>Zur See</u> gilt das gleiche für alle kriegerischen oder
als solche zu deutenden Handlungen.

Die defensiven Massnahmen der <u>Luftwaffe</u> sind <u>zu-
nächst</u> auf die unbedingte Abwehr feindl. Luftangriffe an
der Reichsgrenze zu beschränken, wobei so lange als mög-
lich die Grenze der neutralen Staaten bei der Abwehr ein-
zelner Flugzeuge und kleinerer Einheiten zu achten ist.
Erst wenn beim Einsatz stärkerer franz. und engl. Angriffs-
verbände über die neutralen Staaten gegen deutsches Gebiet die Luftverteidigung im Westen nicht mehr gesichert
ist, ist die Abwehr auch über diesem neutralen Gebiet frei-
zugeben.

Schnellste Orientierung des OKW über jede Verletzung
der Neutralität dritter Staaten durch die Westgegner ist
besonders wichtig.

4.) <u>Eröffnen England und Frankreich die Feindseligkeiten</u>
gegen Deutschland, so ist es Aufgabe der im Westen ope-
rierenden Teile der Wehrmacht, unter möglichster Schonung
der Kräfte die Voraussetzungen für den siegreichen Ab-
schluss der Operationen gegen Polen zu erhalten. Im Rah-
men dieser Aufgabe sind die feindl. Streitkräfte und de-
ren wehrwirtschaftl. Kraftquellen nach Kräften zu schädi-
gen. Den Befehl zum Beginn von <u>Angriffs</u>handlungen behalte
ich mir in jedem Fall vor.

- 3 -

C-126 a

Das <u>Heer</u> hält den Westwall und trifft Vorbereitun-
gen, dessen Umfassung im Norden - unter Verletzung belg.
oder holländ. Gebietes durch die Westmächte - zu verhindern. Rücken franz. Kräfte in Luxemburg ein, so bleibt
die Sprengung der Grenzbrücken freigegeben.

Die <u>Kriegsmarine</u> führt Handelskrieg mit dem Schwer-
punkt gegen England. Zur Verstärkung der Wirkung kann
mit der Erklärung von Gefahrenzonen gerechnet werden.
OKM meldet, in welchen Seegebieten und in welchem Umfang
Gefahrenzonen für zweckmässig gehalten werden. Der Wort-
laut für eine öffentl. Erklärung ist im Benehmen mit dem
Ausw. Amte vorzubereiten und mir über OKW zur Genehmigung vorzulegen.

Die Ostsee ist gegen feindl. Einbruch zu sichern.
Die Entscheidung, ob zu diesem Zwecke die Ostsee-Eingänge
mit Minen gesperrt werden dürfen, trifft Ob.d.M. bleibt vorbehalten.

Die <u>Luftwaffe</u> hat in erster Linie den Einsatz der
franz. und engl. Luftwaffe gegen das deutsche Heer und
den deutschen Lebensraum zu verhindern.

Bei der Kampfführung gegen England ist der Einsatz
der Luftwaffe zur Störung der engl. Seezufuhr, der
Rüstungsindustrie, der Truppentransporte nach Frankreich
vorzubereiten. Günstige Gelegenheit zu einem wirkungs-
vollen Angriff gegen massierte engl. Flotteneinheiten,
insbes. gegen Schlachtschiffe und Flugzeugträger ist aus-

- 4 -

As early as 1928, plans had been considered for a potential German invasion of Poland. Known as 'Case White' (or '*Fall Weiss*'), the plan was based on a three-pronged assault, intended to converge on Warsaw while encircling the main Polish Army. The German strategists had also devised a number of other plans for potential military action against European targets, each distinguished by different colours, but 'Case White' would prove to be the first such plan put into operation.

Date of attack: 1.9.39

This time also applies to operations at Gdynia, in the Bay of Danzig and at the Dirschau Bridge.

3. In the West it is important to leave the responsibility for opening hostilities unmistakably to England and France. Minor violations of the frontier will be dealt with, for the time being, purely as local incidents. The assurances of neutrality given by us to Holland, Belgium, Luxembourg and Switzerland are to be meticulously observed. The Western frontier of Germany will not be crossed by land at any point without my explicit orders. This applies also to all acts of warfare at sea or to acts which might be regarded as such.

The defensive activity of the Air Force will be restricted for the time being to the firm repulse of enemy air attacks on the frontiers of the Reich. In taking action against individual aircraft or small formations, care will be taken to respect the frontiers of neutral countries as far as possible. Only if considerable forces of French or British bombers are employed against German territory across neutral areas will the Air Force be permitted to go into defensive action over neutral soil.

It is particularly important that any infringement of the neutrality of other states by our Western enemies be immediately reported to the High Command of the Armed Forces.

The Directive made it clear that Hitler fully expected retaliatory action by Britain and France, in accordance with their military alliance with Poland. However, his hope was that Poland could be fully annexed before any of his Western opponents became involved. The recognition and respect of other countries' neutrality was therefore crucial in order to avoid immediate declarations of war against Germany which would cause detriment to the Polish operation.

4. Should England and France open hostilities against Germany, it will be the duty of the Armed Forces operating in the West, while conserving their strength as much as possible, to maintain conditions for the successful conclusion of operations against Poland. Within these limits enemy forces and war potential will be damaged as much as possible. The right to order offensive operations is reserved absolutely to me.

The Army will occupy the West Wall and will take steps to secure it from being outflanked in the north, through the violation by the Western powers of Belgian or Dutch territory. Should French forces invade Luxembourg the bridges on the frontier may be blown up.

The Navy will operate against merchant shipping, with England as the focal point. In order to increase the effect, the declaration of danger zones may be expected. The Naval High Command will report on the areas which it is desirable to classify as danger zones and on their extent. The text of a public declaration in this matter is to be drawn up in collaboration with the Foreign Office and to be submitted to me for approval through the High Command of the Armed Forces. The Baltic Sea is to be secured against enemy intrusion. Commander-in-Chief Navy will decide whether the entrances to the Baltic should be mined for this purpose.

This naval blockade of British merchant shipping mirrors the German strategy adopted in the First World War, which was to starve the country into submission while stripping it of the imported supplies necessary to wage war. Hitler's separate plan to invade Britain, codenamed 'Sea Lion', would depend upon German air superiority:

The Air Force is, first of all, to prevent action by the French and English Air Forces against the German Army and German territory. In operations against England the task of the Air Force is to take measures to dislocate English imports, the armaments industry, and the transport of troops to France. Any favourable opportunity of an effective attack on concentrated units of the English Navy, particularly on battleships or aircraft carriers, will be exploited. The decision regarding attacks on London is reserved to me. Attacks on the English homeland are to be prepared, bearing in mind that inconclusive results with insufficient forces are to be avoided in all circumstances.

The German invasion of Poland launched on 1 September 1939 and was soon accompanied by a Soviet invasion from

C-126a

zunutzen. Angriffe gegen London bleiben meiner Entscheidung vorbehalten.

Die Angriffe gegen das engl. Mutterland sind unter dem Gesichtspunkt vorzubereiten, dass unzureichender Erfolg mit Teilkräften unter allen Umständen zu vermeiden ist.

Verteiler:

OKH	1. Ausf.
OKM	2. "
R.d.L.u.Ob.d.L.	3. "
OKW:	
Chef WFA	4. "
L	5.-8. "

German troops breaking the border barrier in the Polish town of Sopot (Zoppot) on the morning of 1 September 1939. The Soviet invasion of Poland would soon follow, beginning on 17 September.

The final page of the Führer Directive, bearing Hitler's signature.

the east, beginning on 17 September. By 6 October the campaign was effectively over, with Poland annexed and split between the two invaders.

Over 70 further Führer Directives would be issued over the course of the Second World War, but none were arguably as important as the first, which served as the spark to ignite the conflict. On 3 September 1939 both Britain and France declared war on Germany and British troops were soon sent across the Channel, readying themselves for the expected German invasion. While that attack would not come until May 1940, the conditions had been put in place for the war to spread into a truly global conflict.

Polish civilians, guarded by German soldiers, are forced to leave the burning village of Goworowo on 9 September 1939. The village was captured by elements of the 'Kempf' Panzer Division.

The Polish capital Warsaw was captured by the German Army on 27 September 1939. This street scene, photographed in October 1939 during the occupation, shows clearly the extensive damage from aerial bombing which had been inflicted on the city while it was besieged.

CHAPTER FOUR

The Battle of the River Plate

Plan Tracking the Cruiser *Admiral Graf Spee*

13 December 1939

Once the war had begun, the German Navy started to implement an aggressive strategy against enemy merchant shipping. Their capital cruiser *Admiral Graf Spee* had been particularly busy since September 1939, raiding merchant shipping lanes throughout the South Atlantic. Between then and the beginning of December, the ship had sunk eight merchant vessels, resulting in very significant losses of cargo. The British Admiralty quickly put plans into operation to protect its commercial shipping by removing the *Graf Spee* threat, and assigned this responsibility to Force G, the South American Cruiser Squadron. Commanded by Commodore Henry Harwood, the Force consisted of the light cruisers HMS *Ajax* (his flagship) and HMS *Achilles*, alongside the heavy cruiser HMS *Exeter*. *Graf Spee* was one of the German Navy's few capital ships, and as such it was deemed acceptable to risk three British cruisers if it meant a chance to sink the important German vessel.

On 2 December 1939, Harwood took HMS *Ajax* north from the Falkland Islands, bound for the River Plate estuary. As the widest river in the world, running along the border between Argentina and Uruguay, the River Plate was an important trading route for merchant shipping. It was therefore a likely location for *Graf Spee* to be lying in wait, looking for opportunities to attack. Harwood was also aware that in six days' time it was to be the 25th anniversary of the Battle of the Falklands, one of the decisive British naval victories of the First World War. He suspected that the Germans might attempt to avenge their earlier defeat in that area.

During the afternoon of 2 December, a coded signal arrived in *Ajax*'s wireless room, addressed to Harwood and marked 'Immediate'. It informed him that the merchant ship *Doric Star* had been attacked and sunk by an unidentified pocket battleship off the coast of South Africa. Then, shortly before dawn, Harwood was handed another 'Immediate' signal: this time an unknown ship had been attacked by a pocket battleship 170 miles south-west of *Doric Star*'s position at 5am. While this German raider was not yet identified as *Graf Spee* and still more than 3,000 miles from any of the South American focal areas, Harwood recognised that the enemy's objective may well also be the valuable shipping located off the coast of South America. It was here in these congested shipping lanes that the Germans could do the most damage.

Plan by Commodore Henry Harwood sketching the likely location of the German battleship *Admiral Graf Spee*, 2 December 1939. The plan has been hastily scribbled on a sheet from a standard Naval message pad, indicating that Harwood simply grabbed whatever paper happened to be near at hand in order to record his calculations.

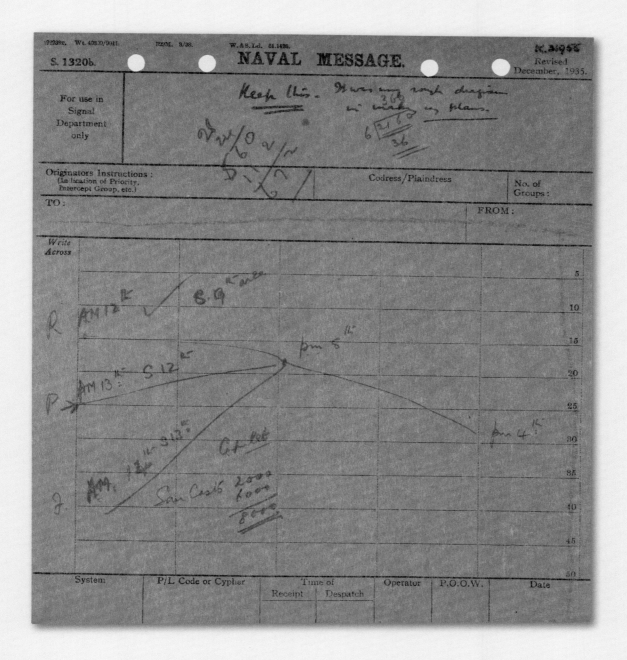

In the chartroom of HMS *Ajax*, Henry Harwood and his staff pored over a chart of the South Atlantic, on which they plotted the last known position of the German threat. Presuming a cruising rate of 15 knots, which turned out to be a remarkably accurate estimate of the speed of *Graf Spee*, Harwood worked out on his signal pad how long it would take the raider to reach the important shipping lanes.

By deciphering the document's abbreviations, we can see that Harwood estimated that the German ship could reach Rio de Janeiro ('R' in the left margin) by the morning of 12 December, the River Plate ('P') by the morning of 13 December or the Falkland Islands ('F') by 14 December. The 'S' stands for *Admiral Scheer,* which was still the supposed name of the German raider; it was not until late in the morning of the day of their encounter that the ship was correctly identified as *Graf Spee*. The references to *Capulet* and *San Casto* are to two tankers carrying 6,000 and 2,000 tons of oil respectively. They were en route to the Falklands at that time and Harwood planned to bring them into the Plate area so that they could be available for refuelling the British cruisers if so required.

Considering the options available to him, Harwood decided that the River Plate was the key area to defend with its larger number of merchant ships and the valuable grain and meat trade which used the route. At 1.15pm on 3 December, he therefore signalled the South American Cruiser Squadron to sail to that location, concentrating his force and establishing their position before the expected arrival of the raider. The three British cruisers met at the estuary on 12 December, and prepared themselves for what would become known as the Battle of the River Plate.

At 6.10am the following day, HMS *Exeter* spotted *Graf Spee* to the north-west and sailed to intercept her. *Graf Spee*'s captain, Hans Langsdorff, decided to engage the enemy but only realised too late that he was in fact about to face three British ships at once. The British put their battle plan into operation, attacking the German vessel from both sides and splitting their own force in order to prevent the Germans from concentrating their fire. *Ajax*, *Achilles* and *Exeter* all opened fire, with *Graf Spee*

Rear Admiral Sir Henry Harwood (shown left) with the British Minister to Uruguay, Eugen Millington-Drake, after his arrival at Montevideo, 3 January 1940.

retaliating in kind. *Exeter* suffered the most immediate damage, but during the battle managed to inflict a decisive blow on *Graf Spee*: one of her shells penetrated the fuel processing area of the German ship, leaving her with insufficient fuel to return home. There were no German reinforcements available, nor any friendly naval bases which she could reach in order to repair her damage, with the only port available being the neutral one of Montevideo. The battle continued for around an hour, but *Graf Spee* finally fled to the south-west beneath a smoke screen.

Pursued by the British ships, *Graf Spee* entered Montevideo harbour in the early hours of 14 December. Although Uruguay was a neutral country, it had a significant British background and favoured the Allies. This factor, combined with false information fed to the Germans which suggested that the British were assembling a major naval force outside the harbour, led Captain Langsdorff to despair. His ship had already used up two thirds of her ammunition and was in no state to fight her way out of the harbour. He therefore ordered the ship to be scuttled in the River Plate estuary on 17 December. The crew were taken to Argentina, while Langsdorff himself committed suicide in shame two days later.

The result of the Battle of the River Plate and scuttling of *Graf Spee* proved a particular embarrassment for Germany, and a major propaganda success for Britain. The South Atlantic was now safer for merchant shipping, while morale had been boosted by an important Allied naval victory achieved early on in the conflict. This otherwise uneventful period was known as the 'Phoney War', yet the River Plate battle had served to show that the Germans were not as unstoppable as might first have been thought. The story of how a German capital ship was destroyed due to the ingenuity of Henry Harwood predicting the enemy's route, combined with British inventiveness in deceiving the enemy about the strength of the opposition awaiting them outside Montevideo harbour, was later turned into a successful post-war film, cementing its place in popular history.

A handwritten situation report dated 17.00 hours on Saturday 16 [December 1939], taken from the notice board of HMS *Cumberland*. The report describes the position of *Graf Spee* in Montevideo, and the measures taken to prevent her escape from the port unnoticed.

SITUATION at 1700 Sat 16

GRAF SPEE. Still at anchor in MONTEVIDEO; she provisioned this morning. The URUGUAYAN govt: now say they will give her 72 hours from the time when they finished their survey of the damage; this means that SPEE would not be interned before 1800 on Sunday 17th. She can, of course, leave at any time she likes before then unless a British Merchant ship sails; if this happens she is supposed to wait for 24 hours before she can leave. It is, however, doubtful whether the URUGUAYANS have the power to prevent her sailing.

URUGUAYAN experts are onboard the SPEE to see that she only works on jobs to make herself sea worthy; she is not allowed to increase her fighting efficiency in any way

US. We are hanging about outside, concentrated. Various measures have been taken to ensure that she is reported leaving, but as the signals sometimes take up to 2 hours to get through, we have to be prepared to bump into her at short notice. Our motorboat, equipped with wireless has been prepared to patrol off the entrance if required.

THE ACTION. AJAX & ACHILLES were firing for 81 minutes & at one time were as close as 8000 yards. SPEE used her 11" mainly against EXETER but occasionally gave the others a dose.

In addition to probable damage resulting from numerous holes which have been reported in the prow

The German battleship *Graf Spee* in flames
after being scuttled in Montevideo harbour,
17 December 1939. The wreck was broken
up for scrap later in the war, but much
remained beneath the shallow waters of the
harbour until larger sections were raised
in 2004 and 2006.

CHAPTER FIVE

Rationing
Ministry of Food Coupon Book

from 8 January 1940

At the beginning of the Second World War, Britain's population was approaching 50 million. In order to feed this number the country had to rely on imports from overseas which were almost exclusively delivered by sea. Aswe have already seen with the threat of the Admiral *Graf Spee*, Germany was quick to adopt the strategy of intercepting merchant ships bound for the United Kingdom. This campaign would aim to starve the country's population into submission while also limiting supplies of other imported commodities such as industrial raw materials and fuel, which were essential for Britain's war effort. The fight for survival between German raiders and U-boats and Allied convoys was christened the Battle of the Atlantic by Churchill, who later declared that it was the only battle that genuinely frightened him throughout the war, due to the catastrophic consequences of not being able to feed the country.

Soon after war's outbreak, the British government introduced rationing for key goods which were likely to become scarce. This would ensure that limited commodities were distributed equally among the population, preventing those on a low income from suffering when demand pushed prices high. Those supplies which were obtained exclusively from overseas were the first to be targeted, with petrol being rationed almost immediately and, by 1942, requisitioned for exclusive use in military vehicles.

Food rationing, which inevitably would prove to be the restriction felt most by the British population, began in January 1940 with limits placed on the purchase of butter, sugar and bacon. Other commodities such as meat, lard, milk, cheese, tea, jam and canned goods were soon added to the list, so that by August 1942 the foods not being rationed were largely only bread, vegetables and fresh fruit. The amount and variety of the latter were limited to what could be grown domestically and some fruit, in particular bananas and lemons, were largely unheard of in Britain until after the war. The government promoted a 'Dig for Victory' scheme to persuade civilians to turn their private gardens and common land into allotments, encouraging home-grown produce to supplement rationed foodstuffs.

The most important element of the rationing scheme was the Ration Book, consisting of individual coupons which could be presented in certain registered shops. These books

Ministry of Food Ration Book issued to Queen Mary, the Queen Mother, in 1944. The address is given as Marlborough House, which had been her London residence since 1936.

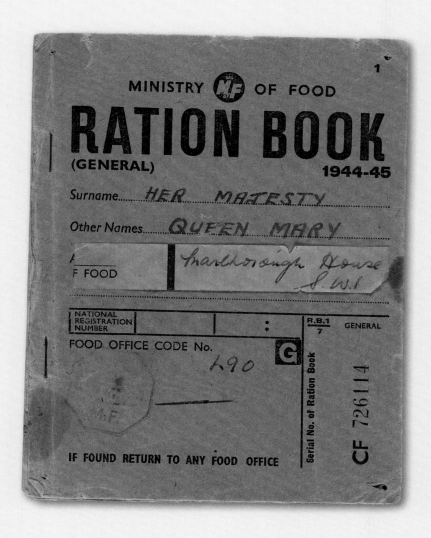

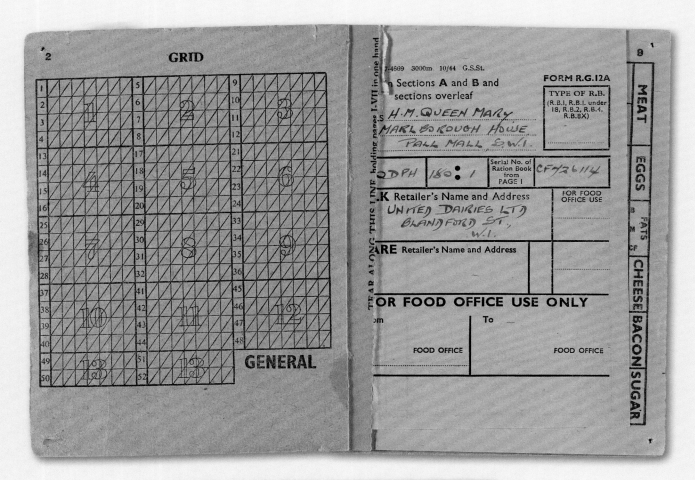

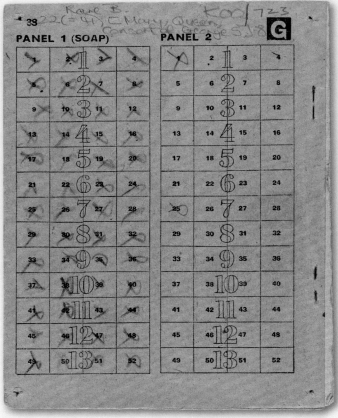

swiftly became an essential part of life, stored carefully in a wallet or purse so that they could be used during every shopping trip. Goods would be bought with money in the usual way, with the ration coupons either marked or removed to indicate that the allotted amount had been issued. Every person in the country was issued with a ration book, with special versions produced for pregnant women and children up to the age of sixteen which allowed them more generous allowances of commodities such as meat, milk and eggs. Some individuals employed in key reserved occupations (such as agricultural workers or railway staff) were also eligible for additional benefits.

As the war progressed, shortages became commonplace and it was not unusual to see long queues of customers outside shops, every person eager to obtain their allotted ration before stocks ran out. Mrs Alice Annis of Clacton-on-Sea wrote to her son on 4 March 1943:

> We haven't had to queue up for fish lately — plenty of that each day now for a time, but to get a cake this morning I had to queue up. I got one but I don't know what it's like. ¼ lb of fat don't go far so we must buy cakes. Sometimes you can get plenty but no sweeteners in the little cakes, so they are not worth buying. It will be nice when the war is over to go in a shop and get what you want and get served right away.
>
> I met Mrs Smith the other day and her son sent her some lemons and oranges from South Africa, but when she got the parcel someone had [had] first pick and she had two little lemons stuck in one corner and a small orange in the centre. She felt mad about it. It's the fault of not doing the parcel up well.

The constantly high demand for commodities led to the creation of a widespread illegal 'black market' in goods, operated by petty criminals. By March 1941, some 2,300 people had been prosecuted and severely penalised for such acts.

Due to the restrictive nature of rationing it was, understandably, an unpopular aspect of life in wartime Britain. But it did serve a very useful purpose by bringing the population together in a shared experience, all suffering the same privations for the war effort. Every person, regardless of their background or social class, was subject to identical restrictions. Not even the Royal Family were exempt.

Shown on page 43 is the ration book issued to Queen Mary, widow of King George V and mother to the then-reigning monarch, King George VI. Although the upper classes were subject to the same rationing as everybody else, it was not unusual for the rich to own large estates on which food could be grown or livestock kept. Winston Churchill's estate at Chartwell, for instance, included a farm that furnished many foodstuffs in quantities which ordinary mortals could only dream about. For this reason, those in rural areas were certainly in a more advantageous position than those living in towns.

⟨ These images of the inside and back of the ration book show that some coupons have been removed in exchange for an allowance of food, while other pages have been marked to indicate that the appropriate ration has been issued for that period.

∧ This official photograph taken for the Ministry of Information shows the weekly ration of sugar, tea, margarine, 'national butter', lard, eggs, bacon and cheese as issued to an adult in Britain during 1942.

From June 1941, new coupon books were issued to cover clothes rationing. The increased demand for textiles for military use meant that clothing manufacturers had to shift their resources, both in terms of raw material and workers, towards the war effort. Clothing and footwear were often in short supply, but rationing sought to ensure a more equal distribution across the population.

As with attempts to maximise usage of available food, the government tried to encourage ingenuity and creativeness among the population through a 'Make Do and Mend' campaign. Women in particular were encouraged to adapt and repair existing clothes, while coming up with resourceful means of creating new clothing with the limited materials available to them. Mrs Esmée Mascall from Chester recalled how clothing coupons could be allocated to the best advantage:

> Allowing 33 coupons for half the year, in summer one could afford one dress (7 coupons), one blouse and skirt (12 coupons), a 'short jacket or coat under 28 inches in length' (11 coupons), one pair of stockings and a pair of ankle-length socks. Undies would apparently have to be made from black-out materials dyed black.
>
> In winter you would of course give priority to a warm coat (16 or 14 coupons according to sex) and a woollen dress (11 coupons) or a man's jacket (13) but you wouldn't get round the rules by knitting your undies, nightgowns, etc. because knitting wool now required one coupon for 2 ounces!
>
> Of course what actually followed was that we went on wearing our old clothes endlessly, until the rules became a little less stringent.

Although largely unpopular, rationing proved an essential way to control supplies throughout the war and it was not until the early 1950s that international trade began to return to normal, allowing most Ration Books to be consigned to the bin. However, for that generation who had experienced the many wartime restrictions on food and clothing, the principles of 'make do and mend' and avoidance of unnecessary food wastage would remain important characteristics of their everyday life.

< In this photograph from 1945, a queue of women wait to buy cakes from Williamson's baker and confectioner. The queue snakes out of the shop and along Wood Green High Road in London.

British propaganda was aimed largely at the home front, where the control of food and other essentials was a crucial element in keeping the war effort going. These posters both stress the importance of not wasting food, in support of the rationing arrangements.

CHAPTER SIX

Dunkirk
Beach Evacuation Plan

26 May – 4 June 1940

The German invasion of Poland, beginning on 1 September 1939, had led to both Britain and France declaring war against Germany. In doing so, they were fulfilling the promise they had made to support Poland in the event of such an attack, yet this obligation was initially met in purely political terms – not militarily. Both of the Allied countries preferred to adopt a longer-term military strategy by accelerating their re-armament and beginning to mobilise their forces in readiness for a ground attack against Germany.

The next few months became known as the 'Phoney War' for the lack of any wide-scale military campaigning in Western Europe. While the French went on the offensive by marching into the Saar region of Germany on 7 September, this was a relatively limited action intended only as an initial probe of the German front line defences. By 16 September the Germans had taken over Poland fully and could redistribute troops to properly reinforce their western defences, sending the French forces back to their defensive Maginot Line. Meanwhile, a British Expeditionary Force (BEF) arrived in France in September and started to assemble along the border with Belgium. Consisting of a relatively small body of 158,000 troops

the British contingent formed only ten per cent of the total Allied soldiers present on the western front at this time.

This period of relative inactivity was to change on 9 April 1940, when Germany launched a full scale invasion of Denmark and Norway. British and French troops started to land a few days later to help the Norwegian forces stop the German attack, yet the speed of the invasion overwhelmed them and, by the beginning of May, both southern and central parts of Norway were in German hands.

The Germans followed up this success by launching an invasion of France and the Low Countries on 10 May, attacking France, Belgium, Luxembourg and the Netherlands. The initial German plan consisted of a *Blitzkrieg* ('lightning war') advance into the Ardennes region, successfully cutting off the Allied units which had advanced into Belgium to meet the German attack which was expected there. The speed and efficiency of the main German assault meant that the Allied troops were forced back to the coast, and it soon became obvious that their only escape would be a mass evacuation from the Continent.

This sketch, showing the evacuation plan for units of the British Expeditionary Force (BEF) to escape from Dunkirk, was kept by Captain Ken Theobald of the 5th Battalion Royal West Kent Regiment. His unit was evacuated on 28 May 1940.

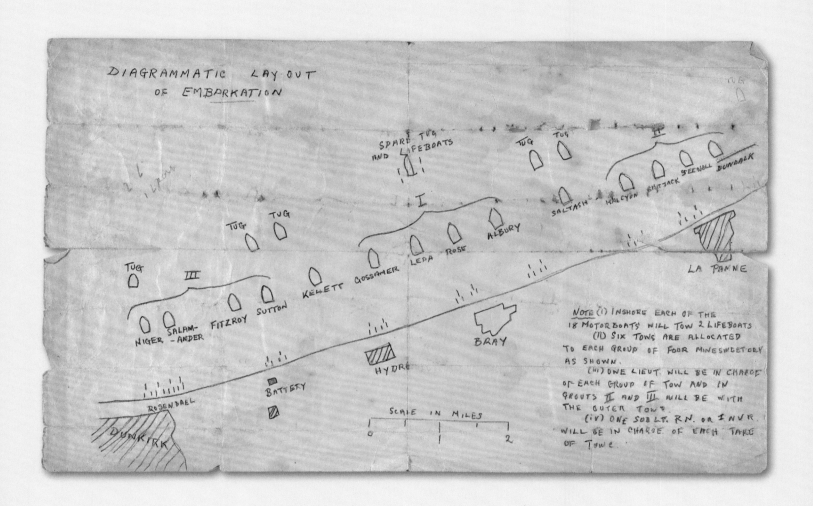

DIAGRAMMATIC LAY OUT
OF EMBARKATION

SPARE TUG
AND LIFEBOATS

TUG   TUG

SALTASH   HALCYON   SKIPJACK   STEENALL   DUNDALK

TUG   TUG

ALBURY

LEDA   ROSE

KELLETT   GOSSAMER

LA PANNE

TUG   III

SUTTON

SALAM-
NIGER   -ANDER   FITZROY

BRAY

HYDRO

BATTERY

ROSENDAEL

DUNKIRK

SCALE IN MILES

0   1   2

NOTE (i) INSHORE EACH OF THE
18 MOTORBOATS WILL TOW 2 LIFEBOATS.
   (ii) SIX TOWS ARE ALLOCATED
TO EACH GROUP OF FOUR MINESWEEPERS
AS SHOWN.
   (iii) ONE LIEUT WILL BE IN CHARGE
OF EACH GROUP OF TOW AND IN
GROUPS II AND III WILL BE WITH
THE OUTER TOWS.
   (iv) ONE SUB LT. R.N. OR I N V R.
WILL BE IN CHARGE OF EACH TAIL
OF TOWS.

To B Coy
From MUNE

A 8   26

Carriers report Tannay and WEST
edge of wood clear of enemy ⊙ they
also report BRIDGE 279406 blown ⊙
Endeavour to establish your line
on the canal from blown
bridge to 287392 ⊙ Bn LEFT
Bdy now altered and runs
Rd June ISBERGUES in a
straight line to to FORET 3039
thence exclusive LA CROIX MAIRESSE
thence 340423 — LE PRE A VIN to
LA COURONNE 4144 ⊙ R. BERKS
already in position hold line to
our SOUTH ⊙ I am endeavouring to
arrange for canal to be held from
your LEFT to HAVERSKERQUE ⊙
You will establish posts at PLAIN
HAUTE and THIENNES which will
be held ⊙ Bn HQ= Rd June.
349427 ⊙ Relay post 340423 closing

To. 4 Pl.   and please inform D Coy
From. MUNE

A 8   26

In reply to your number 3 ⊙ B Coy
was NOT intended to take over Road
WEST from LA CROIX MAIRESSE ⊙
When D Coy are in touch with
2 Dw. at or about LA CROIX
MAIRESSE you will return to Bn.
HQ area now at Rd June. 349427 ⊙
Bring back report from D Coy whether
MGs can be usefully employed in
their area ⊙ MG fire against B Coy
is believed to have come from
BOESEGHEM

Capt + Adj.
1955

To B Coy
From MUNE

A 1   27

Responsibility for establishing
posts NW of canal is withdrawn
from you ⊙ You will make good
the line of canal already detailed
and ensure that all houses from
BRIDGE 279406 to mill TANNAY
are clear of the enemy ⊙ To
support you in this I am sending
one sec. carrier Pl. under your
command ⊙ Please send back any
definitely located targets for
artillery or places you would like
shot up ⊙ Am arranging shoots
on BOESEGHEM and PECQUEUR

Capt + Adj.
6625

To C Coy.   28   A 1

In reply to TK1 David has
just come through LA MOTTE 044 ⊙
in difficulties at 355442 ⊙ No
information about troops on our left
flank ⊙ If pressed you may
withdraw area present Bn HQs ⊙
If general withdrawal is ordered
make through BOIS D'AVALE to
NE corner of WOOD thence LE
PARADIS and final RV FLETRE
4151 ⊙ Still no news of ration

Capt + Adj.
0800

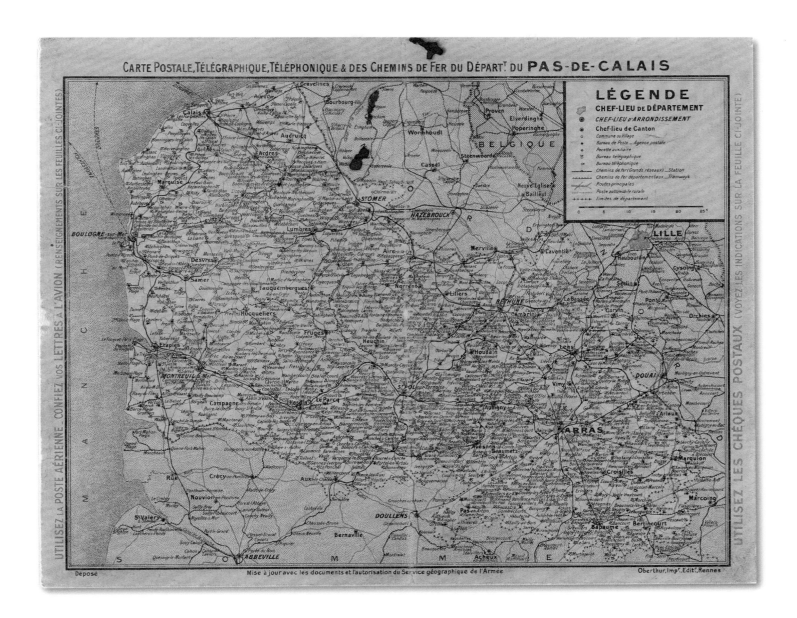

Carte Postale,Télégraphique,Téléphonique & des Chemins de Fer du Départ.ᵗ du **PAS-DE-CALAIS**

LÉGENDE

Mise à jour avec les documents et l'autorisation du Service géographique de l'Armée

Pages from Captain Theobald's field notebook, including carbon copy messages sent during his unit's retreat to Dunkirk. The 5th Royal West Kents were acting as a rearguard while other troops of the BEF made for Dunkirk. These messages, dating from the last few days of May 1940, refer to blown bridges and the German forces advancing swiftly behind them.

This map sheet of the Pas-de-Calais area of France was originally displayed in a French post office in May 1940. It was 'liberated' by a Royal Engineer during the BEF's retreat to Dunkirk in order to help them find their way to the evacuation point.

The 5th Battalion Royal West Kent Regiment were one such unit who received orders to withdraw from Belgium, via the Nieppe forest region located on the border with France. Their Adjutant was Captain Ken Theobald, who recalled how his Company were told to hold a rearguard position at Flétre:

> We found no sign of the rest of the brigade whose withdrawal we had been covering. We were told to make our way to Dunkirk for evacuation. We found out afterwards that when we arrived at Flétre, Brigade Headquarters was already on its way to England! Whenever we came to a bridge there always seemed to be a Corporal of the Royal Engineers waiting to blow it up. One in particular was particularly helpful. We had a choice of two roads to the coast and he recommended that we take the northern route. When others had taken a southern route he had heard considerable firing.
>
> Some of the carbon copies of messages I wrote in my field message book still survive. It is unfortunate that some of them were spoiled through immersion in the sea when we waded out to the small boats. The numbers 26, 27 and 28 on the messages refer to the day on which they were written, that is the 26th, 27th and 28th May 1940.

As these field messages indicate, the retreat of the BEF, along with Canadian, French and Belgian troops, was complicated by the urgency and chaos of such an unforeseen emergency:

> The maps with which we were issued were supposed to be 1 inch to the mile, but seemed to have little of the detail expected in a map of that size. Colonel Brown, who had travelled extensively in France, suddenly rumbled to the fact that they were really a quarter inch to the mile motoring maps blown up to one inch!

⟨ Ships holding position off the beaches at Dunkirk. Smoke billows from burning oil storage tanks, deliberately ignited by the fleeing Allies in order to prevent such a useful resource falling into the hands of the invading Germans, c.3 June 1940.

The constant stream of refugees interrupted our progress. We had scares about the German fifth column being mixed up with these refugees and having arms concealed in perambulators. Once or twice suspicious prams were investigated but we were considerably embarrassed by only finding babies and having to cope with irate mothers.

Our withdrawal to Dunkirk from the Forest of Nieppe was reasonably orderly with little interference and few casualties. My main trouble was tiredness! Whenever we halted, most of the troops just collapsed on the ground and went to sleep – particularly at night. As Adjutant, however, I was trying to keep track of everybody which meant no sleep for me and no opportunity to do such things as change my socks.

The port of Dunkirk was the main focus for the retreating troops, and its beaches would serve as the main evacuation point to transport hundreds of thousands of Allied soldiers back to the safety of England. Planning for Operation 'Dynamo' began on 20 May, with ships gathering at Dover in readiness for the evacuation. In order to help the ferrying of troops from the beaches to the large transport ships, a call was put out for any small civilian craft to be made available for such a job; within weeks, nearly 400 such 'little ships' had been voluntarily offered. Although troops had been leaving the French coast as and when the opportunity permitted, the full evacuation started on 27 May. Ken Theobald and his 5th Royal West Kents arrived at Dunkirk the following day:

We stayed on the beach for some hours, when small rowing boats came to our section of the beach to take us off. The C.O. and I saw everybody taken off in small parties to the larger ships lying off the coast. Our stay on the beaches was the usual wartime mixture of periods when nothing was happening interspersed with sudden periods of frenzied activity involving shelling and strafing from aircraft.

Having seen the Battalion, less A Company, off the beach the C.O. and I waded waist-deep into the sea to the next rowing boat and were taken on board the Kingfisher, I believe a fishery protection ship of the Royal Navy. Just after we were on board four shells landed short of the ship. Shortly afterwards four

more shells arrived from a German battery on shore and landed just the other side of us. 'We've just been bracketed,' said the Skipper. 'It's about time we moved.' He promptly set sail and four shells landed exactly where we had been a few moments before! I had had very little rest for the past four days and after drinking a very welcome cup of tea laced with, I think, probably rum, I just went to sleep on the deck. I understand a bomb from a German aircraft scored a near miss which shook things, but I was blissfully unaware of it!

My main memory of my last few moments of Dunkirk is the appalling column of black smoke rising from burning oil dumps that had been deliberately set on fire to deny the enemy the use of the oil, and the sight of an anti-aircraft battery where the gunners had destroyed their guns by then firing another round from the breech. The result was that the barrels split and curved over looking like peeling bananas.

By 4 June, some 288,000 soldiers (including 193,000 from the BEF) had been evacuated by a fleet of over 800 boats. In total, 66,426 soldiers had been lost by the BEF during their short campaign in France, whether killed, wounded or captured, along with an enormous amount of tanks, vehicles and equipment which the evacuating army had been forced to discard. On a smaller scale, a similar situation had arisen in Norway with Allied forces evacuating the now German-occupied country at the beginning of June. It would take some time to reconstitute Britain's Army, while the immediate future would see the threat of an imminent German invasion. The United Kingdom had effectively become a besieged island.

Rescued troops shown on board the destroyer HMS *Vanquisher* on their way back to Britain from Dunkirk. Ships were filled to the brim with evacuated soldiers, necessitating each man to find space for himself either above or below deck, 29 May 1940.

CHAPTER SEVEN

The Battle of Britain

Douglas Bader's Flying Report

7 February 1940

One of the most memorable personalities associated with the Second World War was Douglas Bader. As a prominent fighter ace of the Royal Air Force, Bader's contribution proved instrumental in winning the Battle of Britain and his reputation as a disabled war hero inspired many, both during the conflict and for many years afterwards. Yet Bader's career was far from straightforward and, following a disastrous incident shortly after qualifying, a report on his flying abilities in February 1940 would prove crucial in determining his future.

The eighteen-year-old Douglas Bader began his flying service in 1928, when he attended the Royal Air Force College at Cranwell in Lincolnshire to train for a commission. Excelling at sports, he came close to expulsion on several occasions due to participation in forbidden activities such as motorcycle racing, a popular activity amongst the cadets. But it was Bader's admiration for the fighter aces of the First World War which inspired him to work hard towards following their example. He was finally commissioned in July 1930 and posted to No 23 Squadron RAF at Kenley, in Surrey.

Bader soon earned a reputation as a daredevil keen to perform dangerous aerobatic manoeuvres, and on multiple occasions was criticised for doing so by his superiors. On 14 December 1931, he was attempting some low-level aerobatics in a Bulldog aircraft, apparently in response to a dare, only for the aircraft wing to clip the ground and cause him to crash. As a result of the serious injuries Bader sustained, both of his legs had to be amputated. After a lengthy and painful year-long convalescence, Bader slowly recovered his health and was fitted with two artificial tin legs. Demonstrating incredible stoicism, he taught himself to adapt to his new limbs and was soon able to walk, drive and eventually fly once again. However, despite an RAF medical examination declaring him fit for service, Bader was ultimately invalided out of the service in May 1933 and forced to enter civilian employment.

It was the Munich Crisis of 1938 and the very real possibility of a European war which inspired Bader to appeal to the Air Ministry to permit him to return to operational flying. However, despite his best efforts, it would not be until October 1939 that he received a telegram instructing him to report for a selection board.

Central Flying School report confirming Douglas Bader's fitness to return to active service as a pilot, 7 February 1940. The positive outcome of this report ensured that Bader could apply his impressive flying skills to the defence of the country in the imminent Battle of Britain, fought in the skies over England.

ROYAL AIR FORCE.

Form 364.

Central Flying School report on an Officer or Airman Pilot undergoing training or test.

(See Instructions over.)

Name F/O D.R.S. BADER.   Unit No 19 (F) SQADRON

Rank FLYING OFFICER   No.

Purpose and duration of training/test—From 27 NOVEMBER 1939 to 7 FEBRUARY 1940
REFRESHER COURSE.

1. FLYING TIMES :—

Type of Aircraft.	DUAL.		SOLO.		Totals.	
	Day.	Night.	Day.	Night.		
1. TUTOR.	1.20	0.50	13.10	0.30	Dual	7.50
2. HARVARD	1.30	—	—		Solo	33.40
3. MASTER	3.40	0.45	3.25	0.30		
BATTLE.	—	—	5.35	—	Grand Total	41.30
MOTH MINOR.	—	—	2.45	—		
4. LYSANDER	—	—	2.05	—	Total flying experience :	
6. HURRICANE.	—	—	5.15	0.55		
5. HART	0.30	—	—	—	641.30 .	

2. OTHER TRAINING :—

Subject		Marks obtained.	% Total.
Link Trainer Time 2 hours 30 mins			
1. Navigation		100	
2. Airmanship		100	
3. Meteorology		100	
4. Theory of Flight		100	
5. Flight Technical Administration ...		100	

3. Assessment of Ability :—

(a) as pilot EXCEPTIONAL

(b) as pilot-navigator

(c) in aerobatics

(d) in instrument/cloud flying

(e) as flying instructor

4. Remarks by C.F.I. 'E' Flight —

This officer is an exceptionally good pilot and has had no difficulty either by day or night with modern type aircraft. Amongst types flown by day are Harvard, Battle, Lysander, Moth Minor, Hurricane, Tutor — by night Tutor, Master and Hurricane. He is a very keen pilot and should be ideally suited both in flying qualifications and temperament to single seater fighter. It is recommended that his flying be confined to single engined aircraft & to those fitted with hand brakes.
R.A.a. Leigh S/L. OC 'E' Flight

5. Remarks by Commandant OC "X" Flight.

I entirely agree 26.1.40. with the above remarks. When flying with this officer it is quite impossible to even imagine that he had two artificial legs. He is full of confidence and possesses excellent judgement and air sense. His general flying (including aerobatics) is very smooth and accurate. I have never met a more enthusiastic pilot. He lives for flying.
S/L. OC "X" Flight CFS 22.2.40.

Recommended for

Remarks by OC. Refresher Squadron with this report.
I am in full agreement with this report.

Signature G.H. Stainforth A/Cdr/Cmdr,

Date 22-2-40   Commandant Central Flying School.

(1609) Wt. 37510—2947 10,000 4/36 T.S. 667.

Found to be medically fit apart from his artificial legs, Bader was then sent to the Central Flying School at Upavon, in Wiltshire, where he was to undertake a two-part refresher course in order to confirm that he possessed the necessary skills to fly modern aircraft.

After he easily passed the initial test, in late November the Air Ministry confirmed that Bader would return to the active list as a regular, keeping his former rank of Flying Officer. However, he was also told that he would need to pass the full refresher course before being assigned to an operational squadron. Completing this final test would therefore be of crucial importance.

Despite his existing experience, Bader still had a lot of fresh things to learn and new aircraft to fly. Over the next few weeks he had to adapt to 'flying blind' [relying purely on the aircraft's instrumentation in order to simulate poor observation conditions] as well as night flying. He flew modern aircraft including the Fairey Battle, a relatively high-performance single-engine light bomber; the Miles Master, a fast low-wing monoplane with a top speed of 290 mph; and the Hawker Hurricane, the superbly fast fighter aircraft, which Bader would come to prefer over the more graceful Spitfire.

By 7 February the refresher course was complete and Bader's instructors provided their final report on his abilities as a pilot. The first assessment was provided by Squadron Leader Rupert Leigh:

> This officer is an exceptionally good pilot and has had no difficulty either by day or night with modern type aircraft. Amongst types flown by day are Harvard, Battle, Lysander, Moth Minor, Hurricane, Tutor – by night Tutor, Master and Hurricane. He is a very keen pilot and should be ideally suited both in flying qualifications and temperament to single seater fighters. It is recommended that his flying be confined to single-engine aircraft and to those fitted with hand brakes.

The reference to hand-operated air brakes relates to the limitations experienced when flying with artificial legs, to which Squadron Leader Cox then also made reference in his summary:

> I entirely agree with the above remarks. When flying with this officer it is quite impossible to even imagine that he has two artificial legs. He is full of confidence and possesses excellent judgement and air sense. His general flying (including aerobatics) is very smooth and accurate. I have never met a more enthusiastic pilot. He lives for flying.

It was a superb assessment of Douglas Bader's skill as a pilot. That same day, he was posted to No. 19 Fighter Squadron, based at RAF Duxford in Cambridgeshire. It had been eight years and two months since his fateful accident and what had threatened to be the end of his flying career. Little did he realise that his true achievements in the air were just about to begin.

Returning to active service, Bader soon saw action in the skies over Dunkirk in May 1940, providing air support to the Allied evacuation from the French beaches. His most famous combat experience, however, would be later that year in the summer months of the Battle of Britain. As the Luftwaffe sent wave after wave of aircraft to bomb British cities into submission, it was up to RAF Fighter Command to defend the country. It was the first major campaign in history to be fought entirely in the air. From when he took over command of the unit in June 1940 until the end of the year, No. 242 Squadron RAF claimed 67 aerial victories for the loss of 6 of its own pilots. By the end of October the Germans had failed in their attempts to achieve air superiority and a clear turning point in the war had been reached. Britain had shown that it could withstand such devastating attacks, and the German plans for an invasion of Britain were shelved indefinitely. For his services during the Battle of Britain, Bader was awarded the Distinguished Flying Cross alongside nine of his fellow pilots from 242 Squadron.

However, despite this success Bader's wartime flying days were numbered. While on an offensive patrol over the French coast on 9 August 1941, his Spitfire suffered serious damage and he was forced to bail out. While he believed that he had suffered a mid-air collision with a German Messerschmitt, modern research suggests that he may have been the victim of friendly fire. Either way, he parachuted into occupied France to be taken prisoner immediately, spending the rest of the war in captivity.

Squadron Leader Douglas Bader DSO DFC, Commanding Officer of No.242 Squadron, Royal Air Force, seated on the cockpit of his Hawker Hurricane. This photograph was taken in October 1940 at the height of the Battle of Britain, when Bader's Squadron was based at RAF Duxford, now part of Imperial War Museums.

Bader soon established a troublesome reputation as a frequent escaper, and was eventually moved in August 1942 to the 'escape-proof' Oflag IV-C at Colditz Castle, where he remained until liberation in 1945.

Douglas Bader became one of the true heroes of the Second World War, and inspired many by his courage in defying his disability. The post-war era saw his legend confirmed, firstly in 1954 by a best-selling book based on his life written by Paul Brickhill, and then by an award-winning film adaption two years later, both titled *Reach for the Sky*. A controversial figure in later life for his forthright and often unfashionable political opinions, Bader remained one of the key British personalities of the war and his inspirational contribution to winning the Battle of Britain has never been forgotten.

Squadron Leader Douglas Bader (centre) and fellow pilots of No.242 (Canadian) Squadron RAF, Eric Ball and Willie McKnight, admire the nose art on Bader's Hawker Hurricane at Duxford, October 1940.

The entrance to Colditz Castle, designated Oflag IV-C during the Second World War, where Allied officers were held under high security. As one of the more high-profile residents of the castle, Douglas Bader spent a considerable part of his time as a prisoner of war here, from August 1942 until his liberation in April 1945.

CHAPTER EIGHT

Invasion Fears

If the Invader Comes Leaflet

18 June 1940

While the likelihood of a German invasion had been secretly discussed by the British government since the start of the war, the threat only began to be considered seriously in the spring of 1940. The Germans had made numerous territorial expansions across Europe, invading Norway on 9 April before entering France on 10 May, and British Expeditionary Forces had been sent to both countries to assist in their defence. Despite some initial successes during the Norwegian campaign, the overall strength of the German Blitzkrieg attacks soon sent the defenders into retreat, and Allied troops were ultimately withdrawn from both countries at the end of May and beginning of June. Britain was now cut off from the rest of Western Europe.

Efforts to prepare for an imminent invasion of Britain now became top of the government's agenda. A considerable amount of equipment and troops had been lost following the evacuation from Dunkirk and so work towards reconstituting the country's fighting strength continued, ensuring that an adequate defensive force was in place. Key to this work were the Local Defence Volunteers, more commonly known as the Home Guard. Largely consisting of men who were not subject to conscription due to their age or reserved occupation, the scheme had already been announced on 14 May; within two months, some 1.5 million men had volunteered to protect their country.

Further measures were also put into place. Large parts of Britain around the south and east coast were deemed Defence Areas, which visitors would require a permit to enter. Fields, parks and golf courses were scattered with improvised hazards in order to prevent enemy gliders landing; tank traps and concrete bunkers were constructed across the countryside; and signposts, railway station names and other information likely to aid a German invader were hastily removed.

However, the most important element in preparing the country for an invasion would be to ensure the support and obedience of the population. The Ministry of Information formed a special Emergency Planning Committee on 22 May which began to devise a publicity campaign to ensure that the public was appropriately prepared for the possibility of a German invasion. While the spread of uncertainty and fear was to be avoided at all costs, the invasion scare would actually prove beneficial in keeping the British public alert and supportive to the overall war effort.

Liaising with the War Office and Ministry of Home Security, the Ministry of Information issued a printed

If the Invader Comes leaflet, printed on 18 June 1940 and distributed widely across Britain.

Issued by the Ministry of Information in co-operation with the War Office and the Ministry of Home Security.

If the
INVADER
comes

WHAT TO DO — AND HOW TO DO IT

THE Germans threaten to invade Great Britain. If they do so they will be driven out by our Navy, our Army and our Air Force. Yet the ordinary men and women of the civilian population will also have their part to play. Hitler's invasions of Poland, Holland and Belgium were greatly helped by the fact that the civilian population was taken by surprise. They did not know what to do when the moment came. *You must not be taken by surprise.* This leaflet tells you what general line you should take. More detailed instructions will be given you when the danger comes nearer. Meanwhile, read these instructions carefully and be prepared to carry them out.

I

When Holland and Belgium were invaded, the civilian population fled from their homes. They crowded on the roads, in cars, in carts, on bicycles and on foot, and so helped the enemy by preventing their own armies from advancing against the invaders. You must not allow that to happen here. Your first rule, therefore, is :—

(1) IF THE GERMANS COME, BY PARACHUTE, AEROPLANE OR SHIP, YOU MUST REMAIN WHERE YOU ARE. THE ORDER IS " STAY PUT ".

If the Commander in Chief decides that the place where you live must be evacuated, he will tell you when and how to leave. Until you

receive such orders you must remain where you are. If you run away, you will be exposed to far greater danger because you will be machine-gunned from the air as were civilians in Holland and Belgium, and you will also block the roads by which our own armies will advance to turn the Germans out.

II

There is another method which the Germans adopt in their invasion. They make use of the civilian population in order to create confusion and panic. They spread false rumours and issue false instructions. In order to prevent this, you should obey the second rule, which is as follows :—

(2) DO NOT BELIEVE RUMOURS AND DO NOT SPREAD THEM. WHEN YOU RECEIVE AN ORDER, MAKE QUITE SURE THAT IT IS A TRUE ORDER AND NOT A FAKED ORDER. MOST OF YOU KNOW YOUR POLICEMEN AND YOUR A.R.P. WARDENS BY SIGHT, YOU CAN TRUST THEM. IF YOU KEEP YOUR HEADS, YOU CAN ALSO TELL WHETHER A MILITARY OFFICER IS REALLY BRITISH OR ONLY PRETENDING TO BE SO. IF IN DOUBT ASK THE POLICE-MAN OR THE A.R.P. WARDEN. USE YOUR COMMON SENSE.

III

The Army, the Air Force and the Local Defence Volunteers cannot be everywhere at once. The ordinary man and woman must be on the watch. If you see anything suspicious, do not rush round telling your neighbours all about it. Go at once to the nearest policeman, police-station, or military officer and tell them exactly what you saw. Train yourself to notice the exact time and place where you saw anything suspicious, and try to give exact information. Try to check your facts. The sort of report which a military or police officer wants from you is something like this :—

> "At 5.30 p.m. to-night I saw twenty cyclists come into Little Squashborough from the direction of Great Mudtown. They carried some sort of automatic rifle or gun. I did not see anything like artillery. They were in grey uniforms."

Be calm, quick and exact. The third rule, therefore, is as follows :—

(3) KEEP WATCH. IF YOU SEE ANYTHING SUSPICIOUS, NOTE IT CAREFULLY AND GO AT ONCE TO THE NEAREST POLICE OFFICER OR STATION, OR TO THE NEAREST MILITARY OFFICER. DO NOT RUSH ABOUT SPREADING VAGUE RUMOURS. GO QUICKLY TO THE NEAREST AUTHORITY AND GIVE HIM THE FACTS.

IV

Remember that if parachutists come down near your home, they will not be feeling at all brave. They will not know where they are, they will have no food, they will not know where their companions are. They will want you to give them food, means of transport and maps. They will want you to tell them where they have landed, where their comrades are, and where our own soldiers are. The fourth rule, therefore, is as follows :—

(4) DO NOT GIVE ANY GERMAN ANYTHING. DO NOT TELL HIM ANYTHING. HIDE YOUR FOOD AND YOUR BICYCLES. HIDE YOUR MAPS. SEE THAT THE ENEMY GETS NO PETROL. IF YOU HAVE A CAR OR MOTOR BICYCLE, PUT IT OUT OF ACTION WHEN NOT IN USE. IT IS NOT ENOUGH TO REMOVE THE IGNITION KEY; YOU MUST MAKE IT USELESS TO ANYONE EXCEPT YOURSELF.

IF YOU ARE A GARAGE PROPRIETOR, YOU MUST WORK OUT A PLAN TO PROTECT YOUR STOCK OF PETROL AND YOUR CUSTOMERS' CARS. REMEMBER THAT TRANSPORT AND PETROL WILL BE THE INVADER'S MAIN DIFFICULTIES. MAKE SURE THAT NO INVADER WILL BE ABLE TO GET HOLD OF YOUR CARS, PETROL, MAPS OR BICYCLES.

V

You may be asked by Army and Air Force officers to help in many ways. For instance, the time may come when you will receive orders to block roads or streets in order to prevent the enemy from advancing. Never block a road unless you are told which one you must block. Then you can help by felling trees, wiring them together or blocking the roads with cars. Here, therefore, is the fifth rule :—

(5) BE READY TO HELP THE MILITARY IN ANY WAY. BUT DO NOT BLOCK ROADS UNTIL ORDERED TO DO SO BY THE MILITARY OR L.D.V. AUTHORITIES.

VI

If you are in charge of a factory, store or other works, organise its defence at once. If you are a worker, make sure that you understand the system of defence that has been organised and know what part you have to play in it. Remember always that parachutists and fifth column men are powerless against any organised resistance. They can only succeed if they can create disorganisation. Make certain that no suspicious strangers enter your premises.

You must know in advance who is to take command, who is to be second in command, and how orders are to be transmitted. This chain of command must be built up and you will probably find that ex-officers or N.C.O.'s, who have been in emergencies before, are the best people to undertake such command. The sixth rule is therefore as follows :—

(6) IN FACTORIES AND SHOPS, ALL MANAGERS AND WORKMEN SHOULD ORGANISE SOME SYSTEM NOW BY WHICH A SUDDEN ATTACK CAN BE RESISTED.

VII

The six rules which you have now read give you a general idea of what to do in the event of invasion. More detailed instructions may, when the time comes, be given you by the Military and Police Authorities and by the Local Defence Volunteers; they will NOT be given over the wireless as that might convey information to the enemy. These instructions must be obeyed at once.

Remember always that the best defence of Great Britain is the courage of her men and women. Here is your seventh rule :—

(7) THINK BEFORE YOU ACT. BUT THINK ALWAYS OF YOUR COUNTRY BEFORE YOU THINK OF YOURSELF.

(52194) Wt. / 14,900,000 6/40 Hw.

leaflet on Tuesday, 18 June 1940, entitled *If the Invader Comes: What to Do – and How to Do It.* By that weekend, it had been delivered to every one of the country's 15 million households. Larger versions were printed for display by local authorities as posters, while the press and radio were drafted in to publicise the initiative as much as possible.

The tone of the leaflet was very matter-of-fact, yet gave a clear message to the public:

> The Germans threaten to invade Great Britain. If they do so they will be driven out by our Navy, our Army and our Air Force. Yet the ordinary men and women of the civilian population will also have their part to play... *You must not be taken by surprise.* This leaflet tells you the general line you should take.

Seven key instructions followed, each written boldly in capital letters. In the event of a German invasion, the public should (i) Stay put; (ii) Do not believe or spread rumours; (iii) Remain alert; (iv) Do not help the enemy; (v) Be ready to help the military; (vi) Organise resistance in factories or shops; and (vii) Act in the country's best interests. This guidance was designed to avoid the situations recently witnessed in other European countries where the invaders had taken the civilian populations by surprise, resulting in confusion and uncertainty which in turn led to a quick surrender.

While public reactions to the leaflet were largely positive, it soon became clear that a certain amount of confusion remained, due to the unspecific nature of the instructions given. Many felt that the instruction to 'stay put' was particularly unclear, especially when coupled with the lack of practical advice on how civilians might defend their own homes. This led to a second leaflet being issued in July 1940 entitled *Stay Where You Are*, which stressed the dangers caused by refugees fleeing before an enemy, whilst encouraging civilians to prepare themselves for invasion by volunteering for Local Defence duties.

In the event, German desires for an invasion of Britain were largely exaggerated. Hitler appealed on numerous occasions for peace to be struck with Britain and only really considered invasion as a final resort, once the opportunity for negotiations was obviously past. It was thus that on 16 July 1940 he issued Führer Directive No. 16, setting in motion the planning for a German landing on the south coast of Britain. Codenamed 'Sea Lion', the plan would only be operational if both air and naval superiority over the English Channel could be achieved, and few among the German military hierarchy believed that this could be easily accomplished.

Coupled with this reluctance on the part of the Germans was their unreadiness for a full-scale invasion operation, since a complicated Channel crossing was ill-suited to the *Blitzkrieg* strategy. A sustained *Blitzkrieg* attack on Britain would rely on short, intensive bursts of economic effort for which Germany's war industry was not yet geared up. However the crucial factor in preventing an invasion was the Royal Air Force's victory over the Luftwaffe during the Battle of Britain, which meant that the essential air support necessary to spearhead a German attack was no longer viable. 'Sea Lion' was postponed indefinitely on 17 September 1940.

By this time the Ministry of Information was able to report that 'except in certain areas invasion talk has receded into the background'. Although fading to an extent, the fear of invasion never fully disappeared, however, and was ever-present among the population of Britain due to war rumours and fluctuating morale. To many, the possibility of a German invasion would not fully disappear until the Allies went on the offensive in north-west Europe after the Normandy landings of June 1944.

This reconnaissance photograph taken by Allied aircraft shows quite clearly the mass of German invasion barges moored in Boulogne Harbour, France, in June 1940. These were in preparation for the planned invasion of Britain – Operation 'Sealion'.

Members of the Home Guard in Cromer, Norfolk, stage an attack on an enemy 'tank' – in reality a corrugated iron mock-up – as they defend a concrete road barrier with petrol bombs. This exercise took place between 31 July and 2 August 1940.

A break from instructions for men on a Home Guard Junior Leaders' course in Shropshire. British soldiers dressed in German uniform – in order to represent a more realistic enemy to fight – pause with members of the Home Guard, 20 May 1943.

CHAPTER NINE

The Blitz

Air Raid Precautions (ARP) Documents

7 September 1940 – 11 May 1941

The development of aircraft for the purposes of war had led to the first aerial bombing raids taking place during the First World War. These were largely restricted by the distance needing to be covered by the primitive aircraft of the time, as well as the limited payload they could carry. As aircraft development advanced dramatically during the 1920s and 1930s, however, it became obvious that any future conflict would most likely see a sustained bombing campaign put into operation. In line with this expectation, it therefore made sense for each nation to put into place its own arrangements for civil defence. This began in Britain in 1937 with the setting up of the Air Raid Precautions organisation, usually referred to by its acronym ARP. Organised by local councils, ARP was intended to protect civilians from enemy air raids through a network of wardens, ambulance drivers and rescue parties, who would liaise directly with other emergency services.

Alexander Pettigrew worked at the engineering firm of Babcock and Wilcox, located in Renfrew, some six miles outside of Glasgow. The nearby Clydebank shipyards and other industries based in that area were a clear target for the Luftwaffe. Prior to the outbreak of war, Babcock and Wilcox had organized its own team of ARP volunteers, made up from members of its workforce. The company's first ARP bulletin was dated February 1939, and described the arrangements being put into place in their firm, which would be mirrored by other organisations across the United Kingdom:

> The members of the various services for the works will [be] Senior Wardens, Wardens and their deputies, First Aid Parties, Observers (usually referred to as Fire Watchers) and Messengers in addition to members of special services such as First Aid and Cleansing Centre attendants, Decontamination, Rescue, Demolition, Fire-Fighting and Repair squads, and certain Key Men. The whole scheme will be worked from a Central Control with emergency communications.

> Each employee will have a definite place to go to and should only be absent from his place by permission, or with the knowledge of the official in charge of his section or squad. It will be imperative that the location of every person is known in an emergency, as absence

Cards of this type were delivered to every address administered by Renfrew County Council at the beginning of the war. They were designed not only to inform residents of the local ARP posts and emergency contacts in their area, but also to collect information which would be of use when tackling fires and other damage to homes.

To Householder.

Renfrew County Council _Renfrew_ **Area**

Your A.R.P. Services are :-

Warden _R. Watson_

Address _37 Douglas Road_

Nearest Wardens' Post :-

Address _Paisley Road (Opposite 4)_

First Aid Post :-

Address _Paisley Road_

Report Centre _Police Office_

Rest Centre _Rutherford Hall_

Nearest Stirrup Pump Party :-

Address _Douglas Road_

Nearest Police 'Phone Box :-
For Report Centre, Police, Fire,
Ambulance or Warden.

Address _Cockles Loan_

From Householder.

Address _7, Douglas Road, Renfrew._

Name _Alexander Pettigrew_

No. of Adults _3_ Children
(14 and over)..... (under 14).....—

FIRE APPLIANCES AVAILABLE?

Stirrup Pumps _1_

Other Types _—_

Buckets of Sand _1_, Bags _6_

Buckets of Water _2_

Ladder _none_

Any other _House Steps_

Telephone No. _—_

Where do you go in the event of a raid?
To street shelter

If absent from premises where is key
available?
_With Mrs. Smith, 9, Douglas Road,
Renfrew._

SECTION Nº I.

					1941.-2.	FIRE WAT...

NUMBERS OF HOUSES.	PARTICULARS.	DAY OF WEEK		NIGHT OR DAY.	17TH MARCH. 16TH JUNE. 15TH SEPTR. 15TH DECEMR.	24TH MARCH. 23RD JUNE. 22ND SEPTR. 22ND DECEMBER	31ST MARCH. 30TH JUNE. 29TH SEPTR. 29TH DECEMBER	7TH APRIL. 7TH JULY. 6TH OCTOBER 5TH JANUARY	14TH AP... 14TH JU... 13TH OCT... 12TH JANU...
HOUSES Nºs 1 TO 16. THAT IS – 8 HOUSES EACH SIDE OF ROAD.		MONDAY.	DAY.		MRS DICKIE.	MRS MACKINNON.	MRS McFEE.	MRS McNEILLIE	MRS YOU...
			NIGHT.		MR J DICKIE	MR MACKINNON	MISS J. CUNNINGHAM	MR SCOTT	MR McLEA...
		TUESDAY.	DAY.		MRS McFEE.	MRS McNEILLIE	MRS YOUNG.	MRS WILSON.	MISS A.CUNN...
			NIGHT.		MR YOUNG.	MR McNEILLIE	MR McLEARIE.	MR MURPHY	MR PETTIG...
		WEDNESDAY	DAY.		MRS YOUNG.	MRS WILSON.	MISS A CUNNINGHAM	MRS KIRK	MRS McLO...
			NIGHT.		MISS J. CUNNINGHAM	MR MURPHY	MR PETTIGREW.	MR KIRK.	MR A.J. SM...
		THURSDAY	DAY.		MISS A. CUNNINGHAM	MRS KIRK.	MRS McLEARIE.	MRS SCOTT.	MRS PETTI...
			NIGHT.		MR McLEARIE	MR KIRK.	MR A.J. SMITH.	MR P. SMITH.	MR MACKIN...
		FRIDAY.	DAY.		MRS McLEARIE.	MRS SCOTT.	MRS PETTIGREW.	MRS P. SMITH.	MRS A.J. S...
			NIGHT.		MR PETTIGREW.	MR P. SMITH.	MR MACKINNON.	MR J DICKIE	MR McNEIL...
		SATURDAY	DAY.		MRS PETTIGREW	MRS P. SMITH.	MRS A.J. SMITH.	MRS DICKIE.	MRS MACK...
			NIGHT.		MR A.J. SMITH.	MR J DICKIE.	MR McNEILLIE	MR YOUNG.	MR MURP...
		SUNDAY.	DAY.		MRS A.J. SMITH.	MRS DICKIE.	MRS MACKINNON	MRS McFEE.	MRS McN...
			NIGHT.		MR KERR.	MR YOUNG.	MR KERR.	MR SCOTT.	MR KERR...

...ING — DOUGLAS RD. RENFREW.

SECTION No 1.

...S BEGINNING (MONDAY)

21ST APRIL / 21ST JULY / ?O OCTOBER / ?H JANUARY	28TH APRIL / 28TH JULY / 27TH OCTOBER / 26TH JANUARY	5TH MAY / 4TH AUGUST / 3RD NOVEMBER / 2ND FEBRUARY	12TH MAY / 11TH AUGUST / 10TH NOVEMBER / 9TH FEBRUARY	19TH MAY / 18TH AUGUST / 17TH NOVEMBER / 16TH FEBRUARY	26TH MAY / 25TH AUGUST / 24TH NOVEMBER / 23RD FEBRUARY	2ND JUNE / 1ST SEPTR / 1ST DECEMBER / 2ND MARCH	9TH JUNE / 8TH SEPTR / 8TH DECEMBER / 9TH MARCH	NIGHT OR DAY	DAY OF WEEK
MRS WILSON	MISS A.CUNNINGHAM	MRS KIRK	MRS McLEARIE	MRS SCOTT	MRS PETTIGREW	MRS P.SMITH	MRS A.J.SMITH	DAY	MONDAY
MR KIRK	MR PETTIGREW	MR P.SMITH	MR A.J.SMITH	MR J.DICKIE	MR MACKINNON	MISS J.CUNNINGHAM	MR MURPHY	NIGHT	
MRS KIRK	MRS McLEARIE	MRS SCOTT	MRS PETTIGREW	MRS P.SMITH	MRS A.J.SMITH	MRS DICKIE	MRS MACKINNON	DAY	TUESDAY
MR SCOTT	MR A.J.SMITH	MR J.DICKIE	MR MACKINNON	MR YOUNG	MR MURPHY	MR McLEARIE	MR KIRK	NIGHT	
MRS SCOTT	MRS PETTIGREW	MRS P.SMITH	MRS A.J.SMITH	MRS DICKIE	MRS MACKINNON	MRS McFEE	MRS McNEILLIE	DAY	WEDNESDAY
MR P.SMITH	MR MACKINNON	MR YOUNG	MR McNEILLIE	MISS J.CUNNINGHAM	MR KIRK	MR PETTIGREW	MR SCOTT	NIGHT	
MRS P.SMITH	MRS A.J.SMITH	MRS DICKIE	MRS MACKINNON	MRS McFEE	MRS McNEILLIE	MRS YOUNG	MRS WILSON	DAY	THURSDAY
MR J.DICKIE	MR McNEILLIE	MISS J.CUNNINGHAM	MR MURPHY	MR McLEARIE	MR P.SMITH	MR A.J.SMITH	MR P.SMITH	NIGHT	
MRS DICKIE	MRS MACKINNON	MRS McFEE	MRS McNEILLIE	MRS YOUNG	MRS WILSON	MISS A.CUNNINGHAM	MRS KIRK	DAY	FRIDAY
MR YOUNG	MR MURPHY	MR McLEARIE	MR KIRK	MR PETTIGREW	MR DICKIE	MR MACKINNON	MR McNEILLIE	NIGHT	
MRS McFEE	MRS McNEILLIE	MRS YOUNG	MRS WILSON	MISS A.CUNNINGHAM	MRS KIRK	MRS McLEARIE	MRS SCOTT	DAY	SATURDAY
MISS J.CUNNINGHAM	MR KIRK	MR PETTIGREW	MR P.SMITH	MR A.J.SMITH	MR YOUNG	MR SCOTT	MISS J.CUNNINGHAM	NIGHT	
MRS YOUNG	MRS WILSON	MISS A.CUNNINGHAM	MRS KIRK	MRS McLEARIE	MRS SCOTT	MRS PETTIGREW	MRS P.SMITH	DAY	SUNDAY
MR McLEARIE	MR KERR	MR SCOTT	MR KERR	MR SCOTT	MR KERR	MR McNEILLIE	MR KERR	NIGHT	

Rota for fire watching duties in Douglas Road, Renfrew, between March 1941 and March 1942. Such locally-organised schedules were crucial in order to ensure constant vigilance in case of fires breaking out due to bombing. This example originates from a group of neighbours, but similar rotas were arranged by businesses and the occupants of larger buildings.

in a roll call may mean that the absentee is in danger or is injured or needs help in some way. A search in war conditions might endanger many lives. From the outset, therefore, each employee should realize the importance of being in his place or reporting his location to the nearest warden.

ARP duties for workers were often two-fold. Not only were they expected to adopt procedures at their place of employment, but there was also an expectation that they would contribute to local ARP activities too, organised by their local County Council. While a small number of key ARP workers were paid for their services, the vast majority undertook the job on a voluntary basis in addition to their regular work. The documents shown here reveal how Alexander Pettigrew was involved in regular fire-watching duties on behalf of his street. Organised on a daily rota, the street's residents would remain alert throughout the day or night in order to keep a look out for enemy aircraft and the first signs of bombing. Cards were issued to each householder to inform them of their nearest emergency contacts, whether the ARP Warden Post, the First Aid Post, or the nearest Police Telephone Box. Equally, each resident was expected to inform their local warden of the number of appliances they had available in their home to counter a fire, whether it was a stirrup pump, sand bags or buckets of water.

Once the Germans began to undertake regular bombing raids against British cities, the ARP organisation jumped into action and provided crucial support in protecting life amongst the destruction and chaos of air raids. Air Raid Wardens enforced the 'blackout' which prevented lights attracting enemy bombers at night; managed the sirens which alerted people to incoming aerial attacks; and directed people to shelters. The German bomber offensive against Britain began by concentrating on London, which from September 1940 suffered mass air raids as the Battle of Britain in the skies above reached its conclusion. For 57 days from 7 September 1940 onwards, the capital was bombed every night except one, with an especially fierce daylight raid on 15 September. Switching to night raids the following month, the Luftwaffe then began to target the country's other main industrial cities and seaports.

< One half of a pair of semi-detached houses located in a suburb on the eastern outskirts of London. The other half has been destroyed by a direct hit from a German bomb, 24 September 1940.

Between March and May 1941, the Clydebank region also suffered a period of intense bombing by the Germans. The activity in March was particularly bad, with Renfrew's catholic church of St James being the target for several incendiary bombs which threatened to destroy the building. Fortunately three Polish airmen, present in the church at the time, managed to put out the fires and protect the place of worship, although at great personal cost – two of them were killed at the scene while the other died in hospital the following day.

The Blitz lasted for just over eight months, coming to an end on 11 May 1941 when the Luftwaffe switched its efforts to the Eastern Front to attack Soviet Russia, as Operation 'Barbarossa' was launched. The German bombing campaign against Britain ultimately failed because it was unable to adopt a methodical strategy for destroying British industry. Rather than concentrating on particular areas, the targets changed constantly, diluting the effectiveness of the damage caused. For three years the civilian population experienced a respite, but the aerial threat would resume in June 1944 with the advent of Hitler's 'V' weapons – flying bombs and rockets which would be largely directed at London and Belgium.

All civilians were in the same boat during the Blitz, doing their bit to defend the home front from enemy attack, and as such the communal spirit was stressed wherever possible in order to ensure that people helped their neighbours and collectively overcame the threat. By the end of the Blitz over 40,000 British civilians had been killed as a direct result of German bombing, with 46,000 injured and a million homes damaged, yet the country had battled through it. This 'Blitz Spirit' in the face of adversity is still remembered today as an important characteristic of the war on the home front.

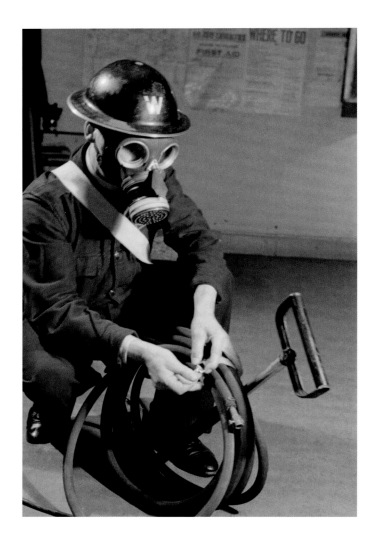

An ARP Warden wearing a gas mask tidies the hose of his stirrup pump at an ARP post in Britain, 1940.

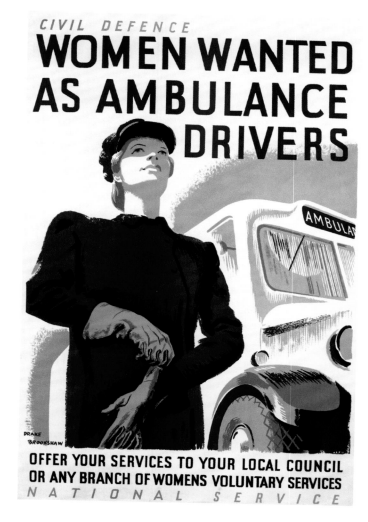

As these recruitment posters from around 1940 show, both men and women were targeted for ARP work, while specific campaigns were aimed at those men over the age of 30 who could contribute to the war effort as firemen or in the other emergency services.

CHAPTER TEN

The Fall of Singapore
The Governor's Final Broadcast

31 January 1942

At the southern tip of the Malay Peninsula lies the island of Singapore. For many decades, Singapore's importance to the British was as a military base designed to protect their colonies and economic interests in the Far East. Nicknamed 'the Gibraltar of the East', Singapore's military fortress was considered impregnable and, since the early nineteenth century, had developed into an important trading post with a booming population.

At this time, Japan remained the great military threat in the Far East and British military planners had considered the likely strategy which the Imperial Japanese Army might follow if attacking British interests. A certain over-confidence existed on the part of the British, who placed greater importance on their naval presence in the region as opposed to defending the island of Singapore itself in a purely military sense. Ultimately, Britain would suffer from being faced by an enemy who relied on the strength and mobility of infantry soldiers for its fighting effort rather than concentrating its resources on a more conventional naval attack.

On the morning of 7 December 1941, the Japanese launched a surprise attack on the United States naval base located at Pearl Harbor, Hawaii. Shortly before 8am local time, hundreds of Japanese aircraft targeted the base and caused immense destruction to ships and aircraft, leading to huge loss of life. 2,403 Americans were killed and 1,178 others wounded. The operation was a preventative one designed to put the US Pacific Fleet out of commission, thereby ensuring that it was unable to interfere with the larger Japanese assault planned for South-East Asia.

Virtually concurrent with this attack, the Japanese began a massive invasion of the Malay Peninsula and Thailand. Strategic bombing of Singapore also began and, while the attack on Malaya was initially resisted by the British Indian Army and other Commonwealth units, the speed and ferocity of the invaders meant that they quickly swept southwards. Singapore's main naval force, headed by the capital ships HMS *Prince of Wales* and HMS *Repulse,* sailed north to oppose enemy landings along the Malayan coast, yet both ships were sunk by Japanese aircraft on 10 December, leaving the coast open to amphibious landings.

This and subsequent images in this chapter show the handwritten draft of Sir Shenton Thomas' final radio broadcast to the people of Singapore, 31 January 1942. The handwritten note at the top of the document indicates that the text is likely to have been retained for later publication.

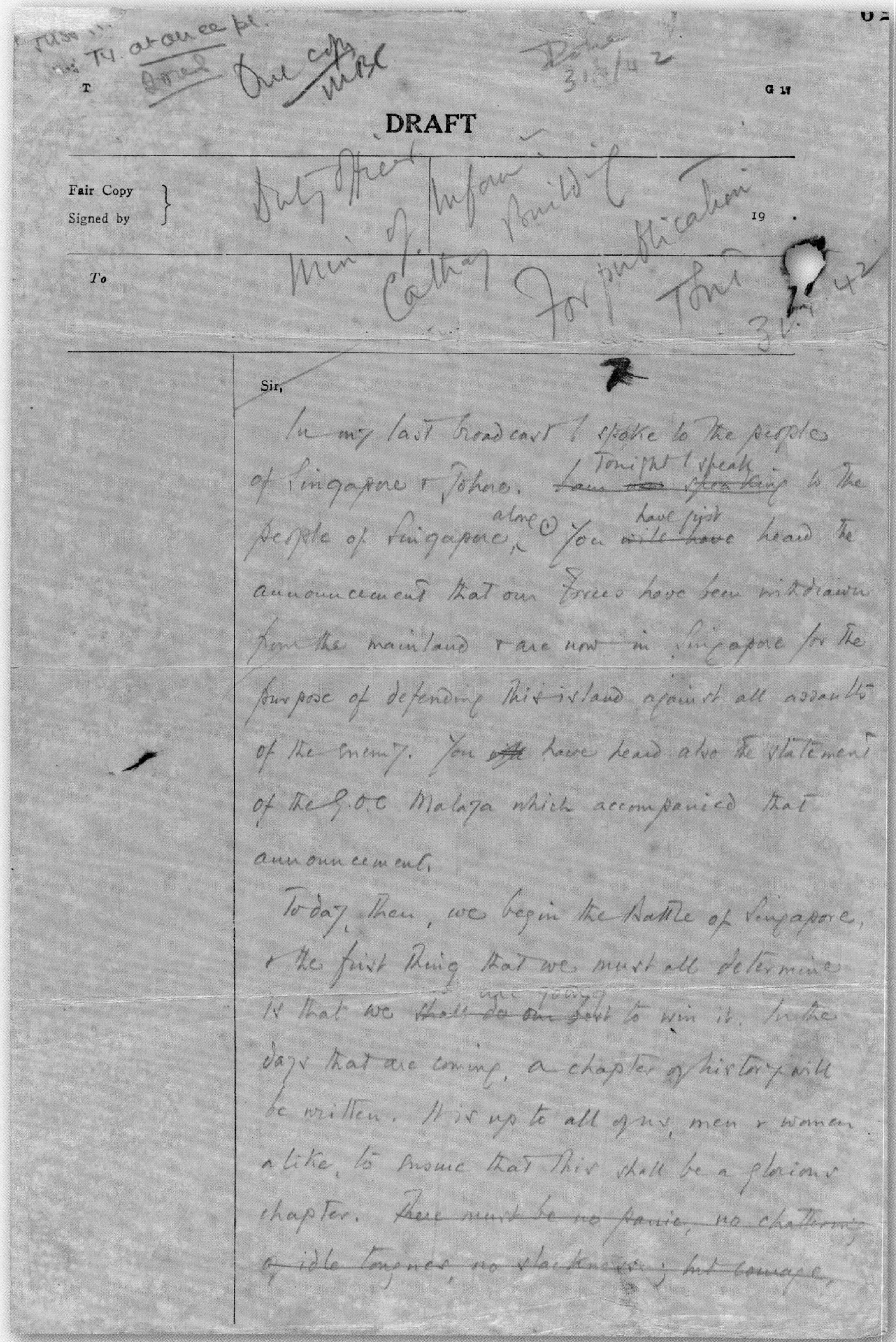
Issued ... at once pl.

One copy MBC

Done 31/1/42

T

G 17

DRAFT

Fair Copy
Signed by

Duty Officer
Min. of Inform.
Cathay Building

19

To

For publication
Tonight 31.1.42

Sir,

In my last broadcast I spoke to the people of Singapore & Johore. ~~I am now speaking~~ Tonight I speak to the people of Singapore alone. You ~~will have~~ have just heard the announcement that our forces have been withdrawn from the mainland & are now in Singapore for the purpose of defending this island against all assaults of the enemy. You ~~will~~ have heard also the statement of the G.O.C. Malaya which accompanied that announcement.

Today, then, we begin the Battle of Singapore, & the first thing that we must all determine is that we ~~shall do our best~~ are going to win it. In the days that are coming, a chapter of history will be written. It is up to all of us, men & women alike, to ensure that this shall be a glorious chapter. ~~There must be no panic, no chattering of idle tongues, no slackness; but courage,~~

Forced into retreat, the final Commonwealth forces reached Singapore on 31 January 1942 and blew up the causeway linking the island to Johore, the southernmost Malay state. Singapore was now isolated and alone.

Governor of the Straits Settlements, which included Singapore, was Sir Shenton Thomas. He had served in this position since 1934 and had warned against the likelihood of a Japanese invasion of the Malayan Peninsula, describing the country as the 'dollar arsenal of the Empire' due to the tin mines and extensive rubber plantations which made the territory a rich prize. His regular radio broadcasts throughout the Malayan campaign had been aimed to inspire fortitude in the face of the Japanese attack, and it was with a heavy heart that he began his final speech on the evening of 31 January 1942:

In my last broadcast I spoke to the people of Singapore and Johore. Tonight I speak to the people of Singapore alone. You have just heard the announcement that our forces have been withdrawn from the mainland and are now in Singapore for the purpose of defending this island against all assaults of the enemy.

Today, then, we begin the Battle of Singapore, and the first thing that we must all determine is that we are going to win it. In the days that are coming, a chapter of history will be written. It is up to all of us, men and women alike, to ensure that this shall be a glorious chapter.

The G.O.C [General Officer Commanding] has told you that our forces are here, and will stay here, to carry out the high task of defending this island, to fight until

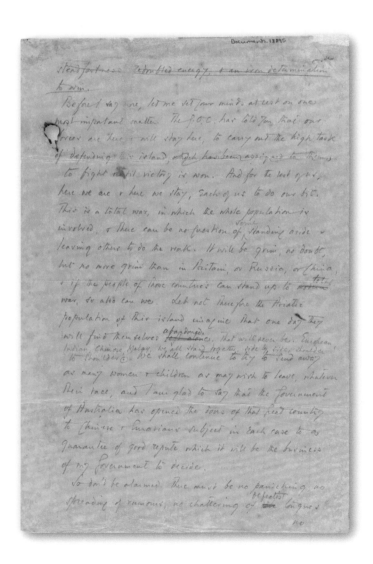

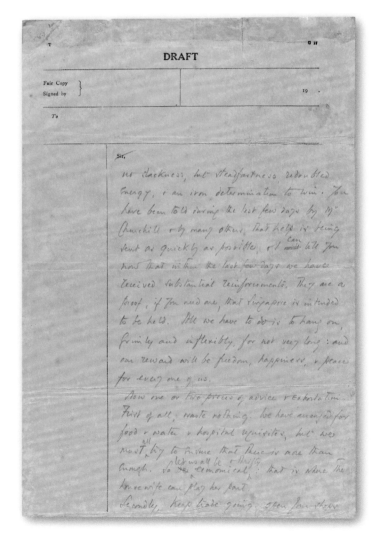

victory is won. And for the rest of us, here we are and here we stay, each of us to do our bit. This is a total war, in which the whole population is involved, and there can be no question of some standing aside and leaving others to do the work. It will be grim, no doubt, but no more grim than in Britain, or Russia, or China, and if the people of those countries can stand up to the total war, so also can we. Let not therefore the Asiatic population of this island imagine that one day they will find themselves abandoned. That will never be. European, Indian, Chinese, Malay, we all stand together, side by side, shoulder to shoulder.

All we have to do is hang on, firmly and inflexibly, for not very long: and our reward will be freedom, happiness and peace for every one of us.

Thomas proceeded to offer some practical instruction to those besieged on the island. While a final push by the Japanese to invade Singapore and complete their invasion of Malaysia was inevitable, the population had to prepare itself as best it could for the final battle:

We have arranged for food and water and hospital requisites, but we must all try to ensure that there is more than enough. So let us all be economical and thrifty: that is where the housewife can play her part.

Secondly, keep trade going. Open your shops and sell to those who need food.

Thirdly, work hard. Work as you never worked before... A sufficient supply of labour is vital: see that it is

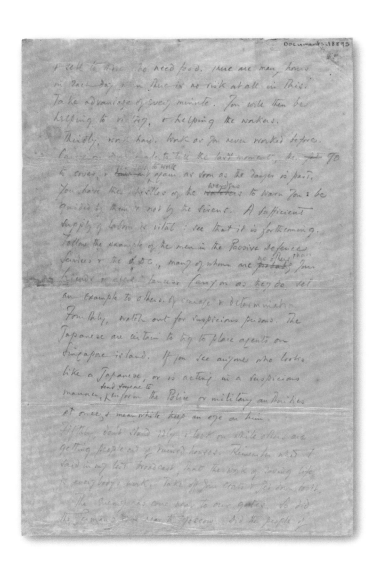

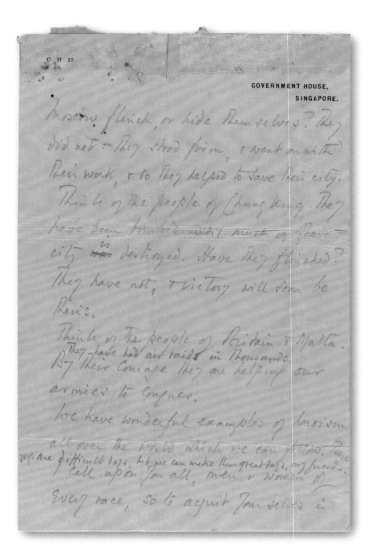

forthcoming. Follow the example of the men in the Passive Defence Services and the LDC [Local Defence Corps], many of whom are no others than your friends and acquaintances. Carry on as they do, set an example to others of courage and determination.

Fourthly, watch out for suspicious persons. The Japanese are certain to try to place agents on Singapore Island. If you see anyone who looks like a Japanese, or is acting in a suspicious manner, send someone to inform the Police or military authorities at once, and meanwhile keep an eye on him.

Fifthly, don't stand idly and look on while others are getting people out of ruined houses... the work of saving life is everybody's work.

Thomas ended his speech with a patriotic call to duty:

We have wonderful examples of heroism all over the world which we can follow. These days are difficult days, but we can make them great days, my friends. I call upon you all, men and women of every race, so to acquit yourselves in the days to come that, when victory is won, the people of Singapore will be judged worthy to be classed with the people of London, Chungking and Moscow. We have a great and a glorious opportunity: let us take it with both hands. Singapore must stand. It shall stand.

Destroying the causeway delayed the Japanese for over a week, but their invasion of the island began on 8 February. Boasting both air and sea superiority and more advanced military hardware, the Japanese victory was swift, and Singapore fell on 15 February 1942. It was the largest military surrender in British history. Winston Churchill expressed the disappointment and disbelief of many when he observed that 'We have so many men in Singapore, so many men – they should have done better.' Although the British preparations for a Japanese invasion and their conduct of the Malayan campaign had been poor,

British soldiers push a car into the harbour at Singapore in the days immediately before the surrender on 15 February 1942. This was part of a plan to destroy all property which would have proved useful to the Japanese.

Firefighters tackle blazing railway stock at Singapore docks after a Japanese air raid, January/February 1942.

Portrait photograph of Sir Shenton Thomas, taken in 1932 when he was appointed Governor of the Gold Coast (National Portrait Gallery).

Singapore could never have held out while surrounded on all sides and with a large civilian population that would easily have been starved into submission.

Sir Shenton Thomas entered captivity along with the rest of the civilian and military population. While initially imprisoned on the island in Changi Prison, he was eventually transferred to Formosa (now Taiwan) in August 1942 where he would remain until the end of the war. The manuscript draft of the governor's broadcast shown here was recovered by a clerk from an office in Government House in February 1942. Realising the document's historical importance as the last message broadcast by Thomas, the sheets were kept as an important wartime memento.

Singapore formally surrendered on 15 February 1942 and the island was occupied by the Japanese for the remainder of the war. Shown here are Japanese troops marching through Fullerton Square, Singapore, during the period of occupation.

CHAPTER ELEVEN

Civilian Internment in the Far East

The Changi Register

29 April 1942

Following the fall of Singapore in February 1942, the Japanese detained some 3,000 civilians in Changi Gaol, the island's existing prison accommodation located on its eastern peninsula. The prison was in fact more of a complex of buildings, as the main gaol had only been built to house 600 prisoners. The Japanese therefore took over the British Army's Selerang Barracks nearby, as well as other suitable buildings which were converted into prisoner of war and internment camps. Soon what became known as Changi Camp had taken over a massive area of 25 square kilometres. Since the Changi peninsula had been the main military base on the island during British rule, it was well suited to keep the civilian and military prisoners in safe custody.

The speed of the Japanese invasion had meant that a very large civilian population remained on the island once it had fallen into the enemy's hands. Within days of the fall of Singapore on 15 February 1942, all those of European descent were required to register and were put into temporary accommodation, being transferred to Changi at the beginning of March. Around 2,500 civilians would largely remain in captivity there for the next three and a half years, suffering from malnutrition, sickness and sometimes brutal treatment by their guards. Captured Allied troops, who were categorised separately as prisoners of war, were also held within the Changi complex of camps but in many cases ultimately transported to work camps elsewhere in Singapore and Malaya, most infamously to build the Burma – Siam Railway.

The civilian prisoners remained largely responsible for their own administration, and throughout their daily lives strived to make the most of a bad situation. Gardens were dug, concert parties set up and even an educational programme introduced. Internees were separated by gender; no contact between husbands and wives was permitted for the first 15 months of internment, with only occasional, very limited opportunities provided thereafter.

In order to facilitate their administrative responsibilities, the civilian internees in Changi set about compiling a detailed register of every man, woman or child held in the camp. Begun on (or soon after) 29 April 1942 and carefully typed on large sheets of paper which were ultimately bound into book form, the register was regularly amended by hand to note things such as deaths and discharges when they occurred. The name, age, marital status and occupation of each internee was carefully noted, together with their respective next of kin. The Register was arranged into three parts (each listing either men, women

A typical page from the register compiled by the civilian internees of Changi internment Camp, Singapore, 29 April 1942 – 1945

Number	Name	Age	Married or Single	Occupation (If not in employment, insert business, professional, etc. qualifications in brackets)	Name & Postal Address of Spouse, or (in case of children) of Parents	Name & Postal Address of Next-of-Kin who is not interned	Remarks
1256	McMICHAEL, WILLIAM Alexander. Intd. 23.2.02.	46	M	Planter.	Mrs S.M.McMichael, c/o National Provincial Bank, 19 Cromwell Place, London, England.	Mrs S.M.McMichael, c/o National Provincial Bank, 19 Cromwell Place, London, England.	Died in Camp hospital 20.1.03.
1257	McMILLAN, Kenneth. Intd. 17.2.02.	61	S	Mechanical Engineer (Retired).		Mrs F.Belcher, Box 104, Roblin, Manitoba, Canada.	PW&I C.H/23.
1258	McMULLAN, William. Intd. 6.4.02.	49	M	Printer.	Mrs E.McMullan, c/o Mrs Podger, Dower House, Bitton, Glos., England.	Mrs E.McMullan, c/o Mrs Podger, Dower House, Bitton, Glos., England.	no
1259	McNAMARA, Francis Knyvett. Intd. 5.3.02.	30	S	Police Officer.		Mrs B.Foley, 22 Heene Way, Worthing, Sussex, England.	XN/UK/1259 Int.R.C. Kuala Kangsar
1260	McNICOL, John. Intd. 17.2.02.	65	M	Planter.	Mrs S.McNicol, c/o T. Macara, 20 Denton Road, Stroud Green, London, England.	T.Macara, 20 Denton Road, Stroud Green, London, England.	XN/UK/1714 Lew & Ladas, Tecoma...
1261	McNULTY, Jeremiah Oswald. Intd. 17.2.02.	26	M	Chartered Accountant.	Mrs J.O.McNulty, c/o Bank of New South Wales, Sydney, Australia.	Mrs J.O.McNulty, c/o Bank of New South Wales, Sydney, Australia.	J/N/1281 Treasury, John Buben
1262	McPHEE, Thomas McAlpine. Intd. 17.2.02.	44	M	Engineer - Civil & Mining.	Mrs B.McPhee, 1 Knowe Terrace, Giffnock, Scotland.	Mrs B.McPhee, 1 Knowe Terrace, Giffnock, Scotland.	庚午嗎所蘇雀中。 XN/UK/2...
1263	McRAE, Robert. Intd. 23.2.02.	45	S	Engineer-Mechanical + Substitute Automobile Dealer		Mrs McRae (Mother), 12 Forrest Road, Queen's Gate, Aberdeen.	XN/UK/... 12, Forrest Rd., Aberdeen, Scotland
1264	McSWAN, David Marrison. Intd. 23.2.02.	48	M	Govt. Medical Service.	Mrs D.M.McSwan, Mansfield, Muckhart, Dollar, Perthshire, Scotland.	Mrs D.M.McSwan, Mansfield, Muckhart, Dollar, Perthshire, Scotland.	XN/UK/1760 33, Woodhall Rd., ... Edinburgh
1265	MEAKIN, William James. Intd. 17.2.02.	17	S	Merchant Seaman.		Mrs A.Meakin, 13 Park Ave. Chorlton, Manchester, England.	no
1266	MEARNS, James Godsman. Intd. 17.2.02.	40	S	Rubber Planter.		Mrs J.G.Mearns (Mother), 135 Mid Stocket Road, Aberdeen, Scotland.	XN/UK/1183 15, Mid Stocket Rd., Aberdeen Scotland
1267	MEARS, Henry Montford. Intd. 24.2.02.	52	M	Rubber Planter.	Mrs E.Mears, c/o Miss Anderson, 9 Gt.Western Place, Aberdeen, Scotland.	Mrs E.Mears, c/o Miss Anderson, 9 Gt.Western Place, Aberdeen, Scotland.	no
1268	MEDCALFE-MOORE, John. Intd. 1.4.02.	30	M	Radio Engineer.	Mrs M.Medcalfe-Moore, 1225 West 14th Ave., Vancouver, British Columbia, Canada.	Mrs A.Moore, 3 Howard Road, Olton, Birmingham, England.	266/17 Telecommunications Dept. Penang
1269	MEKIE, David Eric Cameron. Intd. 25.3.02.	40	M	Surgeon.	Mrs Mekie, c/o Bank of New South Wales, Perth, W.Australia.	Mrs Mekie, c/o Knott, 42 Argyle Place, Edinburgh, Scotland.	no
1270	MENZIES, Thomas Hutchison. Intd. 17.2.02.	56	M	Planter.	Mrs M.A.Menzies, c/o I.C. Menzies, 22 Rutland St., Edinburgh, Scotland.	I.C.Menzies, 22 Rutland Street, Edinburgh, Scotland.	N/XN/AN29 the Shetland Bank, Liverpool?
1271	MENZIES, William Henry. Intd. 17.2.02.	43	S	Company Representative.		Mrs W.Menzies, Gershoiling, 19 Havelock St., Helensburgh, Dumbartonshire, Scotland.	no
1272	MERRIFIELD, George James. Intd. 17.2.02.	37	S	Prison Officer.		Mrs A.Merrifield, Ditcheat Mr.Evercreech, Bath, Somerset, England.	XN/UK/... Prison Malacca

or children below the age of thirteen) and subdivided by nationality. The way in which the information was ordered allows it to now be interpreted in many useful ways.

The different nationalities alone tell their own stories. The largest numbers were of course for British internees, with 282 women and over 2,000 men. The number of the latter was increased on 3 June 1942 after 19 Southern Irish men asked to be transferred to the list of British nationals. Australians were the next largest group with 23 women and 127 men, then Eurasians (those of mixed European and Asian ancestry) with 23 and 101 respectively. As well as representatives from other Dominion countries, Changi held a single internee from each of Malta, Mauritius and the British West Indies. The Register records ten American men as internees, although not included in their number was the boxer Al Rivers. A sportsman well-known in the late 1930s, Rivers registered under his true name of Alexander Wercolor and declared himself Ukrainian, presumably in the hope of obtaining better treatment as a neutral.

The oldest internee recorded appears to have been the 79-year-old barrister Frances John Bryant, while the youngest was the one-month-old Alexander John Clark. Alexander would lose his claim to fame on 14 June 1942, when details of the two-week-old John Morris were added.

With regard to the internees' occupations, it was perhaps predictable that the majority had worked in government, whether it was the Malayan Civil Service, the judiciary, the police and prisons, the health services, post offices or railways. Despite having been ordered to leave the island prior to occupation due to their technical knowledge, some had been employed by the Harbour and Marine authorities. As well as those who had worked on rubber plantations, in tin mines, as ministers, lawyers and accountants, there were department store managers, opticians and journalists. Some of the more unusual trades included a Dutch violin teacher, a swimming pool superintendent and a piano tuner. One gentleman of no fixed abode simply described himself as a traveller. The great and the good received the same treatment as everybody else. Sir Shenton Thomas, whose occupation was given as Governor of the Straits Settlement, was listed as internee number 1780 between Thomas John Thomas (school master) and William Percival Thomas (Master Mariner).

The civilian internees were moved out of Changi Gaol in May 1944 to a camp at Sime Road, to make room for an influx of military prisoners who had survived constructing the Burma Railway. As Sime Road was larger than the Gaol, just over a thousand more people were interned including the British Jewish community of Singapore. Although the British would remain the majority nationality of internees in Singapore throughout the war, the final roll call of civilian prisoners when the war ended in August 1945 would include more than twenty different nationalities, emphasising the international composition of the Allies.

This unique watercolour painting by Miss Gladys Tompkins, a civilian internee at Changi Camp, Singapore, shows an outside view of the Gaol.

from Rose Garden - Changi Prison 1942 - 1944

Photographs of life inside Japanese internment camps are incredibly rare. This image shows prisoners queuing for food inside Sime Road camp, where many internees from Changi were sent towards the end of the war. The emaciated physique of the internees is evident as they await their daily ration.

Metal food bowl used by Mrs Lyra Brooks
while interned in Changi. Utensils of this kind
were often inscribed with the letters 'CP'
meaning 'Changi Prison', but internees would
often use whatever resources were at hand. ∧

These shorts were handmade by Vincent
Beck whilst he was held as a civilian internee
in Changi. Adequate clothing was often in
short supply and internees would therefore
have to use their initiative and ingenuity in
order to create their own from whatever
supplies could be obtained. 〉

CHAPTER TWELVE

The Battle of El Alamein

Winston Churchill's 'End of the Beginning' Speech

10 November 1942

The year 1942 was arguably the lowest point of the war for Britain. It was marked by a series of military setbacks and disappointments, beginning in February in the Far East with the loss of Singapore to the Japanese. Meanwhile, the main campaign being fought by the British was in North Africa. Since the end of 1940 the British Eighth Army had been fighting in the Western Desert, firstly against Italian forces who had invaded Egypt in September that year, but subsequently against the German Afrika Korps which had landed in Libya in January 1941. The Axis forces under the command of General Erwin Rommel pushed the British back towards Egypt, besieging the port of Tobruk for nine months before the British could push the enemy back. Recovering their momentum the following year, the Germans and Italians resumed their attack, capturing Tobruk and forcing the British into Egypt where they made a stand at El Alamein.

An initial, unsuccessful attempt to force the British out of their defensive position at El Alamein took place in July 1942, before the Eighth Army were reinforced and went on the offensive on 23 October. This Second Battle of El Alamein saw the fighting turn in favour of the British, who by 10 November had forced Rommel's army into retreat.

By a fortuitous coincidence the annual Lord Mayor's Banquet at the Mansion House was to be held on 10 November, when the news from North Africa was at its most positive. During the banquet the incumbent Prime Minister traditionally delivers a keynote speech, and 1942's address would therefore be a particularly important one, providing Winston Churchill with an opportunity to celebrate the first really significant British victory of the war and define it as a turning point in the conflict. Widely reported and broadcast, Churchill's speech would be remembered as one of his most important.

The copy of the Mansion House speech shown here, which remains in the care of the Imperial War Museum, is a draft bearing amendments in Churchill's own hand. While largely similar to the speech as delivered, it includes some interesting deviations which illustrate Churchill's thought-processes and skill at honing a speech of this kind to the best advantage.

Draft page from the speech delivered by British Prime Minister Winston Churchill at the Mansion House on 10 November 1942. The text, typed by Churchill's secretary Elizabeth Nel, is spaced appropriately to suit the Prime Minister's vocal delivery. The blue and red ink amendments are in Churchill's own hand.

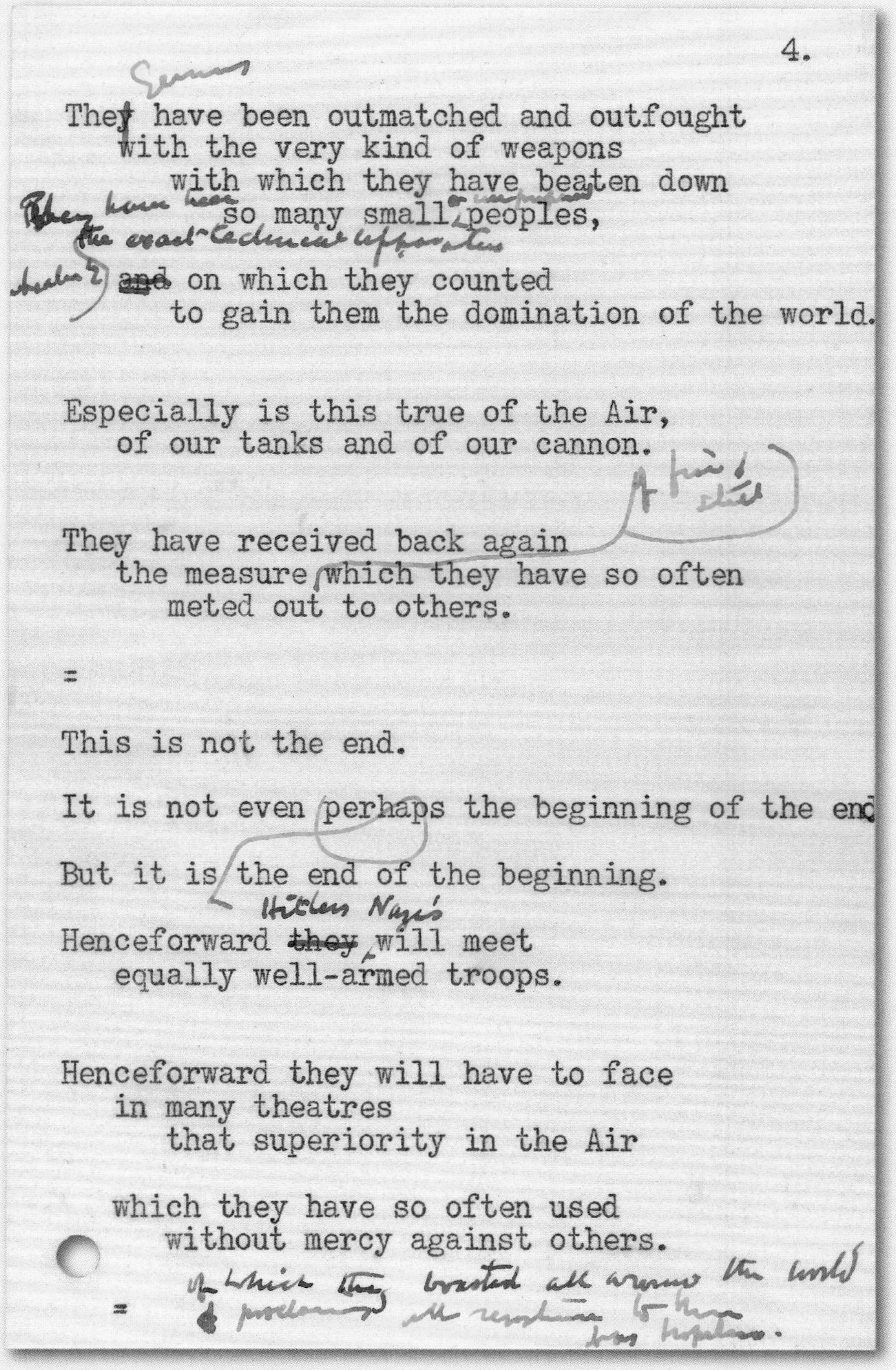

4.

Germans

They have been outmatched and outfought
   with the very kind of weapons
      with which they have beaten down
      so many small peoples,
  and on which they counted
      to gain them the domination of the world.

Especially is this true of the Air,
   of our tanks and of our cannon.

They have received back again
   the measure which they have so often
      meted out to others.

=

This is not the end.

It is not even perhaps the beginning of the end

But it is the end of the beginning.

     Hitlers Nazis
Henceforward ~~they~~ will meet
   equally well-armed troops.

Henceforward they will have to face
   in many theatres
      that superiority in the Air

   which they have so often used
      without mercy against others.
=

Churchill began by setting the scene, acknowledging that up to now the British war record had been a disappointment. He compared the present war with the earlier conflict of 1914–1918 by admitting that, up to this point, British successes had been few and far between.

> In our wars the episodes are usually adverse, but the final result is satisfactory... In the last war up till almost the end we met with continual disappointments and with disasters far more bloody than anything we have experienced so far in this; but in the end all opportunities fell together and our foes submitted themselves to our will. We have not so far in this war taken on many German prisoners as they have British, but they will no doubt come in in droves at the end, as they did last time.

For in the last few days, following the British successes in North Africa, the tide had turned. As far as Churchill was concerned, the importance of the victory at El Alamein lay not just in territorial gains but rather in the larger beneficial effect on the country's confidence and morale:

> I have never promised anything but blood, tears, toil and sweat. Now, however, we have a new experience. We have victory. A remarkable and definite victory. A bright gleam has caught the helmets of our soldiers and warmed and cheered all our hearts...

> This battle was not fought for the sake of gaining positions or desert territory. General Alexander and General Montgomery fought it with one single idea – to destroy the armed force of the enemy, and to destroy it at the place where its disaster would be most far-reaching.

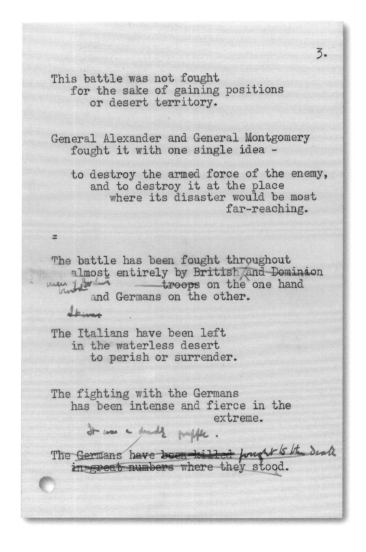

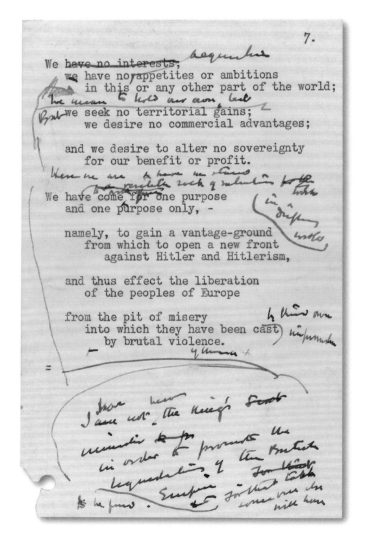

His handwritten amendments to the speech show how numerous phrases were changed, with the language simplified into a more 'Churchillian' style, appealing to his audience's deepest emotions and invoking a sense of national pride:

> The battle has been fought throughout almost entirely by ~~British and Dominion troops~~ men of British blood on the one hand and Germans on the other. The Italians have been left in the waterless desert to perish or surrender. The fighting with the Germans has been intense and fierce in the extreme. ~~The Germans have been killed in great numbers where they stood.~~ It was a deadly grapple.

Even the phrase which has become one of Churchill's most famous quotes sees a final amendment in order to improve its rhythm and make the statement more memorable:

This is not the end. It is not even ~~perhaps~~ the beginning of the end. But it is (perhaps) the end of the beginning.

To celebrate the victory at El Alamein and emphasise its importance, Downing Street promptly issued a decree that church bells were to be rung prior to morning service on Sunday 15 November. The significance of this edict lies in the fact that the ringing of church bells had been banned since June 1940, unless to give warning of an imminent German invasion. For a population used to wartime

⌄ A selection of pages – with handwritten amendments – from Churchill's speech.

restrictions, one can only imagine the uplifting feeling of this brief return to normality.

The future did indeed seem brighter than before. Two days before Churchill's speech, the Allied invasion of Axis-controlled North Africa had begun under the codename of Operation 'Torch', and the Italians and Germans would ultimately be driven out of Libya and suffer final defeat in Tunisia. This would mark the opening of the much longed-for second front, relieving pressure on the Soviet forces fighting for the Allies on the Eastern Front whilst also preparing the way for an invasion of southern Europe the following year.

Churchill attracted controversy throughout his career, yet was a hugely respected statesman whose qualities of sober steadfastness and determination, often combined with a dry wit, proved to be exactly what Britain needed to inspire its population to fight. While some modern studies have argued that Churchill's speeches were not as widely regarded at the time as is now commonly thought, it certainly remained the case that his detractors were greatly outnumbered by those who saw him as an inspiring war leader. Churchill's speeches and oratory played a crucial role in establishing him as the face of British resoluteness, and would inspire further victories over the subsequent years of the war.

Winston Churchill makes a radio address from his desk at 10 Downing Street, wearing one of his famous 'siren suits', June 1942.

'Australians storm a strongpoint'. A posed portrait of Australian troops advancing during the Second Battle of El Alamein, 3 September 1942. It was this Allied victory in North Africa which inspired Churchill's speech.

Sherman tanks of the 9th Queen's Royal Lancers during the Battle of El Alamein, 5 November 1942.

CHAPTER THIRTEEN

The Eastern Front
Adolf Hitler's Stalingrad Signal

26 November 1942

Hitler's attitude towards the Soviet Union was governed by Nazi ideas of racial purity (which portrayed Slavic people as inferior), coupled with the *Lebensraum* concept of repopulating annexed territories with German speakers. The Bolshevik Soviet Union was anathema to National Socialism, and the most western areas of Soviet territory were targeted for takeover by the expanding Third Reich. This would provide the Reich with important agricultural land and oil reserves, together with an enormous amount of slave labour. The earlier Nazi-Soviet Pact, a neutrality agreement designed in part to facilitate the mutual-annexation of Poland, was effectively terminated on 22 June 1941 when Operation 'Barbarossa' was launched – the German invasion of the Soviet Union.

Barbarossa proved to be one of the largest military campaigns ever put into operation, involving an invasion force of some 4 million Axis troops attacking over a massive 1,800 mile front. The Germans achieved great initial success, capturing important economic areas of the Ukraine before moving towards Moscow. But it was during their attack on the besieged Russian capital that the German advance was halted in October, and a ferocious Russian counter-offensive at the end of the year drove the German Army from the city, forcing them into a war of attrition.

As winter closed in, bringing respite to the campaign, Hitler could assess the German progress on the Eastern Front. They had established a long but stable front line and, despite suffering heavy losses in the Battle of Moscow, the Nazis remained numerically strong. Barbarossa had shown that a wide large-scale attack was unlikely to succeed against the Russians, and the Germans therefore decided on a more concentrated attack towards the south, targeting the oil fields of the Caucasus.

Although originally planned to begin in May 1942, the Axis attack was delayed by other operations including the Second Battle of Kharkov. Here, an attack by the Red Army was foiled by a successful Axis counter-offensive, leading to significant Soviet casualties. But it was not therefore until 28 June that Army Group South began its advance into southern Russia. Initially the advance was overwhelmingly successful, and by the end of July they had crossed the River Don.

Signal sent by Adolf Hitler to inspire his troops besieged in Stalingrad, 26 November 1942. The document has been personally 'signed' with Hitler's name by his Chief Wehrmacht Adjutant, General Rudolf Schmundt.

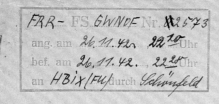

26. 11. 1942.

Soldaten der 6. Armee und der 4.Panzer-Armee !

Der Kampf um S t a l i n g r a d geht seinem Höhepunkt entgegen.

Der Feind ist im Rücken der deutschen Truppen durchgebrochen und versucht nunmehr verzweifelt, dieses für ihn ausschlaggebende Bollwerk an der Wolga wieder in seinen Besitz zu bringen.

Mit mir sind in diesen schweren Stunden die Gedanken des ganzen deutschen Volkes bei Euch !

Jhr müsst die unter der Führung tatkräftiger Generale mit soviel Blut eroberte Position Stalingrad unter allen Umständen halten !

Es muss unser unabänderlicher Entschluss sein: dass, so wie im Frühjahr bei Charkow, auch dieser Durchbruch des Russen am Ende durch die eingeleiteten

It is perhaps this initial success which encouraged Hitler to step in and personally change the plan for the campaign, an act which in hindsight may have cost the Germans ultimate victory. Hitler decided to split his Army Group South into two halves – the first (Army Group A) would continue south towards the Caucasus as planned, while the other force (Army Group B) would mount a concentrated attack on the city of Stalingrad and the River Volga. The destruction of a key centre of Soviet industry and the opportunity to block the important transport route of the Volga were clear motivations, while the capture of a city which bore the name of the Soviet leader would prove particularly significant. In addition, Hitler decided to add the 4th Panzer Army to the main southern attack. This only caused traffic jams and confusion, which led him to then reverse the decision and direct the 4th Panzers towards Stalingrad instead. This delayed the German advance by at least a week and allowed the Russians to rally themselves in readiness for the attack; everybody, both military and civilian, was called to take up arms in defence of their country.

By the end of August, Army Group A had advanced significantly into the Caucasus, but any further progress was thwarted by their poor supply lines. Meanwhile Army Group B reached the outskirts of Stalingrad on 23 August and began their sustained attack on the city. An intensive months-long bombing campaign by the Luftwaffe soon reduced much of the city to rubble, but the Axis forces met a strong Soviet resistance within the crumbling buildings and rubble-strewn streets. With both sides throwing reinforcements into the battle, any German progress in the advance was slow, and both sides suffered enormous losses.

A Russian counter-attack was launched on 19 November which saw the Red Army attempt to target the weaker forces defending the Axis flanks. This led to the German 6th Army and 4th Panzer Army being effectively encircled and cut off within Stalingrad. The situation was desperate and Hitler issued a signal, shown here, designed to inspire and encourage his troops. Printed in the large typeface characteristic of the Führer, the signal was signed in Hitler's name by his Chief Wehrmacht Adjutant, General Rudolf Schmundt:

Soldiers of the 6th Army and of the 4th Panzer Army!

The Battle for Stalingrad is approaching its climax.

The enemy has broken through behind the German troops and is now desperately seeking to recapture this crucial stronghold on the Volga.

In these difficult hours my thoughts and those of the entire German people are with you!

You must in all circumstances hold the Stalingrad position, which has been taken under the leadership of enterprising generals with the loss of so much blood!

It must be our firm decision that this breakthrough by the Russians, like the one in Kharkov in the spring, will in the end and by the means adopted result in their annihilation.

Everything that lies in my power will be done to support you in your heroic struggle.

This support came in the form of repeated military attempts to break the encirclement, coupled with the dropping of air supplies to the besieged Axis troops. Yet the stalemate could not be broken and the Battle of Stalingrad continued for two further months, only reaching a conclusion at the beginning of February 1943, once the Germans had run out of food and ammunition. What was left of the German 6th Army and 4th Panzers surrendered. From this point on, there was no doubt at all that the Germans had been beaten on the Eastern Front.

The Battle of Stalingrad had lasted for five months, one week and three days, and would be remembered as the longest and most bloody campaign of the Second World War. Soviet casualties amounted to 1.1 million, of whom nearly half a million died. The Axis forces also lost over half a million men, either killed or captured. The admiration earned by the Russians in opposing the invasion of their homeland inspired other resisters to the Nazi regime, while Hitler's clear failure to win on the Eastern Front would mark the beginning of the end for the Third Reich.

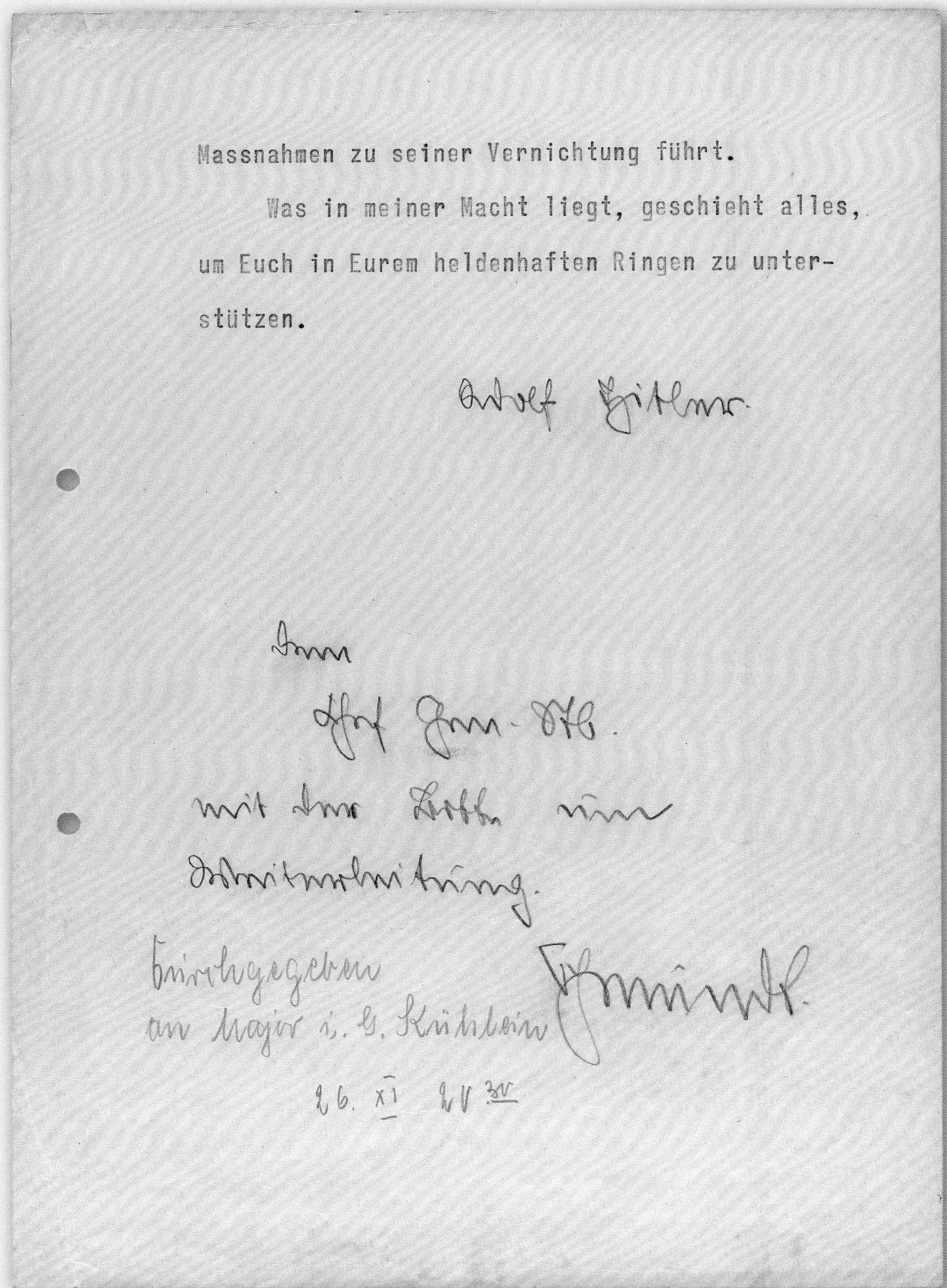

Massnahmen zu seiner Vernichtung führt.

Was in meiner Macht liegt, geschieht alles, um Euch in Eurem heldenhaften Ringen zu unterstützen.

Adolf Hitler

Dem

Chef Gen-Stb.

mit der Bitte um

Weiterleitung.

Schmundt

Durchgegeben
an Major i. G. Kühlein

26. XI 24 30

Soviet infantry in action in the ruins of Stalingrad. The nature of the battle meant that much close fighting ensued, with the ruins of the city providing a dangerous environment for the siege.

Hitler, shown here studying campaign maps on 12 September 1939, took a keen personal interest in directing the campaign on the Eastern Front.

A pall of smoke hanging over Stalingrad as German infantry move into the outskirts of the city, September 1942. To capture such a key Russian stronghold would result in a great victory for the Axis powers, yet the battle did not go according to plan.

CHAPTER FOURTEEN

Secret Operations

Operation 'Mincemeat' Plans

4 April 1943

Efficient military planning requires a very high level of secrecy in order to ensure that the enemy is kept in the dark. With this in mind, British Intelligence worked hard throughout the war to establish different strategies for disinformation and deception, aiming to cause confusion within the enemy intelligence services and hide the Allies' real aims and objectives wherever possible.

This need for secrecy had been highlighted by an event which occurred just prior to Operation 'Torch', the Allied invasion of French North Africa in November 1942. A British aircraft crashed off the coast of Spain whilst en route to Gibraltar, and a body and various papers were washed up on shore shortly afterwards. It was later learned that some of the secret papers had been seen and acted upon by the Germans. With this in mind, a 'Trojan Horse' scheme began to be considered within British Intelligence circles which involved a deliberate emulation of this original accident. The initial stages of the deception plan began to be put into place, so that it could be executed once opportunity permitted.

In early 1943 the Allies decided to stage an invasion of the Axis-held island of Sicily, as a first step towards launching a full scale invasion of Italy. Operation 'Husky'

was planned for the beginning of July and would involve a major amphibious and airborne operation. It was absolutely essential that the Germans should not reinforce the island in preparation for the attack.

British Intelligence decided to use their 'Trojan Horse' idea in order to convince the Germans that Sicily was not the intended target for 'Husky'. On 4 April 1943 the following briefing paper was circulated at a high level, marked 'Most Secret':

> It is probable that any document, purporting to be a British official document, which is washed ashore in the Huelva area of Spain will be handed over to the Germans, or at least photographed for them. It is proposed to cause a dead body, dressed in British Officer's uniform, to be washed ashore in the Huelva area together with a bag and other articles as if they had gradually been washed ashore after an aircraft crash while en route to AFHQ from England. All arrangements have been made with the appropriate British authorities in Spain and the body has been

This original briefing paper outlines the deception plan, already given the codename Operation 'Mincemeat', which aimed to mislead the Germans as to the true target for the Allied invasion of Sicily.

OPERATION "MINCEMEAT"

OBJECT

It is desired to place in the hands of the German Intelligence Service some really convincing information which will mislead them as to the objective of HUSKY.

CONSIDERATIONS

2.   It is considered that one way in which this can be effected would be to plant on the enemy a high level document which should disclose:-

(a) what purports to be the real objective.

(b) what purports to be the cover or deception objective.

3.   It is probable that any document, purporting to be a British official document, which is washed ashore in the Huelva area of Spain will be handed over to the Germans, or at least photographed for them.

PLAN

4.   It is proposed to cause a dead body, dressed in British Officer's uniform, to be washed ashore in the Huelva area together with a bag (containing inter alia the document mentioned in para. 2 above) and other articles as if they had gradually been washed ashore after an aircraft crash while en route to A.F.H.Q. from England.

5.   All arrangements have been made with the appropriate British authorities in Spain and the body has been prepared together with all necessary documents and other "properties" to lend verisimilitude. The operation will be carried out by H.M. S/M SERAPH (P.219) (which is commanded by Lt. Jewell, M.B.E., R.N. who has had experience of most secret operations) while en route for Gibraltar after leaving this country on 18th or 19th April.   The probable date of the operation will be 28th April.

6.   The crucial letter from V.C.I.G.S. to General Alexander giving the facts mentioned in para. 2 above is attached.   It has been approved by Colonel Dudley Clarke who is in charge of the deception for HUSKY.   The letter is considered to be one which will be accepted as authentic by the Germans for the following reasons:-

(a) It is passing between persons who are not only "in the know" but also on a high enough level to exclude the possibility of mistake.

(b) The tenor and tone of the letter are such that the Germans are likely to accept it as an "off the record" negotiation between two officers who are personal friends and working in harmony.

(c) The purported real objective is not blatantly mentioned although very clearly indicated.

(d) The Germans will on this occasion be looking for a cover or deception objective and this is given to them.

(e) The purported cover or deception objectives include SICILY which they are already appreciating as one of the most probable of our real objectives, and will also explain our later preparations which may point more clearly to that island.

/Recommendations

MOST SECRET

WARNING: This message must first be paraphrased if it
is essential to communicate it to persons
outside British or Allied Government Services.

MOST SECRET	MESSAGE	151451B/April	IN
FROM F.O.S.		Date 15.4.43.	
		Recd. 1615.	

NAVAL CYPHER 'A.1.' BY T/P   CORRECTION

Addressed Capt.(S) 3 Repeated Admiralty C. in C. Western
Approaches H.Q.C.C. C. in C. Plymouth F.O.I/C.
Gibraltar H.M.S. SERAPH.

IMPORTANT

Capt.(S) 3 is to sail H.M.S. SERAPH for Gibraltar
on 19th April on route ROSE repeated ROSE.   H.M.S. SERAPH
is to be ordered to carry out operation MINCEMEAT in
accordance with verbal orders already received by
Commanding Officer establishing patrol for this purpose
in area between Meridian 006 degs. 30' West and 008 degs.
00' West and North of 036 degs. 40' North.   H.M.S.
SERAPH is to be ordered to report to F.O.I/C. Gibraltar
when operation is completed and to request onward route.

2.   F.O.I/C. Gibraltar is requested to arrange total
bombing restrictions in this area from 0001B 29th April.

151451B.

Advance copy sent Duty Capt. D.O.D.(H)

V.C.N.S.
A.C.N.S.(F)(2)
A.C.N.S.(H)
U.W.R.
N.A.(Mails)
Capt. Pim.
D.O.D.(F)(2)
D.O.D.(H)(2)
D.D.O.D.(M)
Duty Capt.(2)
D.D.I.C.(2)
D. of P.(2)
D.A/S.W.
D.T.D.(M)
Hd. of M.
V.D.
I.P.(2)
D.N.I.(4)
Dep. Contr.   }Bath.
EML.   Hd. of S.W.R. }

This signal outlines the specific role of HMS *Seraph* in delivering its secret cargo. Note how the order specifies that any bombing operations in the relevant area are to be avoided to ensure that the secret mission is not disrupted unexpectedly.

Once the body was 'delivered', this secret signal written by Montagu sought to ensure that the Spanish authorities were aware that the body was carrying papers of some importance which the British wanted to have returned.

Wt. 22293/P6141. 10,500 pads. 9/42. A.G. Ltd. 51-5434.

POSTAGRAM OR MESSAGE (*Delete as necessary*) OUT.

FOR WAR REGISTRY USE ONLY.

PASS TO:—

ADDRESSED   DATE 4. 5. 43.

N.A. MADRID (Personal)   MOST SECRET

IMMEDIATE

~~SECRET.~~
~~CONFIDENTIAL.~~   } *Delete as*
~~NON-CONFIDENTIAL.~~   *necessary*

From D.N.I. (Personal):

Your 021738. Some of papers Major Martin had in his possession are of great importance and secrecy. Make formal demand for all papers and notify me by personal signal immediately of addressees of any official letters recovered. Such letters should be returned addressed to Commodore Rushbrooke, Personal, by fastest safe route and should not repetition not be opened or tampered with in any way. If no official letters are recovered make searching but discreet enquiries at Huelva and Madrid to find whether they were washed ashore and if so what has happened to them.

041321

E.M.Montagu

N.I.D. 12
(Ext. 193)

Approved D.D.N.I.(H)

D.N.I. (2 only)

prepared together with all necessary documents and other 'properties' to lend verisimilitude.

The body would be that of a 34-year-old man named Glyndwr Michael, a homeless labourer who had committed suicide by swallowing rat poison. After having died in a hospital in Fulham on 28 January, his body was removed and kept in great secrecy for several months until required. The operation involved dressing this corpse as a Major in the Royal Marines and giving it the false identity of 'William Martin', complete with appropriate identification documents and other papers which would give the body a personality and fake background. These included a photograph of Major Martin's fiancée, a receipt for an engagement ring, a theatre ticket stub and other evidence indicating that the officer had been alive and well in London just days before the recovery of the body.

The key document intended to be found by the Germans with the body was a letter written by Lieutenant General Sir Archibald Nye, Vice-Chief of the Imperial General Staff, to General Alexander, who was in command of the 18th Army Group in North Africa. This letter suggested that the targets for the forthcoming Allied operation would be Greece and Sardinia, with the real target of Sicily only intended as a feint. As the briefing document explained, it was hoped that the letter would be accepted as authentic by the Germans for the following reasons:

(a) It is passing between persons who are not only 'in the know' but also on a high enough level to exclude the possibility of mistake.

(b) The tenor and tone of the letter are such that the Germans are likely to accept it as an 'off the record' negotiation between two officers who are personal friends and working in harmony.

(c) The purported real objective is not blatantly mentioned although very clearly indicated.

(d) The Germans will on this occasion be looking for a cover or deception objective and this is given to them.

(e) The purported cover or deception objectives include SICILY which they are already appreciating as one of the most probable of our real objectives, and will also explain our later preparations which may point more clearly to that island.

The deception plan, designated Operation 'Mincemeat', was given the official go-ahead by Churchill on 16 April. At 4.30am on 30 April, the body of 'Major Martin' was launched into the sea from the British submarine HMS *Seraph*, and left to drift just over a mile off the southern Spanish coast. A rubber dinghy was also launched at the same time, upside down and with one paddle missing, about half a mile further south. HMS *Seraph* then retired, disappearing beneath the waves.

A short time later a Spanish fisherman saw an object floating in the sea and hailed a small launch close by, which picked up Major Martin's body. The corpse was taken to the naval commandant in Huelva, where a post-mortem examination concluded that the man's death was due to drowning, having fallen into the sea while still alive and been in the water for at least 15 days. The body was then released by the Spanish authorities and buried (as 'Major William Martin') with full military honours in Nuestra Señora cemetery, in Huelva.

The all-important briefcase, containing the 'secret' documents, was in due course returned to Britain via the diplomatic bag. However, on receipt the documents were forensically examined and it was discovered that they had indeed been covertly opened by the Spanish authorities. As was the intention, the information had been read, photographed and passed via Nazi sympathizers to German intelligence representatives in Spain.

The success of Operation 'Mincemeat' can be measured by the confidential minutes recording staff meetings between Hitler and his various commanders. The German naval conference held on 14 May 1943 is particularly relevant:

> The military problem of where the Allies would next strike was still unsolved. While Doenitz was in Italy, however, an Allied order had been discovered and shown to Hitler, pointing to Sardinia and the Peloponnesus as the next Allied objective. At the conference between Hitler and Doenitz, Hitler showed that he accepted this information as true and laid his plans accordingly.

This official notification from Churchill, dated 16 April 1943, authorised Operation 'Mincemeat' to proceed. The body of 'Major Martin' had already been prepared by this time, and it was just a question of receiving the Prime Minister's go-ahead before the deception plan could be executed.

D.N.I.

Lt. Cdr. Montagu.

<u>MOST SECRET</u>

<u>D.N.I.</u>

     The Prime Minister has
approved the proposed plan for
Operation "Mincemeat" and has
directed that General Eisenhower
should be informed of the plan.

     Brigadier Hollis is making
the necessary arrangements in
this connection.   (C.O.S.(43)
77th (O) Conclusions, Item 9)

         Secretary to First Sea Lord.
           16th April, 1943.

By the end of June, the number of German troops sent to Sardinia had been doubled, while seven additional German divisions were transferred to Greece and ten additional divisions to the Balkans. The Allied invasion of Sicily was launched on 9 July and, as had been the intention, proved a huge surprise to the German defenders. In just over a month the island was fully captured by the Allies, and the lack of enemy reinforcements had proven to be a deciding factor in the success. 'Mincemeat' had been well and truly swallowed.

A wartime portrait photograph of Captain Ewen Montagu RNR, one of the key Naval Intelligence officers behind Operation 'Mincemeat'.

HMS *Seraph* returns home to Portsmouth on Christmas Eve 1943. Earlier that year, the submarine had played a crucial role in delivering 'Major Martin' to Spain as part of Operation 'Mincemeat'.

CHAPTER FIFTEEN

Prisoners of War

'Wooden Horse' Escape Documents

29 October 1943

When the Germans constructed the prisoner of war camp designated Stalag Luft III in March 1942, its location near the town of Sagan in modern-day Poland was chosen very purposely. The loose ground consisting of sandy yellow soil would make any tunnelling activities very difficult and ensure that surreptitious disposal of the soil would be nigh on impossible.

Run by the Luftwaffe, the camp was intended to house captured Allied airmen. It was here that Flight Lieutenant Eric Williams arrived in early 1943, having been shot down during a bomber raid over Germany on 17–18 December the previous year. Since then, Williams had gained a reputation as a troublesome prisoner, having escaped briefly from another camp before being recaptured. While it remained the responsibility of every British officer to attempt to escape or cause disruption to his captors, the Germans believed that the high security at Sagan would remove any thoughts of further such disobedience.

Williams would have quickly realised the difficulties faced in attempting to escape from Stalag Luft III. As well as the problems caused by the sandy soil, the camp had been constructed in a very deliberate fashion in order to deter tunnelling. The prisoner accommodation was raised slightly above ground level so as to allow for inspections below each building. In addition, the camp was fitted with seismograph microphones, which could identify the sound of digging – especially when monitored at night.

The plan which Williams instigated, together with his fellow officers Michael Codner and Oliver Philpot, proved to be ingenious. They would create an opportunity for themselves to dig an escape tunnel in plain sight of their captors during daylight hours. A report subsequently written by Philpot describes how they went about putting the plan into operation:

> A hollow vaulting horse, light but strong, was constructed by Wing Commander Maw DFC out of some stolen pieces of wood and the three-ply from Canadian Red Cross boxes. This was carried by four men and used to be placed quite openly close to the wire. Vaulting then took place and when finished the horse was taken back to the canteen building, where it was housed. The horse itself was in fact quite a good athletic horse and the Germans accepted it as such.

Forged identity documents used during the 'Wooden Horse' escape from Stalag Luft III, 29 October 1943. Prisoners of war became extremely skilled at creating impressive forgeries like these, often stealing real documents from which to create convincing fakes.

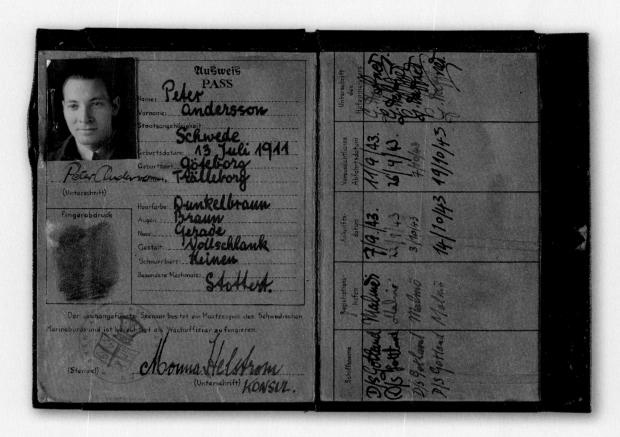

The real object was to have the horse to conceal the entrance to a tunnel, the advantages being twofold: firstly, it was near the wire, secondly, the entrance of the tunnel was thus in a highly original spot – out in the open flat ground in full view of everybody, British and German alike, except that there was nothing to see, since after work was completed the hole was boarded over and carefully covered with sand to resemble the adjacent surface. It could be, and was frequently, walked over.

The method of work was as follows: when the horse was taken out for a vaulting session one of us would be inside in its belly. This person would then open up the trap, work at the tunnel, fill with sand 12 bags (consisting of cut-off trouser legs below the knee) and hang these bags inside the horse. He would then close the trap, taking a long time to cover it over carefully, squeeze himself into one end of the horse, and be carried off.

The problem remained as to how they would dispose of the soil, although once again their ingenuity saved the day. The three officers were aided by their fellow prisoners, comrades who assisted them selflessly in the knowledge that they would not be able to escape themselves:

Disposal of the sand was the usual nightmare difficulty and in all about ten methods were used, two of which were found by the Germans who felt there was something going on but they didn't know what. We settled down to using chiefly the canteen roof and the space under the barber's shop in the canteen. The scheme began on July 8th and was, of course, very slow due to the limited amount of sand which could be removed at any one time. Codner and Williams did the first 40 feet alone, going down in turns, working entirely naked and 'side stroking' the sand down the tunnel to the entrance. The work was tiring and the air was poor.

Throughout we had quite extraordinary luck in evading detection. One day 'Charlie', the German security Unteroffizier, walked up to within 6 feet of the horse when operations were proceeding and suggested that the vaulters would find it easier if they had a springboard. They agreed.

Finally the tunnel was nearing completion and on 29 October 1943 the final stages were completed, as Williams later described:

We had arranged to break the tunnel at 1800 hours in order to catch the Frankfurt train, which departs at 1900 hours. As we still had several feet to dig, Codner went down at 1230 hours and started to dig, filling in the tunnel behind him as he went forward. After the 1630 roll call I went down and crawled up the tunnel to send the loose sand back to Philpot, who remained in the vertical shaft to put the sand into bags to be taken back with the vaulting horse. I found the tunnel thick with steam and very hot, but Codner cheerful but extremely dirty. We all worked without ceasing until 1805 when we emerged.

We managed to reach the woods without being seen by the guard and once there we took off our black camouflage suits and hoods and cleaned one another down. We then walked to the station, where Codner bought two tickets to Frankfurt. In the booking hall of the station I came face to face with the German doctor who had been treating me in the hospital only two days before. Fortunately I had cut off my rather heavy moustache and I was not recognised.

Each man carried with him some forged identity papers, designed to substantiate their individual cover stories. Williams was to pose as a Swedish sailor, with the fake identity documents shown here all created in the camp by using whatever paper and materials were available. The forged documents included his *Ausweis* identity pass, a police permit to travel, a letter permitting him to travel on Reich business and, perhaps most inventively, two personal letters written in French together with an inscribed photograph from his 'girlfriend'.

The men managed to catch their train to Frankfurt, and Williams and Codner then made their way via local trains to the Baltic seaport of Stettin. There they managed to make contact with the local Resistance movement and obtained passage in a ship which took them to Gothenburg in neutral Sweden. They soon met up with Philpot, who had taken a different route, and all three escaped officers were in due course repatriated back home to England.

This photograph of a French girlfriend was part of the fake cover story created by the escaping officers. On the reverse of the photograph was scribbled a basic map of the local area, showing the location of the railway station from where they would attempt to journey to the nearest port.

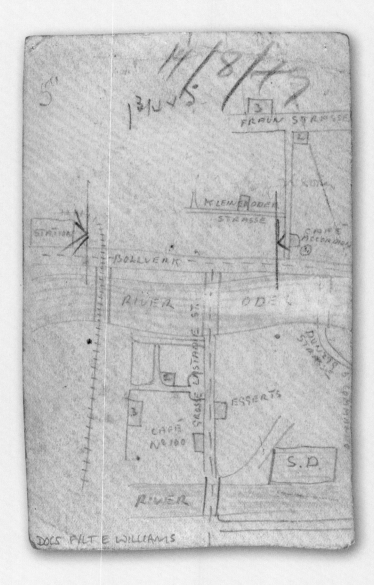

Eric Williams recorded the story of *The Wooden Horse* in a book published in 1949, to be followed the following year by a popular film adaption. However, it was another escape from Stalag Luft III in April 1944 which would become perhaps better known due to the elaborate nature of the plan, the vast number of prisoners who successfully escaped, and the harsh reprisals which followed. This 'Great Escape' was, however, undoubtedly inspired by the actions of Williams, Codner and Philpot, and their ingenious Wooden Horse.

This fake German identity document was created inside the prisoner of war camp for 'Marcel Levasseur' – in reality, Eric Williams. Its issue date was given as 2 September 1943, a month or so before the escape was finally executed.

Compass made for Oliver Philpot by Jerry Dawkins while they were both in captivity in Stalag Luft III. Dawkins, an RAF bomber pilot from Coventry, took two days to make the compass, which utilised parts from a gramophone disc, a gramophone needle, razor blades and broken watches. It was used during the 'Wooden Horse' escape on 29 October 1943.

Shown (left to right) are Michael Codner, Oliver Philpot and Eric Williams who successfully escaped from Stalag Luft III as part of the 'Wooden Horse' plan. Williams would later publish their story as the best-selling book *The Wooden Horse*.

A German guard by one of the watch towers at Stalag Luft III, Sagan.

CHAPTER SIXTEEN

D-Day and the Battle for Normandy

Montgomery's Plans for Operation 'Overlord'

11 Febraury 1944

One of the most anticipated campaigns of the Second World War was an Allied landing in north-west Europe. This was important in order to open up a new front in the west and allow the Allies to fight their way towards Berlin, the heart of the Third Reich. Codenamed 'Overlord', the operation would begin with an amphibious landing on the beaches of Normandy, with the first day of the operation identified as 'D-Day'. It would prove to be an enormous operation, on a scale unlike anything previously seen, and would require meticulous planning.

At the beginning of 1944, the American General Dwight D Eisenhower was appointed overall commander of the Supreme Headquarters Allied Expeditionary Force (SHAEF), while the British General Bernard Montgomery was assigned to take over command of 21st Army Group, initially controlling all ground forces in the campaign. Montgomery (known widely as 'Monty') had gained the reputation of being a successful military leader following his victory at El Alamein in 1942. Although Eisenhower was in charge of the general direction of the campaign, it fell to Monty to present his strategy for the invasion and convince his fellow commanders of its wisdom.

Although a plan for 'Overlord' had already been drawn up in 1943 by Eisenhower's predecessor, Lieutenant General Frederick Morgan, as the Chief of Staff Supreme Allied Commander (COSSAC), Montgomery disagreed with his idea of a three-divisional assault. Despite not being alone in recognising the plan's flaws, Montgomery seemed to be the only person willing to openly question it. Over the first few months of 1944 Monty slowly gained acceptance for his own strategy, although this was a far from straightforward process as he revealed in a private diary entry:

> I arrived in England from Italy on 2 January and it is now 2 April; the past three months have been hard work, and things have not been too easy. The original plan for 'OVERLORD' was wrong; there was little fighting experience in the Army in England; HQ 21 Army Group was very theoretical and many of the more senior staff officers were definitely not good enough for their jobs; many changes had to be made, and quickly. All this has drawn a good deal of adverse comment, and much mud has been slung at me; I have always had enemies and now probably have many more. But the job has been done; 'OVERLORD' is now properly 'teed up' and the plan is good; I have got my HQ well organised, and

General Bernard Montgomery's handwritten plans for Operation 'Overlord', 11 February 1944. In the bottom right of the document is its most important premise – 'the key note of everything to be SIMPLICITY'.

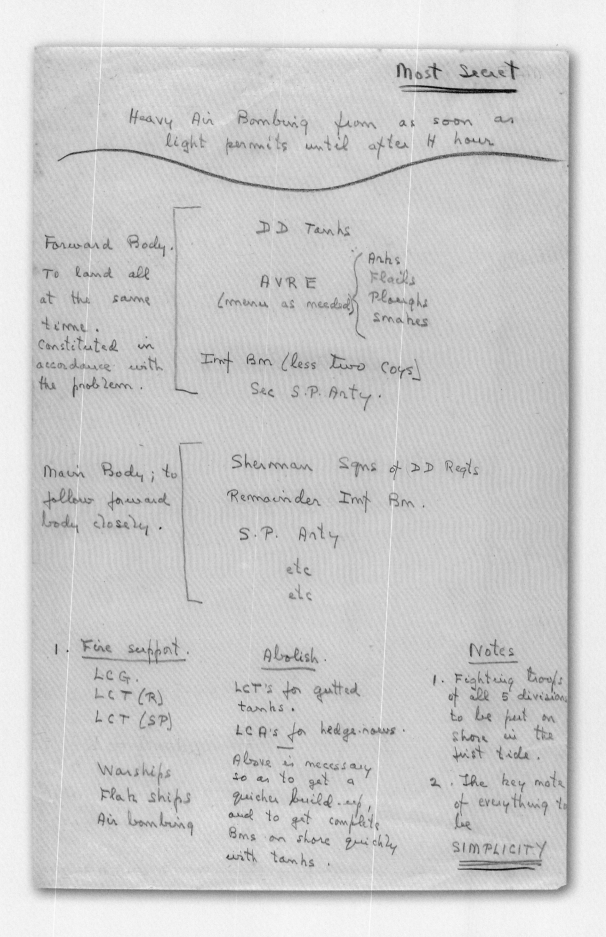

Most Secret

Heavy Air Bombing from as soon as
light permits until after H hour

Forward Body.
To land all
at the same
time.
Constituted in
accordance with
the problem.

DD Tanks

AVRE
(menus as needed)

Arks
Flails
Ploughs
Smokes

Inf Bn (less two Coys)
Sec S.P. Arty.

Main Body; to
follow forward
body closely.

Sherman Sqns of DD Regts
Remainder Inf Bn.
S.P. Arty
etc
etc

1. Fire support.
   LCG.
   LCT (R)
   LCT (SP)

   Warships
   Flak ships
   Air bombing

Abolish.
LCT's for gutted
tanks.
LCA's for hedge-rows.

Above is necessary
so as to get a
quicker build-up,
and to get complete
Bns on shore quickly
with tanks.

Notes
1. Fighting troops
   of all 5 divisions
   to be put on
   shore in the
   first tide.

2. The key note
   of everything to
   be
   SIMPLICITY

have brought in the experienced officers I required... Operation 'OVERLORD' is now in good shape. We have got ANVIL [the Allied invasion of Southern France] relegated to a back seat and got agreement that we must have what we want for 'OVERLORD'.

The draft plan for 'Overlord' shown here is written in Montgomery's own hand and is believed to date from a conference of army commanders held on 11 February 1944 at St Paul's School in London, the 21st Army Group headquarters. Monty's main concern on this occasion was to discuss the tactical approach to the D-Day landings, rather than the ongoing campaign once the beaches were secured. Monty was keen to establish a common understanding of how the landings should be planned, in order to inform the subsequent planning for what was to become the Battle of Normandy.

Rather than the staggered approach of the earlier COSSAC's plan, Montgomery argued for 'fighting troops of all 5 divisions to be put on shore in the first tide'. The forward body of troops were to land together, with supporting weapons and tanks. As many special tanks as possible were to be sent ashore with the first wave of troops; these included Duplex Drive amphibious tanks and AVRE (Armoured Vehicle Royal Engineers) specially adapted for engineering duties. This would make sure that the land battle developed quickly. Also, in contrast to earlier ideas of a 'silent' assault in order to maximise the element of surprise, Montgomery argued for 'heavy air bombing from as soon as light permits'.

Perhaps the most memorable element of Montgomery's strategy was his declaration that 'the key note of everything to be SIMPLICITY'. Rather than an over-complicated plan involving staged assaults on the beaches, unclear command and numerous objectives, Monty pushed for a simple, straightforward strategy of landing as many ground forces as possible in one go, under his own single command.

On 7 April, Montgomery explained his plan to the participating commanders and their staff. As his biographer Nigel Hamilton elucidates, 'It was an amazing demonstration of the manner in which, within twelve weeks, Monty had transformed a contentious (though deeply researched) proposal in which few commanders had any faith into a clear, simple plan, the presentation of which stunned all.'

The Normandy campaign would not be fought with the object of capturing towns (with the exception of the channel ports), but rather to allow the build-up of troops and equipment until the moment when the Americans would be strong enough to start the push south into Brittany, before turning east towards Paris. The German commander responsible for defending the French coastline was Erwin Rommel, whom Monty had previous experience of fighting in North Africa and for whom he continued to hold a good deal of respect. In his speech he personalised the enemy as only 'Rommel', and thereby simplified the whole scenario in a way that both inspired those present and clarified the plan.

Operation 'Overlord' was finally put into action on 6 June 1944. Parachute and glider landings combined with air attacks and naval bombardments, while the main amphibious landing on five beaches proved a great success despite the high cost in casualties. A new European front was soon established, which took a huge amount of pressure off the Red Army fighting the Germans on the Eastern Front. The German position in France soon became untenable. Despite their very significant losses in the first phases of the campaign, the Allies' morale remained high – the stage was set for the advance towards Berlin.

General Sir Bernard Montgomery, 21st Army Group Commander, steps onto Juno Beach at 8.45am on 8 June 1945, after being ferried from his ship.

Film still showing troops from No.4 Commando, 1st Special Service Brigade, coming ashore from landing craft at Sword Beach on 6 June 1944 — D-Day.

Later the same day. Sherman DD tanks of 'B' Squadron, 13th/18th Royal Hussars support infantry and commandos as they advance into Ouistreham, from Sword Beach, on 6 June 1944. Despite sustaining many casualties, the Allies had successfully established themselves in north-west Europe.

CHAPTER SEVENTEEN

Special Operations Executive
Odette Sansom's Arrest Papers

13 May 1944

The Axis occupation in Europe and the overwhelming nature of total war meant that new means to fight needed to be developed. With this in mind, the Special Operations Executive (SOE) was created in July 1940 to spearhead unorthodox methods of warfare behind enemy lines, in support of local resistance movements.

SOE specialised in espionage and sabotage, and operated under extreme secrecy. It used fictitious names of different service branches in order to hide its true purpose, and recruited its operatives in a similarly secret fashion.

In early 1942 a public appeal was made by the Admiralty asking people to send them private photographs or postcards showing the French coastline, ostensibly to build up a useful visual guide to aid the eventual Allied invasion. One individual who chose to respond to the appeal was Odette Sansom, a 30-year-old Frenchwoman, married to an Englishman, who was living with her three children in Somerset. She mistakenly sent her photographs to the War Office rather than the Admiralty, and as such her letter came to the attention of those running SOE.

Odette was considered a useful potential recruit due to her strong patriotism and invaluable French background. She felt guilty that she was enjoying freedom in Britain whilst other members of her family were trapped in occupied France:

> My mother had to run away from her home. It was the second time in her life she had lost everything, because it had been over-run by the Germans and things had happened to the rest of the family. My brother... had been wounded and was in... a military hospital in Paris. Some of our friends were already in captivity. So am I supposed to accept all this sacrifice that other people are making without lifting a finger in a way?

Odette therefore agreed to serve with SOE, and was swiftly enrolled into the First Aid Nursing Yeomanry (FANY) as a cover. Reluctantly leaving her children in the care of a convent school, she began to undertake training as a behind-the-lines operative who would assist groups of resistance fighters acting subversively in occupied France.

Landing on a beach on the south coast of France on the night of 31 October 1942, Odette (operating under the codename of 'Lise') made contact with the local SOE network on the French Riviera and its head, the British officer Captain Peter Churchill (codenamed 'Raoul'). Odette

Gestapo papers relating to the arrest of Special Operations Executive (SOE) agent Odette Sansom and her transfer to Karlsruhe prison on 13 May 1944.

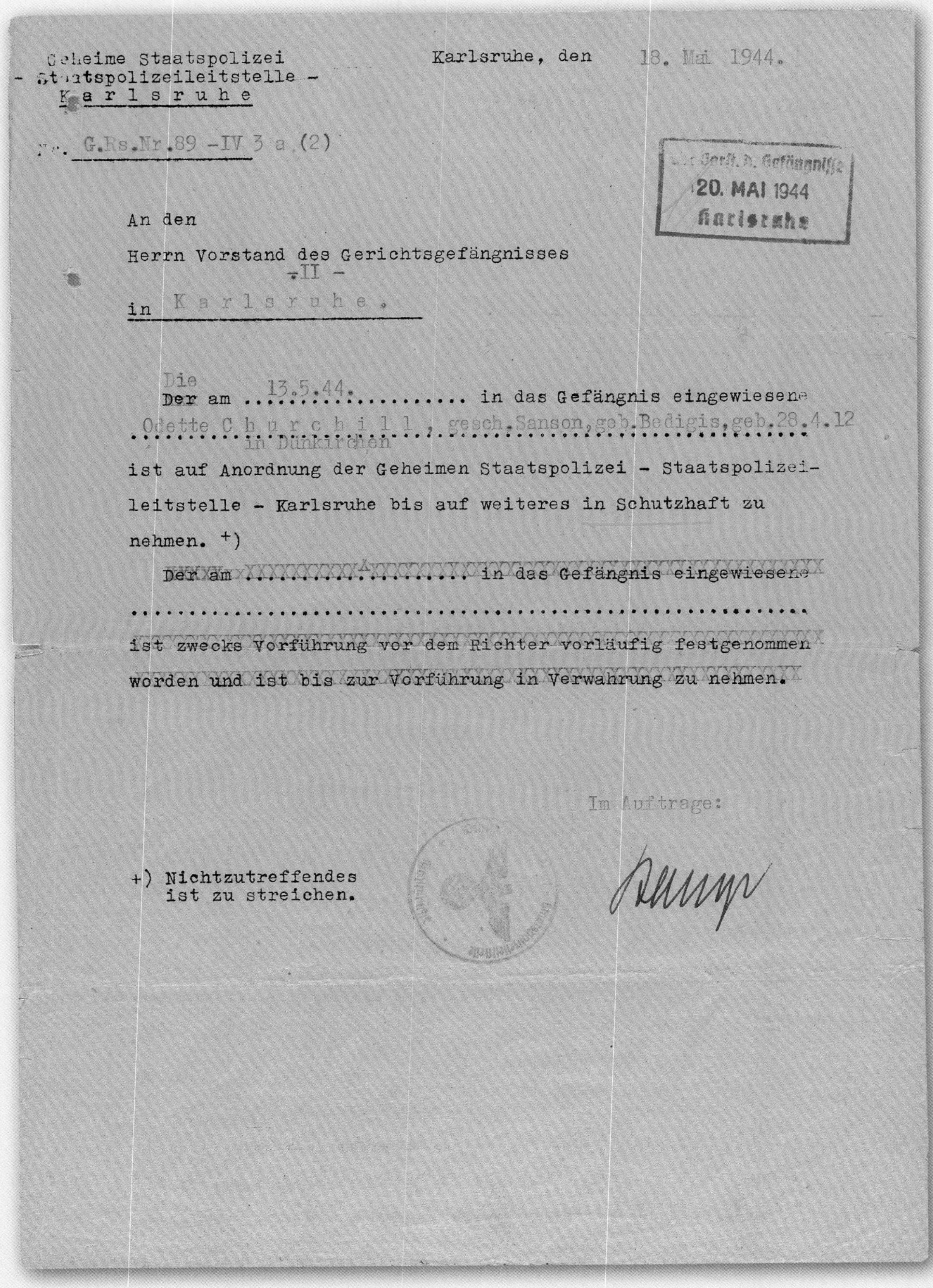

Geheime Staatspolizei   Karlsruhe, den   18. Mai 1944.
- Staatspolizeileitstelle -
   K a r l s r u h e

Nr. G.Rs.Nr.89 -IV 3 a (2)

Geft. d. Gefängnis
20. MAI 1944
Karlsruhe

An den

Herrn Vorstand des Gerichtsgefängnisses
         - II -

in   K a r l s r u h e .

     Die
     Der am ....13.5.44.......... in das Gefängnis eingewiesene
....Odette C h u r c h i l l , gesch.Sanson,geb.Bedigis,geb.28.4.12
.... in Dünkirchen..
ist auf Anordnung der Geheimen Staatspolizei - Staatspolizeileitstelle - Karlsruhe bis auf weiteres in Schutzhaft zu
nehmen. +)
     Der am .... in das Gefängnis eingewiesene
....
ist zwecks Vorführung vor dem Richter vorläufig festgenommen
worden und ist bis zur Vorführung in Verwahrung zu nehmen.

                          Im Auftrage:

+) Nichtzutreffendes
   ist zu streichen.

worked closely with Churchill and Adolphe Rabinovitch, the network's radio operator, and became involved in arranging increasingly dangerous air drops of equipment and supplies. However, after a few months of this perilous work the local SOE network was infiltrated by a German double agent, and this led to the arrest of Odette and Churchill on 16 April 1943. Sticking to their pre-prepared cover story of posing as a married couple, both operatives were sent to Fresnes prison, just south of Paris.

Throughout her captivity, Odette was subjected to frequent and violent interrogation by the Gestapo:

> They wanted to know where our radio operator was, they wanted to know where another British agent who had arrived some little time before had been to and was, where he'd gone to. Yes, they wanted to know things about people they didn't manage to capture.

> I'm not brave or courageous; I just make up my own mind about certain things. I thought there must be a breaking point, even if in your own mind you don't want to break up but physically you're bound to break up after a certain time I suppose. If I can survive the next minute without breaking up this is another minute of life, and if I can feel that way instead of thinking of what's going to happen in half an hour's time.

> Having torn my toe nails they were going to do my fingers... They were stopped because the Commandant came in and he said stop. Then they had burned my back and of course there are many things they can do to me. Now I have lived through those things, had the experience of that... what next is coming? How do I know? I can only hope for the best but I know I've been able to accept this and to survive it.

> I felt it was a duty. I had been brought up all my life with a sense of duty, I had been trained with a sense of duty, I was a woman with a sense of duty to life.

Odette's treatment was harsher than that inflicted on Peter Churchill, who was posing as a nephew of the Prime Minister Winston Churchill and therefore handled differently by the Gestapo. Odette's refusal to give up any useful information led to her transfer to Karlsruhe prison on 13 May 1944, where the surviving Gestapo records shown here indicate that she was to be kept in 'protective custody' until further notice. Although she continued to refuse to disclose anything useful to the Gestapo, the association which she had established between her 'husband' Peter Churchill and the Prime Minister meant that she might still prove to be a useful bargaining chip for the Germans to retain. Despite this, however, she was officially condemned to death in June and the following month transported to Ravensbrück concentration camp, where she would remain for the rest of the war.

At Ravensbrück, Odette's treatment failed to improve. She was kept in solitary confinement for three months in an underground, windowless cell in total darkness, given inadequate food and water, while her cell was made even more uncomfortable by the heating being turned up full:

> They put me in the cell next to the punishment cell. So every evening there used to be women coming to that cell to be beaten. I could count every stroke, I could hear everyone, I could hear the screams. Then, when I was moved a few months after... to a ground floor cell on the other side of the bunker and I was by the side of the crematorium so I could hear what was going on in the crematorium. I was ill then, very ill, they opened the top of my window that much, I could not see through it but the air was made of the cinders of the crematorium. My cell was covered with cinders from the crematorium, pieces of burning hair and, ugh, the smell of it all...

Such horrors only came to an end with the Allied liberation of Ravensbrück. When American troops were a few miles away from the camp, the Commandant Fritz Suhren took Odette with him to the US Army headquarters in order to surrender, thinking that her association with Winston Churchill would benefit his case. However, it was to be the testimony of Odette and other prisoners in the subsequent war crimes trials which would lead to the conviction and execution of Suhren and many other Ravensbrück staff.

In 1946, Odette was awarded the George Cross (GC) in recognition of her refusal to betray her fellow secret agents under torture. The same year her marriage was dissolved, allowing her to marry Peter Churchill who had also managed to survive captivity. When the story of her wartime bravery emerged she became a national heroine, and in 1950 a successful film was made about her life, titled *Odette*. However, she preferred to avoid fame, choosing to accept her GC on behalf of those of her comrades who did not survive.

This order issued by the Gestapo in Karlsruhe was addressed to the prison governor, informing him that Odette was to be transferred to Ravensbrück concentration camp. She would remain in Ravensbrück for the rest of the war.

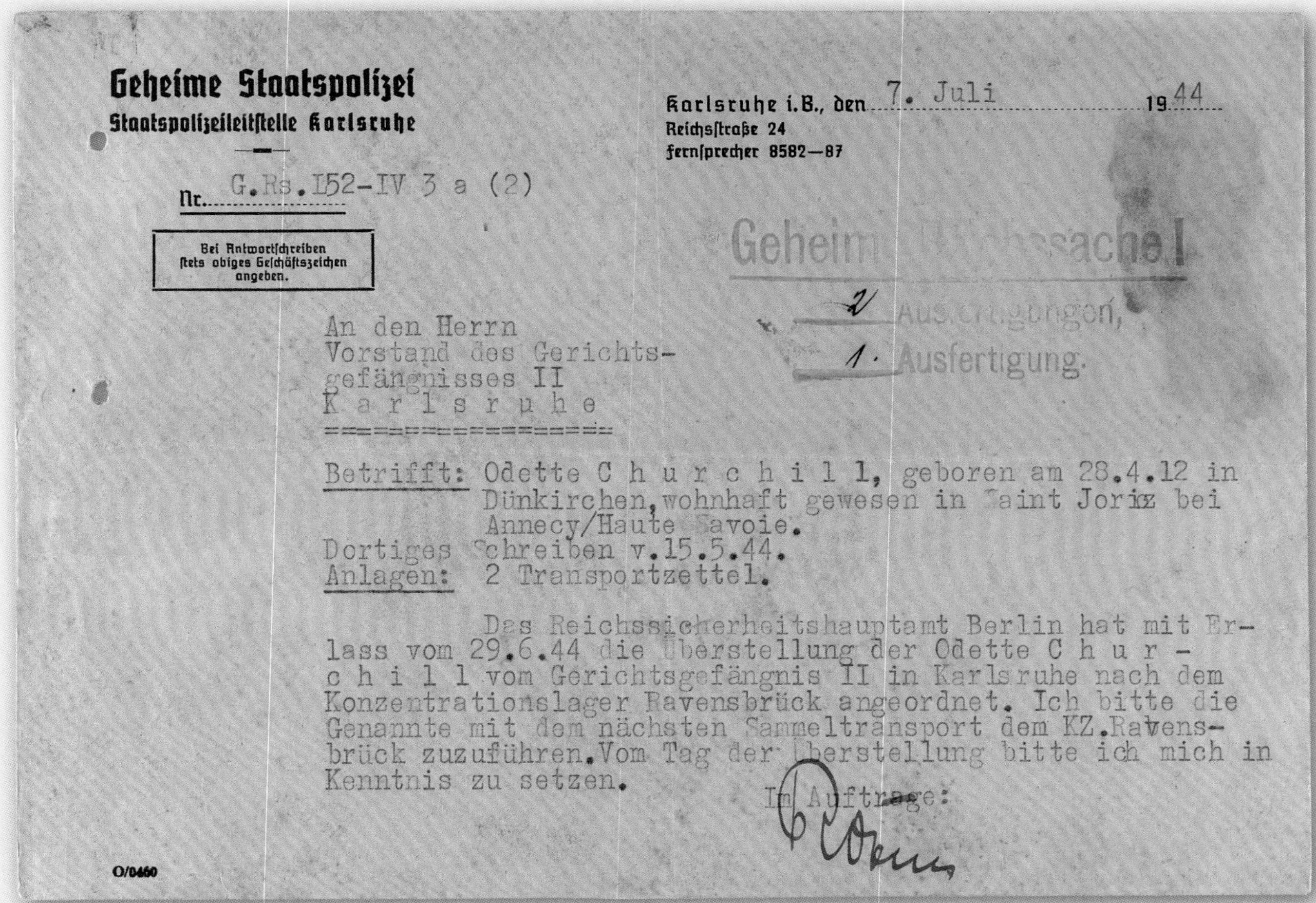

Geheime Staatspolizei

Staatspolizeileitstelle Karlsruhe

Nr. G.Rs.I52-IV 3 a (2)

| Bei Antwortschreiben |
| stets obiges Geschäftszeichen |
| angeben. |

Karlsruhe i.B., den 7. Juli 19 44

Reichsstraße 24
Fernsprecher 8582—87

Geheime Reichssache!

2 Ausfertigen,

1. Ausfertigung.

An den Herrn
Vorstand des Gerichts-
gefängnisses II
K a r l s r u h e
========================

Betrifft: Odette C h u r c h i l l , geboren am 28.4.12 in
          Dünkirchen, wohnhaft gewesen in Saint Joriz bei
          Annecy/Haute Savoie.
Dortiges Schreiben v.15.5.44.
Anlagen: 2 Transportzettel.

          Das Reichssicherheitshauptamt Berlin hat mit Er-
lass vom 29.6.44 die Überstellung der Odette C h u r -
c h i l l vom Gerichtsgefängnis II in Karlsruhe nach dem
Konzentrationslager Ravensbrück angeordnet. Ich bitte die
Genannte mit dem nächsten Sammeltransport dem KZ.Ravens-
brück zuzuführen.Vom Tag der Überstellung bitte ich mich in
Kenntnis zu setzen.

                              Im Auftrage:

O/0460

This small tin, with its contents of a needle and thread, a razor and a piece of broken mirror, was given to Odette Sansom by a German woman in Karlsruhe Prison when Odette was on her way to Ravensbrück Concentration Camp. This was Odette's sole possession during her last year of captivity in Ravensbrück.

Portrait photograph of Odette Sansom, taken in 1946 after she had been repatriated and presented with the highest gallantry award of the George Cross.

CHAPTER EIGHTEEN

The Fall of Berlin
Adolf Hitler's Final Political Testament

29 April 1945

The final testament drafted by Adolf Hitler in the last hours of his life could be considered in many ways as the most symbolic record of the Nazi defeat. No other document represents with such cold blame and vitriolic anger the failure of Hitler and National Socialism.

The initial months of 1945 were characterised by a remarkably successful Russian offensive on the Eastern Front, the Red Army liberating key cities as it moved westwards, progressing nearer and nearer to the German stronghold of Berlin. Having established themselves on the outskirts of the city, on 16 April the Russians commenced what would become known as the Battle of Berlin, the final major offensive of the war in Europe. As the Red Army slowly encircled the city, using intense artillery fire and aided by aerial bombing from the RAF, it became clear to even the most ardent Nazi that the capital of Fascist Germany was about to fall. Any dreams of a triumphant Third Reich were close to ruin.

By 25 April, the decisive stages of the Battle had been fought. With the Soviet encirclement of Berlin complete and the main body of the German IX and XII Armies

completely separated from the city, it was only a matter of time before the city would be in Allied hands.

As the Battle raged above their heads, Hitler and his small court were effectively ensnared in the *Führerbunker*, a thickly protected underground network of rooms located deep beneath the Reich Chancellery. Present alongside Hitler was his lover Eva Braun; Minister of Propaganda Dr Joseph Goebbels with his wife and six children and their adjutant; and Hitler's personal staff including his surgeon, personal adjutants, secretaries and cook. As the dust fell from the low ceiling and the walls shook from the bombardment being unleashed above them, Hitler still believed that the capital of the Reich could never fall with the Führer still resident. He was resolved to stay until the very end.

Communication between the bunker and the outside world was increasingly limited, and any news received in those final weeks of April served only to infuriate Hitler. Reichsmarschall Hermann Göring had sought to assume

This and the following images show pages from the Final Political Testament written by Adolf Hitler. Dated 28 April 1945, this is the last official document he signed. Compare Hitler's signature on the final folio (page 150) to the bolder, more confident way in which he signed the Anglo-German Declaration some seven years earlier, (page 11).

Mein politisches Testament.

      Seit ich 1914 als Freiwilliger meine
bescheidene Kraft im ersten, dem Reich aufgezwungenen
Weltkrieg einsetzte, sind nunmehr über dreissig
Jahre vergangen.

      In diesen drei Jahrzehnten haben mich bei
all meinem Denken, Handeln und Leben nur die Liebe
und Treue zu meinem Volk bewegt. Sie gaben mir die
Kraft, schwerste Entschlüsse zu fassen, wie sie
bisher noch keinem Sterblichen gestellt worden
sind. Ich habe meine Zeit, meine Arbeitskraft
und meine Gesundheit in diesen drei Jahrzehnten
verbraucht.

      Es ist unwahr, dass ich oder irgend-
jemand anderer in Deutschland den Krieg im Jahre

power in Hitler's place, while Reichsführer Heinrich Himmler had attempted to negotiate a surrender deal with the Allies. Hitler considered both acts as treachery against his leadership. Along with the German military failure to protect Berlin, circumstances conspired to make him feel that he had been stabbed in the back by both his armed forces and his closest colleagues. Seemingly ignorant of his own poor leadership, it would be this sense of betrayal that most informed Hitler's final Testament.

On the night of 28 April, Hitler married Eva Braun in a simple ceremony in the bunker, witnessed only by a minister and two others. A small celebration followed, with those present drinking champagne and sharing final conversations. During the party, Hitler disappeared at intervals into an adjoining office in order to dictate to his secretary, Traudl Junge, his Final Will and Testament.

By 4am the following morning two separate documents had been prepared: Hitler's Personal and Political Testaments. The Personal Will was the simpler document, concerning pragmatic matters such as Hitler's marriage, the disposal of his personal property and his impending death. The Political Testament, however, was more of a final political statement intended to act as lasting evidence. Written in order to provide justification for Hitler's acts, it explained why the war had not been won and apportioned blame, whilst looking to the future and appointing his successors to continue the Nazi philosophy.

Three copies of each Testament were typed up, signed and witnessed for delivery to separate destinations: to Field Marshal Ferdinand Schörner (as the newly-appointed Commander-in-Chief of the Army); to Grand Admiral Karl Dönitz (as Hitler's successor as Führer); and, perhaps most tellingly if we consider that the Testament was intended to define its author's place in history, to the Nazi Party Archives in Munich.

The content of the Political Testament reflected Hitler's racial beliefs and willingness to allocate blame. He placed culpability for the current conflict directly on Jewish shoulders, just as his first published testament from 1925, *Mein Kampf*, identified an identical cause for Germany's failures in the First World War:

It is untrue that I, or anybody else in Germany, wanted war in 1939. It was wanted and provoked exclusively by those international politicians who either came of Jewish stock, or worked for Jewish interests. After all my offers of disarmament, posterity cannot place the responsibility for this war on me.

After a six-years' war, which in spite of all the set-backs will one day go down in history as the most glorious and heroic manifestation of a people's will to live, I cannot forsake the city which is the capital of this state... I wish to share the fate that millions of others have accepted and to remain here in the city. Further, I will not fall into the hands of an enemy who requires a new spectacle, exhibited by the Jews, to divert his hysterical masses.

Hitler had fought in the First World War as a soldier and blamed Germany's defeat on the politicians – yet now, as

- 2 -

1939 gewollt haben. Er wurde gewollt und ange-
stiftet ausschliesslich von jenen internationalen
Staatsmännern, die entweder jüdischer Herkunft
waren oder für jüdische Interessen arbeiteten.
Ich habe zuviele Angebote zur Rüstungsbeschrän-
kung und Rüstungsbegrenzung gemacht, die die
Nachwelt nicht auf alle Ewigkeiten wegzuleugnen
vermag, als dass die Verantwortung für den Aus-
bruch dieses Krieges auf mir lasten könnte. Ich
habe weiter nie gewollt, dass nach dem ersten
unseligen Weltkrieg ein zweiter gegen England
oder gar gegen Amerika entsteht. Es werden Jahr-
hunderte vergehen, aber aus den Ruinen unserer
Städte und Kunstdenkmäler wird sich der Hass gegen das, letzten Endes verantwortliche Volk immer wieder erneuern, dem wir das alles zu verdan-
ken haben: Dem internationalen Judentum und seinen
Helfern!

    Ich habe noch drei Tage vor Ausbruch des
deutsch-polnischen Krieges dem britischen Bot-
schafter in Berlin eine Lösung der deutsch-polnischen Probleme vorgeschlagen - ähnlich der im
Falle des Saargebietes unter internationaler
Kontrolle. Auch dieses Angebot kann nicht weg-
geleugnet werden. Es wurde nur

a politician himself, he believed that it was the German Army who had stabbed its country in the back:

> In future may it be a point of honour with German Army officers, as it already is in our Navy, that the surrender of territory and towns is impossible, and that, above all else, commanders must set a shining example of faithful devotion to duty until death.

He proceeded to highlight two of his closest confidantes, who should now be considered as traitors:

> Göring and Himmler, by their secret negotiations with the enemy, without my knowledge or approval, and by their illegal attempts to seize power in the state, quite apart from their treachery to my person, have brought irreparable shame on the country and the whole people.

Hitler proceeded to appoint his successors: the key ones being Dönitz (as Reich President and Supreme-Commander of the Armed Forces), Goebbels (as Reich Chancellor) and his own private secretary Martin Bormann (as Party Chancellor). They were then given their orders to ensure that the Nazi administration continue, whilst being reminded that they were to:

> ...above all else, uphold the racial laws in all their severity, and mercilessly resist the universal poisoner of all nations, international Jewry.

Hitler signed the documents at 4am on 29 April, with the Political Testament witnessed by Goebbels, Bormann and Wehrmacht Generals Hans Krebs and Wilhelm Burgdorf. The personal one was witnessed by Goebbels, Bormann, Krebs and Colonel Nicolaus von Below, Hitler's Luftwaffe adjutant. Signing the documents was the final political act of Hitler's life. He shot himself the following day.

Although despatched with their respective couriers, none of the Testaments were delivered to the intended recipients and it was to be many months before the documents were found by the Allies and properly recognised. The first set to be discovered were those intended for the Munich Archives, and were identified when the courier, Heinz Lorenz, was arrested in Hanover in November 1945. During a routine search, the papers were found sewn into the lining of his clothing. Under interrogation, Lorenz explained about the two other couriers, and these men were soon located by investigators. One man, Willi Johannmeier, unable to complete his mission and afraid to be associated with the documents, had hidden them in a bottle which was then buried in his back garden in the Rhineland town of Iserlohn. It is these two copies of the Private and Political Testaments which are now in the care of the Imperial War Museum.

The third set of documents, those intended for Dönitz and which were accompanied by the certificate of Hitler's marriage to Eva Braun, were found hidden in a trunk after having been concealed by the final courier, Wilhelm Zander. This set is now preserved by the United States National Archives in Washington DC.

jeden einzelnen verpflichtet, immer dem gemeinsamen
Interesse zu dienen und seine eigenen Vorteile dem-
gegenüber zurückzustellen. Von allen Deutschen,
allen Nationalsozialisten, Männern und Frauen
und allen Soldaten der Wehrmacht verlange ich, daß
sie der neuen Regierung und ihren Präsidenten treu
und gehorsam sein werden bis in den Tod.

Vor allem verpflichte ich die Führung der
Nation und die Gefolgschaft zur peinlichen Ein-
haltung der Rassegesetze und zum unbarmherzigen
Widerstand gegen den Weltvergifter aller Völker,
das internationale Judentum.

Gegeben zu Berlin, den 29. April 1945, 4.00 Uhr.

British and Russian troops in the garden of the former Reich Chancellery. The entrance to Hitler's underground bunker can be seen immediately behind them, on the left of the photograph.

Three Soviet soldiers, Privates Alexei Kovalyov, Abdulkhakim Ismailov and Aleksei Goryachev, raise the Soviet flag in victory on the top of the ruined Reichstag building following the fall of Berlin, 2 May 1945. Although Yvgeny Khaldei's photograph was staged and its details altered for Soviet propaganda purposes, it became famous as a symbol of victory over Nazi Germany.

CHAPTER NINETEEN

Victory in Europe
The Lüneburg Heath Surrender Document

4 May 1945

Hitler's Testament had appointed Karl Dönitz as Germany's new President and Joseph Goebbels as its Chancellor, yet Goebbel's suicide shortly after Hitler's own death meant that Dönitz was now the sole leader of the Reich. However, with Hitler's suicide and the military defeats being suffered by the German Army within its own territory, it was clear to all that the war in Europe was in its final stages. The Italian fascist leader Mussolini had been captured and executed on 28 April 1945, while on 2 May the German forces in Italy surrendered. On the same day the Battle of Berlin was over, with the city falling into the hands of the Soviet Red Army.

Dönitz recognised that the war had been lost, but sought for any opportunity to save German troops and refugees from Soviet reprisals in the east. Being aware of the Allied plan to split German territory into various occupied sectors, his tactic was therefore to negotiate a surrender with the Western Allies, but to prolong deliberations in order to allow his people time to seek refuge in the west.

As a head of state, Dönitz felt it was inappropriate to negotiate surrender terms himself, but instead sent in his place a delegation headed by Admiral Hans-Georg von Friedeburg, the new Commander-in-Chief of the German Navy. Arriving by car at the 21st Army Group tactical headquarters located near Lüneburg Heath, a few miles south-east of Hamburg, the delegation met with Field Marshal Bernard Montgomery:

> They were brought to my caravan site and were drawn up under the Union Jack, which was flying proudly in the breeze. I kept them waiting for a few minutes and then came out of my caravan and walked towards them. They all saluted, under the Union Jack. It was a great moment; I knew the Germans had come to surrender and that the war was over.

The Germans' initial offer was to surrender Army Group Vistula, which had unsuccessfully defended Berlin to the east and was now being cut off by Soviet forces. Yet this was refused by Montgomery, who was more concerned with the enemy threatening his own front. He therefore insisted on the unconditional surrender of all German forces to the north and west. Those in the east would need to negotiate a separate surrender with the Soviets. The German forces were split without any cohesion and, as

The Instrument of Surrender for the German Army in Holland, north-west Germany and Denmark, signed on Lüneburg Heath, 4 May 1945.

Instrument of Surrender

of

All German armed forces in HOLLAND, in

northwest Germany including all islands,

and in DENMARK.

1. The German Command agrees to the surrender of all German armed forces in HOLLAND, in northwest GERMANY including the FRISIAN ISLANDS and HELIGOLAND and all other islands, in SCHLESWIG-HOLSTEIN, and in DENMARK, to the C.-in-C. 21 Army Group. *This to include all naval ships in these areas.* These forces to lay down their arms and to surrender unconditionally.

2. All hostilities on land, on sea, or in the air by German forces in the above areas to cease at 0800 hrs. British Double Summer Time on Saturday 5 May 1945.

3. The German command to carry out at once, and without argument or comment, all further orders that will be issued by the Allied Powers on any subject.

4. Disobedience of orders, or failure to comply with them, will be regarded as a breach of these surrender terms and will be dealt with by the Allied Powers in accordance with the accepted laws and usages of war.

5. This instrument of surrender is independent of, without prejudice to, and will be superseded by any general instrument of surrender imposed by or on behalf of the Allied Powers and applicable to Germany and the German armed forces as a whole.

6. This instrument of surrender is written in English and in German.

   The English version is the authentic text.

7. The decision of the Allied Powers will be final if any doubt or dispute arises as to the meaning or interpretation of the surrender terms.

Friedeburg

Kinzel

B. L. Montgomery
Field-Marshal

4 BLM May 1945
1830 hrs

Montgomery himself later observed, 'in the narrowing belt between the eastern and western fronts the confusion was most remarkable.'

Retiring to their own headquarters in order to seek direction from Dönitz, the Germans returned to Lüneburg at 6pm the following day, ready to sign the surrender agreement:

> I took von Friedeburg into my caravan, to see him alone. I asked him if he would sign the full surrender terms as I had demanded; he said he would do so. He was very dejected and I told him to rejoin the others outside... The German delegation went across to the tent, watched by groups of soldiers, war correspondents, photographers, and others – all very excited. They knew it was the end of the war.
>
> I had the surrender document all ready. The arrangements in the tent were very simple – a trestle table covered with an army blanket, an inkpot, an ordinary army pen that you could buy in a shop for twopence. There were two BBC microphones on the table. The Germans stood up as I entered; then we all sat down round the table. The Germans were clearly nervous and one of them took out a cigarette; he wanted to smoke to calm his nerves. I looked at him, and he put the cigarette away.

Along with Montgomery and von Friedeburg, the signatories to the surrender were General Eberhard Kinzel (Chief of Staff to the German Army in the north-west) and his staff officer Major Hans Jochen Friedel, Rear Admiral Gerhard Wagner (Head of the German Navy operational staff) and Colonel Fritz Poleck (representing the German Armed Forces' Supreme Command).

The significance of the surrender was reflected in a daily report sent late that evening to Field Marshal Alan Brooke, the Chief of the Imperial General Staff. In it, Montgomery (famous for abstaining from alcohol) remarked, perhaps reluctantly, 'I was persuaded to drink some champagne at dinner tonight'.

The Lüneburg Heath Instrument of Surrender was momentous. It was the first such capitulation by Germany, covering the key territories of the Netherlands, Denmark and North-West Germany. Two further instruments would be signed to cover the complete and unconditional surrender of Germany on all fronts. The first of these occurred at Reims on 7 May, before a more formal signing ceremony was held in Berlin the following day.

After the Lüneburg Heath surrender document was signed, the original was retained by Montgomery himself and a duplicate copy sent for the official records. By June 1954 the legality of the document's ownership was in question, with the issue being debated in the House of Commons at Prime Minister's Question Time. Declining the suggestion that he should order the Field Marshal to return the original surrender document, Sir Winston Churchill, the then serving PM, memorably remarked:

> It seems to me that Field Marshal Montgomery set a valuable precedent by retaining in his own hand the original document of the battlefield surrender to him at Lüneburg of more than a million well-trained enemy soldiers. The fact that such trophies will hereafter be the personal property of the British Commander-in-Chief in the field should be an incentive to all young officers in the British Army to repeat the episode on the half-million scale whenever the public interest requires.

The document went on public display for the first time in September 1968 when Montgomery presented it to the Imperial War Museum, where it now remains as a permanent donation.

This letter, dated 2 May 1945, from Field Marshal Keitel, Cheif of the German Armed Forces High Command, serves to introduce Admiral von Friedeburg, General Kinzel, Rear Admiral Wagner and Major Friedel as plenipotentiaries authorised to negotiate surrender terms with the British 21st Army Group.

Der Chef   Hauptquartier, den 2.5.1945
des Oberkommandos der
deutschen Wehrmacht

      Ich entsende als Beauftragen des Oberkommandos der
Wehrmacht den Oberbefehlshaber der deutschen Kriegsmarine,
Generaladmiral von Friedeburg, den General der Infanterie
Kinzel, den Konteradmiral Wagner, den Major i.G. Friedel,
sowie Dolmetscher und Kraftfahrer in 4 Kraftwagen zum Oberbefehlshaber der 21. englischen Heeresgruppe. Sie sind be-
vollmächtigt, über militärische Fragen Besprechungen zu
führen und daraus sich ergebende Fragen zu erörtern.

Der Chef
des Oberkommandos der
deutschen Wehrmacht

Generalfeldmarschall

Field Marshal Bernard Montgomery greets the German delegates outside his headquarters at 21st Army Group, 3 May 1945.

The signing of the Instrument of Surrender of the German Armies in the North at Lüneburg Heath, 4 May 1945. Montgomery (seated, centre right) looks over the terms of surrender, watched by Admiral von Friedeburg (middle) and Rear Admiral Gerhard Wagner (left).

A rare colour photograph showing the view down Whitehall on 8 May 1945. The huge crowd is amassing in front of the balcony of the Ministry of Health building, decorated with flags, from where Winston Churchill would address them in his famous VE Day speech.

CHAPTER TWENTY

Final Judgement

Belsen War Crimes Trial Transcripts

17 September 1945

Serving as an emotive epilogue to the Second World War were the series of war crimes trials conducted by the Allied occupation forces against members of the former Nazi regime. Most notable among these proceedings were the trials of those involved with running the various concentration camps in which many hundreds of thousands of victims had been kept in inhumane conditions and, in many cases, systematically murdered.

The Belsen Trial was held at Lüneburg in Lower Saxony, an appropriate location considering that the initial German surrender had been signed on the nearby heath only a few months before. The trial defendants were largely SS personnel and prisoner functionaries who had been involved in operating the concentration camps at Auschwitz and Bergen-Belsen. The trial would be followed in news reports avidly across the world by a public shocked to discover not only the terrible conditions in which prisoners had been held, leading to widespread sickness and malnutrition, but also the true horror of the deliberate atrocities carried out during the war years in the name of the Final Solution. Journalists fed the public's eager appetite to see justice done to those who had previously considered themselves untouchable.

All of the war crimes trials, including the later ones held at Nuremberg and elsewhere, were carried out with the greatest care to follow established legal procedure and to give each defendant a fair hearing. To see justice allocated and to stress the inhumanity of National Socialism was a crucial part of the de-Nazification process which was applied by the occupation forces to all who had previously supported the Hitler regime. The Belsen Trial was held before a British military tribunal, with army officers serving as both judges and counsel. The trial was presided over by six military judges, including Lieutenant Colonel R McLay who, as shown here, made careful handwritten notes throughout the proceedings in support of the official court transcripts.

The first trial of 45 individuals began on 17 September 1945, with the star defendant among them being Josef

This and subsequent images show notes made by Lieutenant Colonel R McLay while serving as a Junior Member of the Court at the Belsen Trial, Lüneburg, 17 September – 17 November 1945. The notes on this first page describe the allegations made against Kramer by his prosecutors, followed by the recollections of the first witness called to give their testimony. Kramer was designated Defendant Number 1.

JOSEF KRAMER

Prosecution

I Recognised in court by Brig Glyn Hughes.
made no attempt to stop S.S. firing at
prisoners on potatoe mound.
no reason for firing.
Delay in carrying out order to help wounded.

At open grave with Brig Glyn Hughes, quite
callous and indifferent.

Not frank when showing Brigadier round, but
unashamed.

Violation of agreement in allowing S.S. to leave rifles
and obstruction of records

Made no effort to help sick. Every effort for himself.

II Singleton recognises No 1 as Kramer. who
stated camp contained habitual criminals felons
and homosexuals. Only admitted political
prisoners in answer to direct question.
Also stated calm at present.
Later stated he was Commandant. (Kramer)
further asked if responsible commandant replied. Yes.
Food twice, turnip soup, bread not always but
whenever possible.
Main water supply off through failure at Hannover
Static tanks in water to get it as best they can.
On observation Witness saw dirty water with
foreign matter floating in it.
Didn't see any more. Kramer didn't mention any
In Kramer's office, seemed confident expressed
no emotion about camp.
Stated by potatoe patch this he could not obey
without fire arms.

Kramer, the Camp Commandant at Bergen-Belsen and previously Auschwitz, who had earned a reputation as 'The Beast of Belsen'. Other high-profile defendants who had also worked at Belsen included the camp doctor Fritz Klein, Deputy Camp Commandant Franz Hössler, and Chief Wardress Elisabeth Volkenrath, who had been in charge of selecting victims for the gas chamber. All of the defendants pleaded not guilty. Leonard Muddeman, a visitor on the first day of the trial, described the anticipation in the room:

> First in the dock this day was Josef Kramer himself. Like all the accused he was identified by a board on his chest with a number. He jumped up briskly like a schoolboy to answer his defending officer's questions although to a layman like myself his answers did not seem to be doing his case much good. His line of defence, as I recall it, was similar to that of other defendants I was to hear that day, namely that circumstances had proved too strong for him, that he could not help himself, that he had orders which he had to obey or be punished himself, that naturally he had disliked what had been going on and had made complaints to higher authority. At the end of his cross-questioning Kramer turned towards the court, thanked it for a fair hearing and expressed his confidence that a just verdict would be pronounced.

> The next defendant heard that day was a Dr Klein, a German born in Rumania, an educated man of ordinary appearance, over middle age, whose job had been to select those who were to be killed in the gas chamber. In a matter of fact way he related how, when a train-load of victims was expected, he would make his way to the station in an ambulance, ride a bicycle or even walk there. He would inspect the latest batch of prisoners drawn up on the platform who had to trail past him and as they did so he would designate which of them were to be set apart for extermination. Like the other defendants he claimed to have played no part in the actual killing of the victims.

> The world was beginning to learn how under the Nazi system nobody apparently was responsible for any of the actual killing. Those on top were to say that they did not know what was going on and those below were to argue that they had only acted under orders. Then there were those who had but an intermediate role in, say, the transport of the tens of thousands of victims. Yet millions died.

Although initially intended to last a few weeks, the trial ran to a full two months:

> The system of interpretation used at Lüneburg was far too slow. Every remark had to be translated into at least two languages for English, German and Polish were spoken here. This procedure was particularly cramping for prosecuting counsel. Colonel B., standing like a boxer taking on all comers, would put a question and have to stand for what seemed an age before he got an answer while the interpreters did their work.

Many observers also argued that the trial had been arranged too quickly, but these lessons would be learned and acted upon in time for subsequent war crimes trials. Final sentencing was carried out on 17 November. Of the 45 defendants tried, 15 were acquitted. The remainder were sentenced to imprisonment, ranging from 1 to 15 years, while 11 defendants were given death sentences by hanging. These last sentences were supervised on 13 December 1945 by the famous British hangman Albert Pierrepoint, who flew to Germany in order to carry out the task. Over the next few years Pierrepoint would be the authorities' executioner of choice, and ended up hanging some 200 war criminals. The considerable fees he received for this work allowed him to buy a public house back in England, which he successfully ran with his wife throughout the post-war years.

A second Belsen Trial was conducted at Lüneburg in June 1946, while the most prominent members of the former Nazi hierarchy were tried before the International Military Tribunal at Nuremburg between November 1945 and October 1946. Further trials followed throughout the late 1940s, including those held in Tokyo which were concerned with war crimes committed in the Far East. Conflicting practices between the German court system and that adopted by other countries led to perhaps the greatest legacy of the Second World War trials – the creation of a permanent International Criminal Court.

KLEIN   Took over milk meat +biscuits from Stan. ①
and ruined them. Not much use. Water + wood
for everyone required.
Overcrowding one of main things.
Went into Camp six with Horstman. Two or three
times on his own.
No papers handed over.
Strength return of disease from interned doctors
No instructions from British Officers. Did not carry
out any more duties.

CROSS
EXAM   Realised that Gas chambers were murder
Not put to work destroyed. Those who could work
Starved, beaten + finally destroyed. Accused said
not right.
Received in hospital people beaten by SS.
Majority beaten by Capos.
Accused made reports to higher fuhrers giving names
of people who had done beating.
Sometimes when chosen to transports in red cross car.
Seen SS women on parade. He divided the
prisoners then handed them over to S.S. Guards.
If prisoners tried to get from one side to the other
Guards put them back.
With exception of four doctors, remainder lived Together.
Does not know where hospital patients who wouldn't
get well, went to
Hungarian transports arriving day + night, Doesn't know
he was told all went to gas chamber.
When spoke to Kramer about water Said "Can't in
any order.
Corpses lying all over Camp.
Duty water of interned doctors.
Medical Store in Camp.

② Klein   very short of medical stores until he took over
Prisoners Same as Auschwitz or any other camp
Belsen not a camp for sick people but a death
Camp.
Re examination
People from Berlin knew what was going on, in
fact sent more more people in.
Court   Enough medical Supplies to cover Camp for 5 days
States   2 to 4000 required medicine
Told food Supplies from Red Cross
Schmidt Never asked for assistance
by anyone.

9 Bat

Josef Kramer, pictured outside his cell, awaiting trial for war crimes, 8 August 1945.

The Belsen war crimes trials were held at the town's sports gymnasium at 30 Lindenstrasse, Lüneburg. The building was converted to a Court of Justice for this specific purpose only ten days before the trials began, (photograph dated 7 September 1945).

Within the image: **ALL PERSONS WILL STAND WHEN THE COURT ENTERS**

This photograph shows the Belsen Trials court in session at Lüneburg in September 1945. Josef Kramer can be seen at the bottom left, front corner of the dock. He wears the number one.

This note was scribbled by Albert Pierrepoint on 13 December 1945 shortly after hanging the 11 war criminals sentenced to death during the Belsen Trial (plus two others for a separate crime). He lists the names and ages of those he hung in the order in which they met their death.

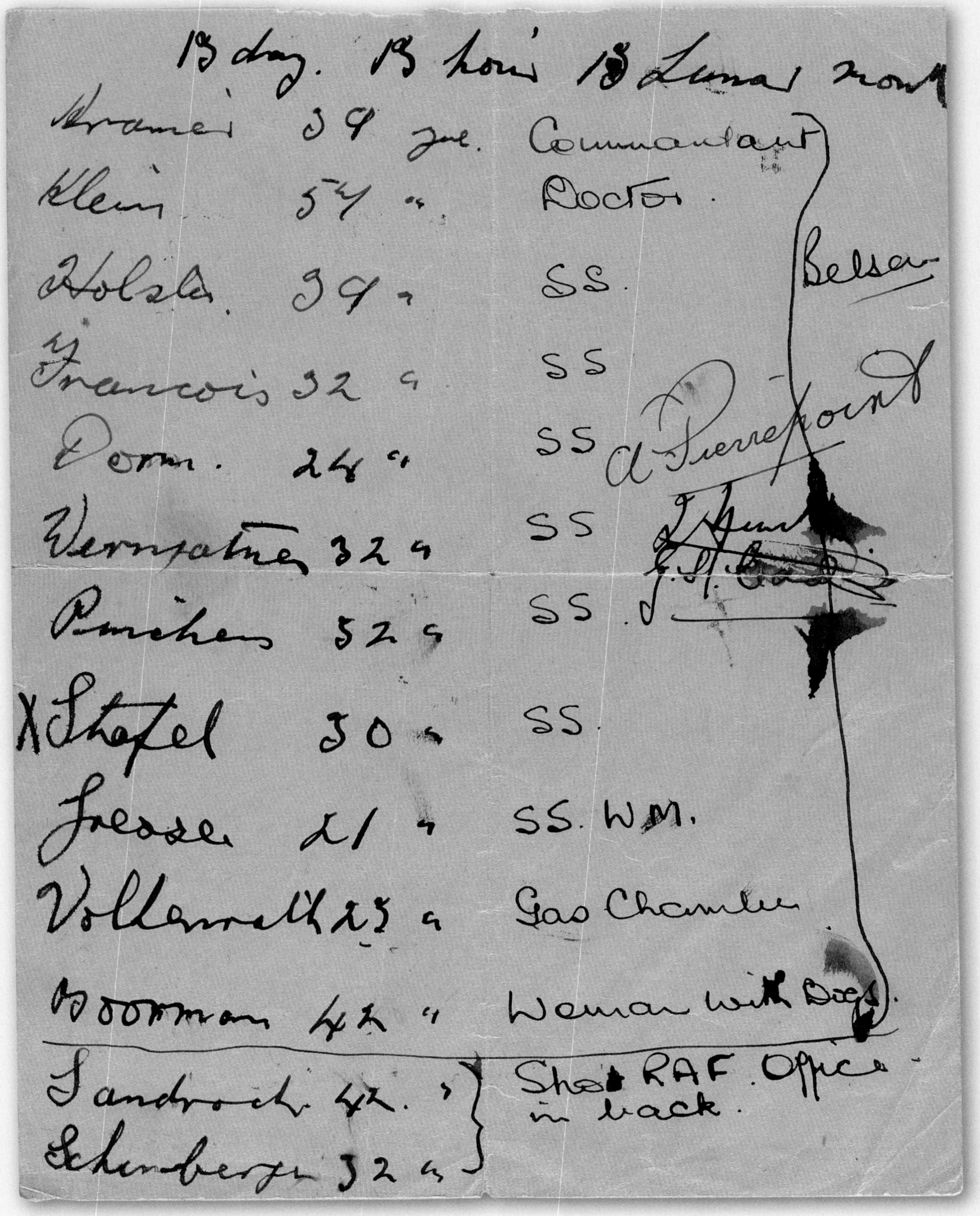

13 day. 13 hour 13 Luna1 mon1

Kramer	39	yr.	Commandant
Klein	54	"	Doctor.
Holsta	39	"	SS.
Francois	32	"	SS
Dorn.	24	"	SS
Vernpatner	32	"	SS
Pinchen	32	"	SS.
X Stapel	30	"	SS.
Freese	21	"	SS. WM.
Vollenrath	23	"	Gas Chamber
Boooman	42	"	Woman with Dogs.
Sandrock	42	" ⎫	Shot RAF. Office
Schemberger	32	" ⎭	in back.

A Pierrepoint

Belsen

The archive store housing the Imperial War Museum's document collection, where the key records featured in this book are permanently preserved.

Sources

IWM COLLECTIONS © IWM unless otherwise stated

BBC radio broadcast of Chamberlain's arrival at Heston
(Sound 4316)
Interview with Odette Hallowes GC (Sound 9478, reel 1)
Private Papers of Mrs A Annis (Documents.21918), courtesy of the
Estate of Mrs A Annis
Private Papers of Miss N Braunschweiger (Documents.15289)
Private Papers of Lieutenant Colonel R McLay (Documents.3597)
Private Papers of Mrs E M Mascall (Documents.11163)
Private Papers of Captain E E S Montagu (Documents.26145),
courtesy of the Estate of Captain E E S Montagu
Private Papers of Field Marshal Viscount Montgomery of Alamein,
M 1118 signal dated 4 May 1945 (Documents.20500, BLM
113/36)
Private Papers of L N Muddeman (Documents.9802)
Private Papers of Colonel F K Theobald (Documents.6713), courtesy
of the Estate of Colonel F K Theobald
Private Papers of Flight Lieutenant Eric Williams (Documents.4077)
'ARP Bulletin No 1' dated 15 February 1939 (Documents.9681)
Central Flying School report on Douglas Bader (Documents.24415)
Chamberlain's air ticket to Munich, 29 September 1938
(Documents.5625)
Changi Internment Camp Register (Documents.8755)
Churchill's Guildhall speech, 10 November 1942
(Documents.24715), reproduced with permission of Curtis
Brown, London on behalf of The Estate of Winston S.
Churchill, © The Estate of Winston S. Churchill
Daily Telegraph, 17 January 1959 (Documents.24332)
Diagram by Commodore H H Harwood RN of the probable
movements of the Admiral Graf Spee, December 1939
(Documents.1458)
Draft of Sir Shenton Thomas' radio broadcast, 31 January 1942
(Documents.18895)
Fuhrer Directive No. 1 for the Conduct of War (Documents.10044)
Hitler's signal regarding the Battle of Stalingrad, 26 November 1942
(Documents.816)
If the Invader Comes leaflet, June 1940 (Documents.8864)
Letter from Keitel dated 2 May 1945 (Documents.5159)
Ministry of Food Ration Book (Documents.24347/A)
The Munich Agreement (Documents.4998)
Note by Albert Pierrepoint (Documents.15557)

PUBLISHED SOURCES

Paul Addison and Jeremy A Crang (eds), Listening to Britain: Home
Intelligence Reports on Britain's Finest Hour May to
September 1940 (London, 2010)
Antony Beevor, The Second World War (London, 2012)
Keith Feiling, The Life of Neville Chamberlain (Hamden Connecticut,
1970)
Nigel Hamilton, Monty: Master of the Battlefield 1942–1944
(London, 1983)
Robert Jackson, Douglas Bader: A Biography (London, 1983)
Roy Jenkins, Churchill (London, 2001)
B L Montgomery, Memoirs (London 1958)
B L Montgomery, Normandy to the Baltic (London 1947)
Denis Richards, The Royal Air Force 1939–1945 Volume I: The Fight
at Odds (London, 1953)
Hugh Sebag-Montefiore, Dunkirk: Fight to the Last Man
(London, 2006)
Penny Summerfield & Corinna Peniston-Bird, Contesting Home
Defence: Men, Women, and the Home Guard in the Second
World War (Manchester, 2007)
Richard Toye, The Roar of the Lion: The Untold Story of Churchill's
World War II Speeches (Oxford, 2013)

Image List

All images © IWM unless otherwise stated. Every effort has been made to contact all copyright holders. The publishers will be glad to make good in future editions any error or omission brought to their attention.

Front cover
Book_Cover_3000

Introduction
IWM SITE Book cover 2962

Chapter One
Documents.4998, NYP 68066, Documents.5625/A © British Airways, reproduced by kind permission of British Airways, D 2239, HU 5509

Chapter Two
Documents.15289/E, Documents.15289/E_1, Documents.15289/C_1, Documents.15289/A_1, Documents.15289/D_1, Documents.15289/F_1, FRA 204717, Documents 15289/B_2

Chapter Three
Documents.10044, HU 56131, HU 8060, HU 5358

Chapter Four
Documents.1458, A 7, Documents.23148_1, A 4

Chapter Five
Documents.24347/A_1, 2 & 3, D 7958, D 25037, Art.IWM PST 20687, Art.IWM PST 2814

Chapter Six
Documents.6713/A_1, Documents.6713/B_3, 4, 5 & 6, Documents.14398/A, C 1720, HU 1152

Chapter Seven
Documents.24415, CH 1406, CH 1412, HU 53912

Chapter Eight
Documents.8664/A_1 & 2, MH 6657, H 2722, H 30177

Chapter Nine
Documents.9681/B_1 & 2, Documents.9681/A, HU 86166, D 3982, Art.IWM PST 13851, Art.IWM PST 13864

Chapter Ten
Documents.18895/A, MH 30186, NPG x84899 Sir Thomas Shenton Whitelegge Thomas by Bassano Ltd © National Portrait Gallery, London, HU 69971 © Estate of Zina Oliver, HU 2787

Chapter Eleven
Documents.8755/A, COL 17, HU 66243, EPH 1452, EPH 37

Chapter Twelve
Documents.24715/A_2, 3, 4, 5 & 6, reproduced with permission of Curtis Brown, London on behalf of The Estate of Winston S. Churchill, © The Estate of Winston S. Churchill, H 20446, E 18972, E 18907

Chapter Thirteen Documents.816/B_1 & 2, NYP 38410, MH 13146, HU 5152

Chapter Fourteen Documents.26145/F, Documents.26145/C, Documents.26145/E, Documents.26145/B, Documents.26145/A courtesy of the Estate of Estate of Captain E E S Montagu, A 21104

Chapter Fifteen Documents.4077/D, F_1, H_1 & 2, E, EPH 6366, HU 21024, Documents.13456/B

Chapter Sixteen Documents.20501/D, B 5174, BU 1184, MH 2013

Chapter Seventeen Documents.8204/A_1, Documents.8204/B_1, EPH 3974, HU 3213

Chapter Eighteen Documents.23985_1 – 10, BU 8730, HU 68178, BU 8634

Chapter Nineteen Documents.5000, Documents.5159, BU 5141, BU 5208, TR 2876

Chapter Twenty Documents.3597/A_1, Documents.3597A_2_1&2, BU 9710, BU 10374, Documents.3597/B_1, Documents.15557/A

Acknowledgements

I should like to thank my IWM colleagues David Fenton, Caitlin Flynn, Madeleine James and Kieran Whitworth, who all made essential contributions to this book. It was their idea in the first place! Also a special thank you to Stephen Walton, for translating the Hitler signal and contributing much-valued historical advice. Thanks also to Stephen Long and Kabir Singh for their work on designing the book.

Heartfelt thanks are also due to Natasha and Henry, plus my chums and colleagues Lucy Donoughue, Bryn Hammond, Peter Hart and Nigel Steel — in different ways you've all given me a huge amount of support during the writing of this book, which I've greatly appreciated.

Creepy
Creatures

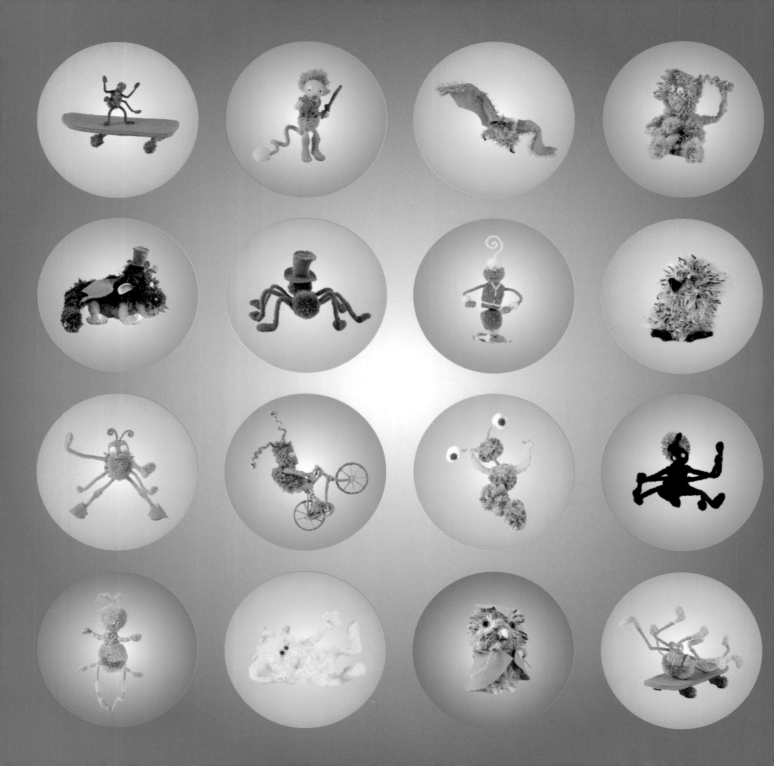

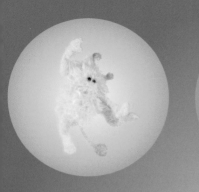

Creepy
Creatures

Julie Sharp

GUILD OF
MASTER CRAFTSMAN
PUBLICATIONS

First published 2006 by **Guild of Master Craftsman Publications Ltd**. Castle Place,
166 High Street, Lewes,
East Sussex BN7 1XU

Text and illustrations © Julie Sharp 2006
© in the Work GMC Publications 2006
Photographs by Anthony Bailey

ISBN-13: 978-1-86108-419-4
ISBN-10: 1-86108-419-6

A catalogue record for this book is available
from the British Library.

Production Manager: Hilary MacCallum
Managing Editor: Gerrie Purcell
Book Editor: Rachel Netherwood
Managing Art Editor: Gilda Pacitti
Designer: Rebecca Mothersole

Set in AvantGarde and TypoUpright
Colour origination by Altaimage
Printed and bound in Singapore by Kyodo

A Note About The Measurements
Conversions are approximate. Use either metric
or imperial; do not mix measurements.

A few words from the author

I find there is always something special about the unique quality of a hand-made object. Making up and developing a technique and new skills can be as much fun as playing with a toy. You will find the characters have a life-like quality experienced through the soft texture and flexible nature of the designs. I have a number of favourites in this book; I wonder what yours will be.

If you are a novice, start with Carmine the Spider, then Shimmie Zing. The easiest yarn-wrapping projects to get started with are Squidge, Ookpik, Owl, then Phlump. Snork and Flippy Floppy are more complex characters to make. The Bonsai Tree House will take the longest to create, but it is well worth the time. The techniques, once you have practised them a few times, will become second nature and will lead you to develop your own designs further.

Go and raid Granny's cupboards; these projects are a great way to use up spare material from a past knitting project and yarn can also be recycled from unravelling an old jumper or cardigan.

Contents

Meet the Characters

Accessories

Meet the Characters

Scant is not creepy at all. He just likes a little attention now and again.

Scant the Ant

What you need:

Materials

* 2oz (50g) ball of brown yarn
* 2oz (50g) ball of heather yarn
* 7in (178mm) grey pipe-cleaner
* 12in (304mm) grey pipe-cleaners x 3
* ⅜in (10mm) glittery pompoms x 2

Tools

* Craft scissors
* Craft/sewing needle
* Small cardboard platform **(see page 128)**

Head

 1 Make a pompom by wrapping the brown yarn around the small cardboard platform 30 times. Then wrap the heather yarn on top of the brown yarn 25 times to create a two-colour pompom. (A)

2 Trim the head pompom into an oval shape and attach a glittery pompom to either side of the head for the eyes. (B)

Body

3 Wrap the brown yarn around the card platform 70 times, then wrap the heather yarn 25 times over the brown, to make up the back end of the ant. (C)

4 Make two pompoms for the middle section of the body. Wrap the heather yarn around the small cardboard platform 30 times for each pompom. (D)

5 Trim the back pompom into an oval shape and leave a pointed tip at the end. Shape the body pompoms so that they are round. Slide the 7in (178mm) pipe-cleaner through the centre of each pompom to make the spine. Place the spheres between the head and back body pompoms in a line. Leave a ¼in (6mm) space between the back body and the middle of the ant. (E)

6 Sew the spine in place with brown yarn, passing it through each pompom. Position the heather side of the head pompom face down and the heather side of the back body pompom pointing up. Wrap the ¼in (6mm) space between the back body and middle pompoms with brown yarn to blend the separation with the core of the body. (F)

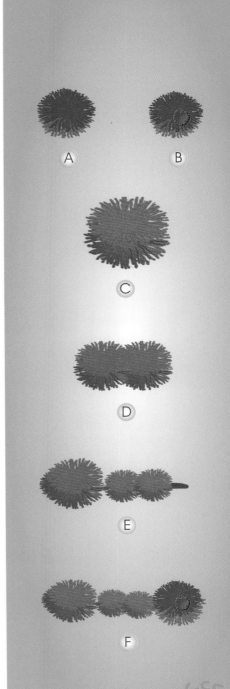

A   B   C   D   E   F

G

H

I

J

K

It's important to watch duels very closely.

Legs

7 Use three full-length pipe-cleaners to make three pod legs and six feet **(see page 147)**. Wrap the feet with three layers of heather yarn. Then cover the legs with three layers of brown yarn. G

8 Bend the pod legs 2in (50mm) from the pod feet. Then curve in the middle section to shape a curve with the body pompoms. H

9 Place a pair of pod legs on the back body pompom, ½in (12mm) from the middle section. Fasten to the bottom of the ant using brown yarn. I Position the second pair of pod legs to the middle section of the body, between the middle two pompoms, and attach with heather yarn. Set the front legs at the front of the middle section and attach with heather yarn. J

10 Weave additional brown yarn to cover the pod leg bars and blend with the pompom texture. Clip the surface of the body to define the body shape. K

*Ookpik is a simple and soft cold weather friend,
who happens to be very well behaved in space.*

Ookpik

What you need:

Materials

* 2oz (50g) ball of beige fluffy fashion yarn
* 1oz (25g) ball of black yarn
* 9in (228mm) black pipe-cleaners x 2
* 6in (152mm) black pipe-cleaners x 2
* ³⁄₈in (10mm) yellow sparkly pompoms x 2

* ³⁄₁₆in (5mm) black sparkly pompoms x 2
* Black sewing thread

Tools

* Craft scissors
* Craft/sewing needle
* Medium cardboard platform **(see page 128)**
* Small cardboard platform

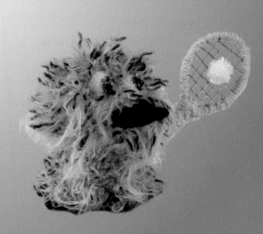

Head

1 Make a pompom by wrapping the beige fluffy yarn around the medium cardboard platform 150 times. Trim the threads to create a rounded head shape. (A)

Body

2 Make a pompom by wrapping the beige fluffy yarn around the medium cardboard platform 120 times. Trim the threads to create a rounded body shape. Clip off enough threads at the bottom of the body to flatten the surface. (B)

Feet

3 Make an Ookpik foot using a 9in (228mm) black pipe-cleaner. Curve the ends and loop them together. Make a triangle shape with three equal sides. Curve the bottom section of the triangle around a pencil to make three claws. (C)–(D) Make another foot in the same way.

4 Use a 3in (76mm) section of pipe-cleaner to place on the centre of each foot. Loop the ends onto the middle claw and heel. (E)

5 Wrap the feet and claws with black yarn, weaving it through the centre crossbars. (F) Sew the feet to the bottom of the body with black yarn, making sure that the claws stick out at the front.

6 Using the black yarn, sew the head to the body, passing the yarn through the middle of each pompom. (G)

We first met on Mars.

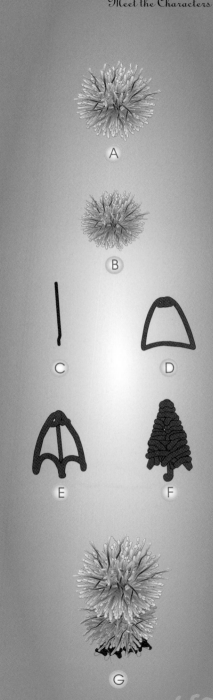

15

Beak

7 Cut the 6in (152mm) pipe-cleaner in half. Fold each piece into a V. Loop the ends in by ¼in (6mm). Place one V on top of the other. (H)–(I)

8 Using black yarn, sew the V-shaped ends together. Wrap black yarn around the rest of the beak, leaving the looped ends free. (J) When all sides are covered with yarn, sew the looped ends into the middle of the head using beige fluffy yarn. (K)

Eyes

9 Attach the black pompoms into the centre of the yellow pompoms with black sewing thread. Attach the eyes above the beak, spacing them evenly apart. (L)–(M)

H   I   J

K

L   M

17

Carmine is an elegant leggy creature.
Although small, she is always well dressed in black.

Carmine the Spider

What you need:

Materials

- ⅜in (10mm) black ready-made pompoms x 2
- ⅝in (15mm) black ready-made pompom
- ³⁄₁₆in (5mm) black ready-made pompom
- ⅛in (3mm) white ready-made pompoms x 2
- ⅝in (15mm) orange glittery ready-made pompom
- 4½in (110mm) black pipe-cleaners x 4
- 1¼in (32mm) black pipe-cleaner
- White sewing thread
- Black sewing thread

Tools

- Craft scissors
- Sewing needle
- Nail clippers

Head

★ Take a glittery orange hair pompom and sew it onto a ³⁄₈in (10mm) black pompom. Attach a ³⁄₁₆in (5mm) black pompom to the centre of the black face pompom for a neck. Position the white pompom eyes on the lower half of the face and secure with white thread. (A)–(C)

Antennae

★ Bend the 1¹⁄₄in (32mm) black pipe-cleaner into a V and loop the ends. Sew to the top of the face underneath the orange pompom with black thread. (D)–(E)

Body

★ Sew a ⁵⁄₈in (15mm) black pompom, for the lower body, to a ³⁄₈in (10mm) black pompom, for the chest area of the body. Sew the head to the top of the body with black sewing thread. (F)

I'm resting on plasma... ooh, nice!

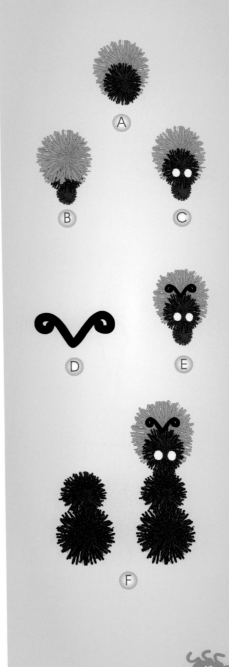

19

Legs

⭐ Make four pairs of legs using the 4½in (110mm) black pipe-cleaners **(see page 148)**. On one pair of legs, fold the legs in the middle and bend the feet forward. Ⓖ

⭐ Connect this pair to the bottom of the spider body in the centre and attach with black sewing thread. Bend the knees 1in (25mm) up from the feet. Taper the area around the ankles using craft scissors to trim the fibres and enhance the difference between the legs and feet. Flatten the feet by clipping fibres from underneath. Ⓗ

⭐ Cut the three remaining pairs of legs in half and loop the ends to connect to the body. Place one set in the middle of the lower body at the sides and sew in place with black thread. Bend the legs 1in (25mm) from the feet. Sew another pair to the middle of the spider between the chest and bottom pompoms. Sew the fourth pair in place at shoulder level. Ⓘ

*With an antenna head that receives and transmits information,
Stikkie always knows what's going on.*

Stikkie the Alien

What you need:

Materials

* 2oz (50g) ball of grey yarn
* 1oz (25g) ball of fluorescent yellow yarn
* 1oz (25g) ball of pale blue yarn
* 12in (304mm) grey pipe-cleaners x 3
* 6in (152mm) grey pipe-cleaner
* ³⁄₁₆in (5mm) green pompoms x 2
* ⅛in (3mm) white pompoms x 2
* White sewing thread
* Silver metallic embroidery thread

Tools

* Craft scissors
* Sewing needle
* Embroidery needle
* Nail clippers
* Small cardboard platform **(see page 128)**
* Pencil

Head

⭐ Wrap the grey yarn around the small card platform 70 times. Wrap the fluorescent yellow yarn on top of the grey yarn 50 times to create a two-colour pompom. Trim it into a rounded shape. Ⓐ

⭐ Cut away some yellow yarn at the front and sides to make a cap. Then shape the rounded top into a tube. Ⓑ Cut a smile line in the front of the grey section in the middle.

⭐ Trim away the yarn under the mouth to enhance the chin. Stitch a band of silver embroidery thread to separate the grey and yellow sections. Sew the green pompoms on the line ½in (13mm) apart with white thread. Attach a white pompom to each eyelid. Ⓒ

Antenna

⭐ Wrap the 6in (152mm) pipe-cleaner with fluorescent yarn. Loop one end and curve the rest into one large swirl. Insert the looped end into the top of the head and sew in place with fluorescent yarn. Trim the yarn into a rounded top. Ⓓ–Ⓔ

Body

⭐ Wrap the grey yarn around the small cardboard platform 140 times. Trim the pompom into a rounded body shape. Cut away the bottom of the body into a flat section. Ⓕ

⭐ Insert a 12in (305mm) pipe-cleaner into the bottom of the head through the middle. Sew in place with grey yarn. Push the other end of the pipe-cleaner into the top of the body pompom. Wrap the neck with four layers of grey yarn. Trim away stray threads around the neck.

⭐ Wrap the grey yarn around the small cardboard platform 120 times. Trim into a rounded shape and cut away a flat area at the top. Insert the pipe-cleaner spine through the middle of the flat bit of the bottom pompom and out by ¾in (19mm). Make a small loop at the end for the pod legs. Ⓖ

⭐ Divide the body pompoms by ¼in (6mm). Coil the silver pipe-cleaner around a pencil. Wrap this around the spine between the pompoms. Clip threads from the waist to smooth and flatten the surface.

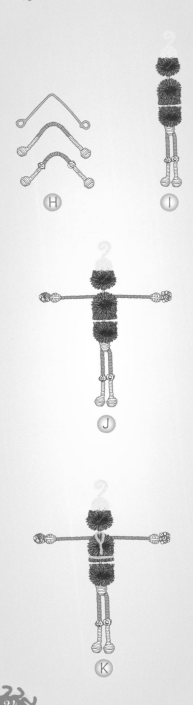

H

I

J

K

Legs

⭐ 9 Use one grey pipe-cleaner to make the pod legs **(see page 147)**. Wrap one layer of pale blue yarn around the feet and 1in (25mm) up the legs. Wrap three layers of yarn around this section to make the tops of the boots. Add vertical strips of yarn around the lumps to secure and decorate the boots. (H)

⭐ 10 Wrap the legs with three layers of grey yarn from the top of the boots upwards. Curve the stick legs in the middle. Hook the bottom of the spine onto the curved leg bar to attach the legs to the body and sew in place with grey yarn. Wrap the bottom of the spine with five layers of pale blue yarn to create a tube shape. Add some vertical stitches to secure in place. (I)

Arms

⭐ 11 Using one grey pipe-cleaner, make the pod arms **(see page 147)**. Wrap the hand loops with grey yarn, then make a thumb bud. Repeat the same process on the other hand, making sure thumbs point in different directions. Wrap the

arms with two layers of grey yarn. Add bobbles to the top of each hand using silver embroidery thread **(see page 139)**. Wrap three layers of pale blue yarn around the wrists, ⅝in (15mm) above the hands. Sew vertical stitches to secure to the arm.

⭐ 12 Connect the middle of the arm bar to the back of the body, ½in (13mm) below the neck. Sew with grey yarn and weave additional thread to the shoulders to cover the arms. Trim stray threads to make a smooth, rounded tubular shape. (J)

Vest

⭐ 13 Thread the embroidery needle with fluorescent yarn. Stitch through the front of Stikkie just below the neck. Sew a large stitch around the neck and reinsert the needle on the opposite side to make one side of a collar band. Reinsert the needle at the same spot and make another stitch on the opposite side of the neck into a V-shaped collar. Add two stitches at the front below the collar. Wrap a single stitch of thread around the waist to make a belt. (K)

Now I have
my very own golden
space module.

25

There are two sides to Gus — he's half fluffy and half smooth.
He has plenty of arms and legs, perfect for hanging around in zero gravity.

Gus the Beetle

What you need:

Materials

* 2oz (50g) ball of sage green yarn
* 2oz (50g) ball of sage green fluffy fashion yarn
* ³⁄₈in (10mm) glittery white ready-made pompoms x 2
* ³⁄₁₆in (5mm) orange ready-made pompoms x 2
* 12in (304mm) yellow or green pipe-cleaners x 3

* 6in (152mm) glittery gold pipe-cleaner
* White sewing thread

Tools

* Craft scissors
* Craft/sewing needle
* Small cardboard platform (see page 128)

My head feels as big and mysterious as space itself when I think about some things.

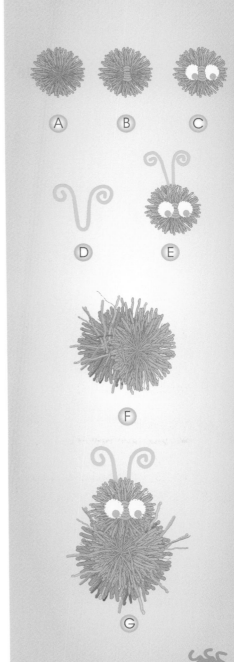

A

B

C

D

E

F

G

Head

★₁ Make a pompom by wrapping the sage green yarn around the small cardboard platform 40 times. Trim away the stray threads and trim the pompom into a circular head shape. Weave an additional cluster of loops into the centre of the face for a nose. A–B

★₂ Sew the white pompoms above the nose, ½in (13mm) apart. Then sew a ³⁄₁₆in (5mm) orange pompom at the bottom of each eye for pupils. C

Antennae

★₃ Bend the gold pipe-cleaner into a V and curl the ends. D Attach them to the top of the head with sage yarn. E

Body

★₄ Make a pompom by wrapping the sage green yarn around the small cardboard platform 60 times. Then wrap the sage green fluffy yarn over the top 60 times. F Trim away stray threads from the fluffy side and even out the overall shape. Trim the front chest of the body by rounding into an oval shape. Connect the body to the head pompom using sage yarn. G

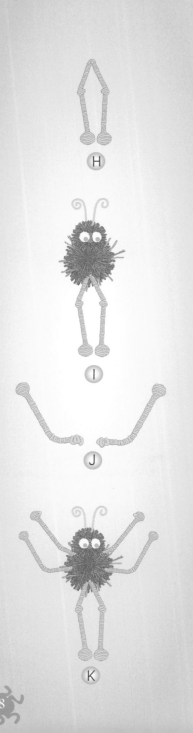

H

I

J

K

Pod legs

5 Use a 12in (304mm) pipe-cleaner and the sage green yarn to make one pair of pod legs and feet **(see page 147)**. Bend the legs in the middle and wrap the knee area with two layers of yarn to make the knee mound shape. H

6 Position the pod legs at the bottom of the body and attach with sage green yarn. I

Pod arms

7 Use a 12in (304mm) pipe-cleaner and the sage green yarn to make one pair of pod arms and hands with thumbs **(see page 147)**. J Set the pod arms with thumbs between the head and shoulder area at the back of the beetle, and sew in place with sage green yarn. Weave additional threads to blend the shoulders into the top of the body. Trim away any excess threads to refine the shape.

8 Make one pair of pod arms without thumbs, for the middle section of the body. Separate the arms into two segments by cutting the pipe-cleaner in the middle. Cut away ½in (13mm) from the end of each separated arm to shorten the arm length. Loop the ends and wrap with sage green yarn.

9 Attach the middle arms into the side of the body midway between the upper arms and legs with sage green yarn. Finish Gus the Beetle by adding more fluffy sage thread to the back, to balance the overall shape. K

A clever creature looks into
space and knows that there
are no limited dimensions.

*Transported all the way from Jupiter,
every fashionable moon abode should have a spider like this.*

Diva the Spider

What you need:

Materials

* 2oz (50g) ball of pink yarn
* 2oz (50g) ball of grey yarn
* 2oz (50g) ball of orange yarn
* $\frac{3}{16}$in (5mm) orange ready-made pompoms x 2
* 12in (304mm) grey pipe-cleaners x 4
* 1$\frac{1}{4}$in (31mm) silver pipe-cleaner
* White sewing thread

Tools

* Craft scissors
* Craft/sewing needle
* Small cardboard platform
  (see page 128)

Body

1   Wrap the grey yarn around the small cardboard platform 25 times. Wrap the pink yarn over the grey 25 times, then wrap another 15 layers of grey yarn, to make a two-coloured pompom. Make another pompom in the same way. (A)

2   Position both pompoms together on a flat surface. Create a V-shape design. Clip off one of the sides of each pompom to make a flat angle and match the V-shape in the centre of the body. Using grey yarn sew the pompoms together matching the pink diagonal strip in the middle of the body. (B)

3   Clip away the bottom of the shape to make a flat, round body. Add woven pink yarn to the pink V to define the shape, then clip surplus strands from the surface of the body.

Head

4   Make a two-coloured pompom by wrapping the grey yarn around the small card platform ten times and wrap ten layers of the pink yarn on top. Trim the pompom into a round shape. Turn the pink side of the head up and attach to the grey section at the front of the body, opposite the point of the pink V. Sew together using grey thread. (C)

Eyes

5   Sew the 3/16in (5mm) orange pompoms to the face with white sewing thread. (D)

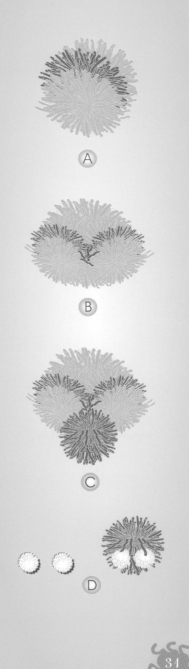

Antennae

★ 6 Bend the 1¼in (31mm) silver pipe-cleaner into a V and curl the ends. Sew the antennae to the lower pink part of the face, using the pink yarn. (E) Trim threads to refine the shape of the head and body. Add thread to smooth the overall shape.

Legs

★ 7 Make a pair of pod legs using a 12in (304mm) grey pipe-cleaner **(see page 147)**. (F)

★ 8 Wrap the tips of the toes and the foot pod with bright orange yarn. Wrap the legs with the grey body yarn. (G)-(H)

★ 9 Fold the pod leg in the middle, and then bend the leg in the middle of each section again to make knees. (I)

★ 10 Make three more pairs of legs in the same way. (J)

You can have lots of legs, but wheels are definitely posher.

★ 11 Attach the legs to the bottom of the body, sewing them equal distances apart using the grey yarn. (K)

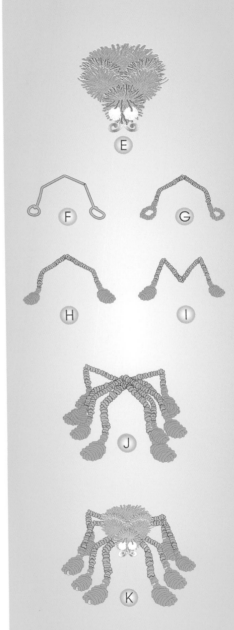

33

Owl is a good-looking chap.
He likes to dress up and pose now and again.

Owl

What you need:

Materials

* 2oz (50g) ball of beige yarn
* 2oz (50g) ball of fluffy beige fashion yarn
* 2oz (50g) ball of fluffy white fashion yarn
* 12in (304mm) white sparkly pipe-cleaners x 2
* $\frac{3}{8}$in (10mm) black pompoms x 2
* 1$\frac{1}{2}$ x 2$\frac{1}{2}$in (38 x 63mm) beige or pale brown felt x 2
* 1$\frac{1}{4}$ x 1$\frac{1}{2}$in (31 x 38mm) beige or pale brown felt x 2
* White sewing thread

Tools

* Craft scissors
* Craft/sewing needle
* Nail clippers
* Medium cardboard platform **(see page 128)**
* Small cardboard platform
* Pencil

Head

⭐ 1   Blend together the fluffy beige fashion yarn and the plain beige fashion yarn. Wrap the blended yarns around the medium card platform 80 times to make a pompom. Wrap the white fluffy fashion yarn 30 times over the top. Trim stray thread to create a rounded head shape. Ⓐ

⭐ 2   Position the black pompoms in the middle of the fluffy white section of the face, about 1½in (38mm) apart. Attach with white sewing thread. Weave additional white fluffy yarn to shape the eye area. Delicately trim excess threads from the eye area to distinguish the eyeballs if necessary. Ⓑ

Body

⭐ 3   Make a pompom using a blend of fluffy beige and plain beige yarn. Wrap it 60 times around the small card platform. Trim the pompom into a round body shape. Ⓒ Sew the head to the body with beige yarn.

Tail

⭐ 4   Wrap a blend of plain and fluffy beige yarn around the small card platform 45 times. Trim stray thread to create a rounded shape. Clip off a small amount of material to flatten the bottom of the tail. Ⓓ Sew the tail to the body using beige yarn.

A

B

C

D

35

E

F

G

H   I

Beak

⭐ 5 Use the sparkly white pipe-cleaner to make a beak **(see page 151)**. Attach it to the middle of the face, 1/2in (13mm) below the eyes, using beige yarn. Ⓔ

Wings

⭐ 6 Use the owl wing template **(page 152)** to cut two sets of wings from the beige felt. Ⓕ Place the smaller piece on top of the larger piece and sew together using white sewing thread. Attach each set of wings to the sides of the owl body at shoulder level using fluffy beige fashion yarn. Ⓖ

Feet

⭐ 7 Make a pair of feet using a white sparkly pipe-cleaner **(see page 151)**. Ⓗ Position them at the bottom of the tail with the claws sticking out. Sew in place with beige yarn. Run the yarn through all sections of the owl to secure the feet and body as one piece. Ⓘ

In my prime, I think it would be fair to say that I was regarded as something of a style icon.

Coily Haired Creature is always wandering off and getting lost.
Thank goodness she's easy to spot in a crowd.

Coily Haired Creature

What you need:

Materials

* 2oz (50g) ball of black yarn
* 2oz (50g) ball of pink yarn
* 2oz (50g) ball of grey yarn
* $\frac{3}{8}$in (10mm) yellow sparkly ready-made pompoms x 2
* $\frac{3}{16}$in (5mm) pink ready-made pompom
* 9in (228mm) black pipe-cleaners x 12
* White sewing thread

Tools

* Craft scissors
* Craft/sewing needle
* Medium cardboard platform **(see page 128)**
* Small cardboard platform
* Marker pen

Head

⭐ 1 Make a spotted pompom by wrapping the pink yarn around the medium cardboard platform 100 times. Wrap 15 layers of grey yarn over the pink, then another 30 layers of pink yarn on top. Wrap another 25 layers of grey yarn over the second pink layer keeping grey threads tightly in one spot. Finish by wrapping the pink yarn 30 times.

⭐ 2 Trim any excess thread to round the shape of the pompom. Weave additional clusters of grey yarn to enhance spots. Ⓐ

Coiled hair

⭐ 3 Wrap a 9in (228mm) black pipe-cleaner with one layer of pink yarn, leaving ¼in (6mm) at one end bare. Fold the black tip into a loop. Coil the wrapped pipe-cleaner around a marker pen to form a spiral. Make nine more coils in the same way. Ⓑ

Body

⭐ 4 Make a pompom by wrapping the black yarn around the small cardboard platform 35 times. Snip away stray thread and trim the pompom into a round shape. Make another pompom in the same way and sew together for the body. Sew the body to the head using black yarn. Ⓒ

⭐ 5 Wrap the black yarn around the small cardboard platform 25 times. Trim it into a round shape and attach it to the back of the body with black yarn. Trim away the threads from the bottom of the body pompoms to make a flat surface.

Feet

⭐ 6 Use two 9in (228mm) black pipe-cleaners to make a pair of three-toed feet **(see page 150)**. Ⓓ Attach the feet to the flat bottom of the body with black yarn. Position the legs together and splay toes on either side of the body at a slight angle. Ⓔ

Ⓐ

Ⓑ

Ⓒ

Ⓓ

Ⓔ

With a bit of gravity a chair always feels more comfortable.

Face

⭐ 7 Attach two yellow sparkly pompoms to the front of the face, ½in (13mm) apart and sew in place with black yarn. Stitch black dots into the centre of each yellow eyeball for pupils. Then weave additional grey thread to the bottom centre of the face. F–G

⭐ 8 Trim threads into a V point for a chin outline. Place the ³⁄₁₆in (5mm) pink pompom below the eyeballs to make a nose, and sew with white sewing thread. Use pink yarn to attach three hair coils around the face. Distribute the remaining seven coils evenly around the head. H

F

G

H

To relieve stress, simply place Squidge in the palm of your hand and squeeze gently. Also terribly useful as a duster.

Squidge

What you need:

Materials

* 2oz (50g) ball of pink fluffy fashion yarn
* 1in (25mm) pink sparkly pompom
* ³⁄₈in (10mm) pink sparkly pompoms x 4
* ³⁄₁₆in (5mm) black sparkly pompoms x 2
* ³⁄₁₆in (5mm) pink pompoms x 10
* 12in (304mm) pink or yellow pipe-cleaners x 5
* White sewing thread
* Black sewing thread

Tools

* Craft scissors
* Craft/sewing needle
* Medium cardboard platform **(see page 128)**
* Small cardboard platform
* Knitting needle

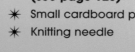

Head

⭐ 1 Make a pompom by wrapping the pink yarn around the small cardboard platform 100 times. Trim the long stray threads to create a round head shape.

Eyes

⭐ 2 Attach the ³⁄₁₆in (5mm) black sparkly pompoms to the middle of the head with black sewing thread, spacing them about ¾in (19mm) apart. Ⓐ

Body

⭐ 3 Make a pompom, wrapping the pink yarn around the medium cardboard platform 150 times. Trim the stray threads to create a round body shape. Ⓑ

⭐ 4 Connect the head pompom on top of the body pompom and sew together using the pink fluffy yarn. Ⓒ

Appendages

⭐ 5 Make a three-claw appendage with a 12in (304mm) pipe-cleaner **(see page 150)**. Ⓓ

⭐ 6 Wrap pink yarn around the finger loops. Wrap three layers of pink yarn around the pipe-cleaner and hands/feet.

⭐ 7 Bend the pipe-cleaners for knee or elbows and add stitches to the bends on one side. Make three more in this way. Ⓔ

Dum de de dum, de de dum dum dum.

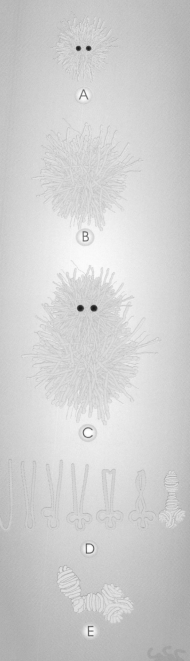

A

B

C

D

E

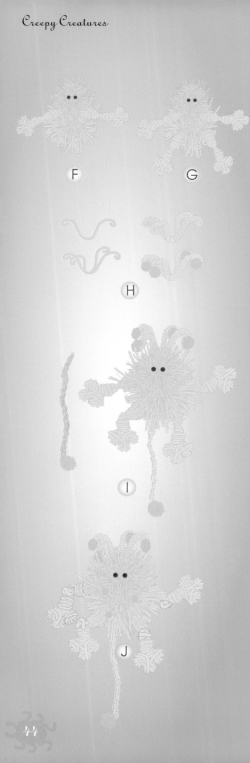

F

G

H

I

J

It's been three light years since I took my vow of silence. Yes, it has definitely paid off.

Arms and shoulders

⭐ 8 Attach the arms to the shoulder area next to the head pompom on either side with pink fluffy yarn. (F)

Feet and legs

⭐ 9 Attach the feet and legs to either side of the lower body and sew in place with pink fluffy yarn. (G)

Hair tentacles

⭐ 10 Cut a 12in (304mm) pipe-cleaner into quarters. Wrap each piece with pink fluffy yarn. Tie the pieces together in a cross shape using the pink fashion yarn. Sew a ⅜in (10mm) pink sparkly pompom to the end of each tentacle with white sewing thread. (H) Attach the four tentacles to the centre of the head with pink fluffy yarn and twist into shape.

Tail

⭐ 11 Plait six strands of the fluffy pink fashion yarn into a 4in (100mm) long braid. Attach the 1in (25mm) pink sparkly pompom to one end of the tail. Sew the other end into the lower half of the back body pompom with fluffy pink fashion yarn. (I)

Body spots

⭐ 12 Sew a random pattern of pink spots over the front and back of the body using the ³⁄₁₆in (5mm) pompoms and white sewing thread. (J)

We know she's thinking
of truly great things.

Dum de de dum,
de de dum dum
dum.

Shimmie Zing is great friends with Carmine. He loves a good party.

Shimmie Zing

What you need:

Materials
- ✳ 4½in (114mm) purple pipe-cleaners x 3
- ✳ ³⁄₁₆in (5mm) glittery purple pompom
- ✳ ⅜in (10mm) glittery purple pompom
- ✳ ⅝in (15mm) glittery purple pompoms x 2
- ✳ ³⁄₁₆in (5mm) glittery green pompom

- ✳ ⅜in (10mm) glittery green pompoms x 2
- ✳ ⅛in (3mm) grey or blue pompoms x 2
- ✳ Green sewing thread
- ✳ Purple sewing thread

Tools
- ✳ Craft scissors
- ✳ Sewing needle
- ✳ Nail clippers

Head

⭐ 1 Sew a ⅜in (10mm) glittery purple pompom to a ³⁄₁₆in (5mm) glittery purple pompom to make the head and neck. Ⓐ

Body

⭐ 2 Sew together two ⅝in (15mm) glittery purple pompoms. Gently trim the sparkles from one of the pompoms to reduce it in size. Ⓑ

⭐ 3 Position two ⅜in (10mm) glittery green pompoms on the front of the body and attach with green sewing thread. Sew the neck and head to the top of the chest pompom. Then place the ³⁄₁₆in (5mm) glittery green pompom at the front of the neck. Sew it in place, securing it to the green tummy area and purple neck. Ⓒ

Legs

⭐ 4 Make a pair of legs using a 4½in (114mm) purple pipe-cleaner. Make a ¼in (6mm) fold at one end. Make another ¼in (6mm) fold and wrap the pipe-cleaner around the first fold to make up the foot. Make another foot in the same way at the other end of the pipe-cleaner. Curve the legs in the middle. Clip away a small area of the pile at the ankle area to shape the legs and feet on both sides. Ⓓ

⭐ 5 Place the legs between the green and purple pompoms at the bottom of the body and sew in place with green or purple thread. Ⓔ

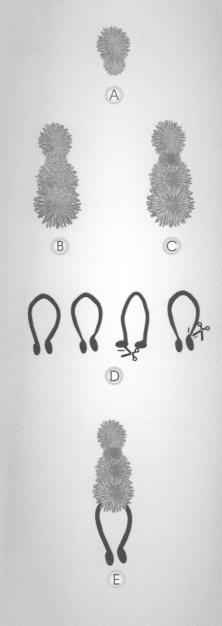

If Shimmie does his Zing, then someone is likely to topple over.

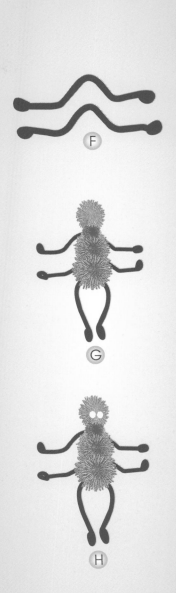

Arms

⭐ **6** Make two pairs of arms in the same way as the legs. Make an elbow fold ⅝in (15mm) above the hands. Ⓕ

⭐ **7** Position one set of arms between the bottom and chest pompoms at the back of the body and sew in place. Place the second pair of arms at the top of the chest, between the purple neck and chest pompom. Sew together and pass the needle through all of the body parts. Ⓖ

⭐ **8** Finish Shimmie Zing by placing two ⅛in (3mm) pompoms onto the lower half of the face. Secure the eyes in place with purple sewing thread. Ⓗ

What a laid-back creature Bobbly Nobbly is.
A pliable fellow, he prefers low gravity for the bouncy effect.

Bobbly Nobbly

What you need:

Materials

* 4oz (100g) ball of multicoloured yarn
* 1oz (25g) ball of white yarn
* 1oz (25g) ball of yellow bobbly yarn
* ⅜in (10mm) blue sparkly ready-made pompoms x 2
* 12in (304mm) yellow pipe-cleaners x 6
* White sewing thread

Tools

* Craft scissors
* Craft/sewing needle
* Nail clippers
* Small cardboard platform **(see page 128)**
* Pencil
* Thick pen

Head

1 Make a pompom by wrapping the multicoloured yarn around the small cardboard platform 100 times. Trim away the stray threads and make the pompom into a round shape. (A)

Chest

2 Wrap the multicoloured yarn around the small cardboard platform 110 times to make a pompom. Trim away the stray threads and make the pompom into a round shape. (B)

Bottom

3 Wrap the multicoloured yarn around the small cardboard platform 100 times to make a pompom. Trim away the stray threads and make the pompom into a round shape. (C)

Tail

4 Make the tail pompom by wrapping the multicoloured yarn around the small cardboard platform 35 times. Trim stray threads and make the pompom into a round shape. Make three more in the same way. (D)

Eyes and stalks

5 Make a pompom by wrapping the white yarn around the small cardboard platform 20 times. Trim stray threads and make a round shape. Make another pompom the same way. Sew a sparkly blue pompom into the centre of each eyeball with white thread.

6 Bend the end of a pipe-cleaner around a pencil to make a 1¼in (31mm) loop. Make a loop at the other end in the same way. Loop the ends around the middle of the pipe-cleaner to secure the bars together.

7 Curve the section in the middle. Wrap each loop with white yarn. Wrap a pink section of multicoloured yarn along the eye stalks, starting beneath the white loops. Cover with two layers of yarn.

8 Sew the middle of the eye stalk to the head with multicoloured yarn. Bend the white loops forward to make little platforms. Attach the white eyeballs onto the eye loop platforms and position the blue pupils forward. Sew in place with white yarn. (E)-(F)

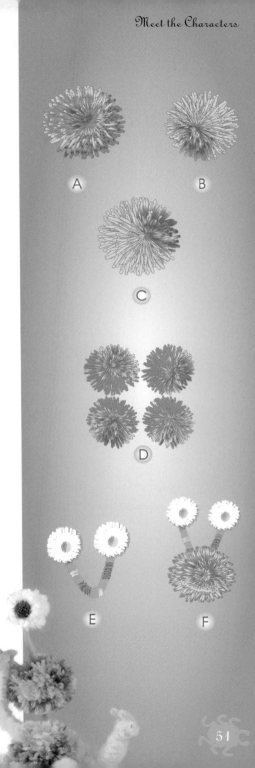

A

B

C

D

E

F

Arms

⭐ **9** Use a 12in (304mm) yellow pipe-cleaner to make a three-claw arm **(see page 150)**. Wrap two layers of yellow bobbly yarn to cover the wrist and arm, but do not wrap the claws. Curve the claws into shape around a thick pen. Make another arm in the same way. Ⓖ

Putting Bobbly Nobbly together

⭐ **10** Push a 12in (304mm) pipe-cleaner through the middle of the chest pompom and out of the top by 2in (50mm). Loop the pipe-cleaner at the bottom of the spine. Wrap with multicoloured thread. Ⓗ Sew the yarn into the centre of the pompom to secure the spine in place. Loop the top end around a pencil. Wrap with an orange section of the multicoloured yarn.

⭐ **11** Insert the arms into either side of the shoulders and attach with multicoloured yarn. Add woven multicoloured yarn to the top of the shoulders to blend the ends of the arms with the body. Trim away stray threads and contour into a rounded shape. Ⓘ

⭐ **12** Place the wrapped spine directly onto the front of the bottom body pompom with the small loop at the bottom. Sew it in place with multicoloured yarn. The spine should be visible at the front. Sew the head to the top orange loop with multicoloured yarn.

⭐ **13** Place a tail pompom onto the centre front of the bottom pompom, and sew together with multicoloured yarn. Sew another pompom on the centre of the second tail pompom. Attach two more in this way. Ⓙ

Bottom tripod

⭐ **14** Use a 12in (304mm) pipe-cleaner to make a pod leg **(see page 147)**. Bend the leg in the middle and curve the looped end to make a bucket shape. Make two more in this way. Connect all three legs at the top by wrapping half a pipe-cleaner around the tips. Wrap bobbly yellow yarn around each pod leg and reinforce the join. Ⓚ

With eyes on stalks
I'm impossible to surprise.

Gleamie Steamie's big ears and long curly tail give this alien mouse perfect equilibrium — handy when travelling by spacecraft.

Gleamie Steamie

What you need:

Materials

* 2oz (50g) ball of turquoise fluffy fashion yarn
* 2oz (50g) ball of turquoise yarn
* 2oz (50g) ball of orange yarn
* 2oz (50g) ball of grey metallic flecked yarn
* 2oz (50g) ball of mint green yarn
* 12in (304mm) grey pipe-cleaners x 4
* $\frac{3}{8}$in (10mm) white pompoms x 2
* $\frac{1}{8}$in (3mm) black pompoms x 2
* $\frac{3}{8}$in (10mm) glittery turquoise pompom
* White sewing thread

Tools

* Craft scissors
* Craft/sewing needle
* Small cardboard platform **(see page 128)**
* Pencil

Head

1 Make a pompom by wrapping the mint green yarn around the small cardboard platform 100 times. (A) Wrap the turquoise fluffy yarn over the mint green band 25 times. Trim the green yarn into an oval shape. Trim the stray threads from the turquoise area and weave a few additional threads to even out the hair. (B)

2 Place the white pompoms in the middle of the face ½in (13mm) apart. Position a black pompom onto each eyeball and sew both in place with white sewing thread. (C) Sew the glittery turquoise pompom ⅜in (10mm) below the eyes with white sewing thread.

Ears

3 Make an ear using 3in (76mm) of pipe-cleaner. Make an oval loop and pinch one end to make a point. (D) Wrap this with mint green yarn and then cover the entire surface of the ear. Make another ear in this way. Sew the ears at the back of the head, 1in (25mm) apart, with mint green yarn. (E)

Arms

4 Take a pipe-cleaner and shape it around a pencil to make a hand loop. Make another hand loop at the other end. Wrap the hands with mint green yarn and make thumb buds (see page 148). Wrap the arms with three layers of orange yarn. (F)

Chest and bottom

5 Make a pompom by wrapping the orange yarn around the small platform 100 times. Trim into a rounded shape. Cut away a flat area on one side for a waistline. (G)

6 Make a grey metallic flecked pompom, wrapping the yarn around the small platform 100 times. Trim into a rounded shape. Cut away a flat area on one side. (H)

Neck

7 Fold a pipe-cleaner in half over a pencil to form a loop. Push the pipe-cleaner through the middle of the orange pompom, leaving 1in (25mm) sticking through the top. (I) Wrap the loop with mint green yarn and the other end with four layers of orange yarn to build up the neck. (J)

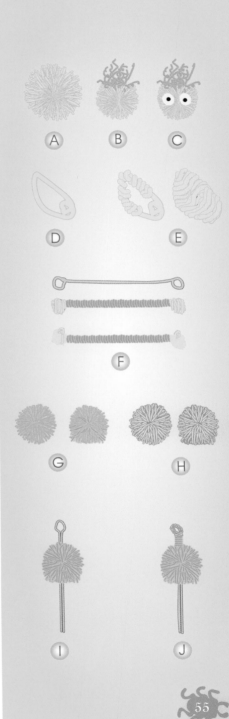

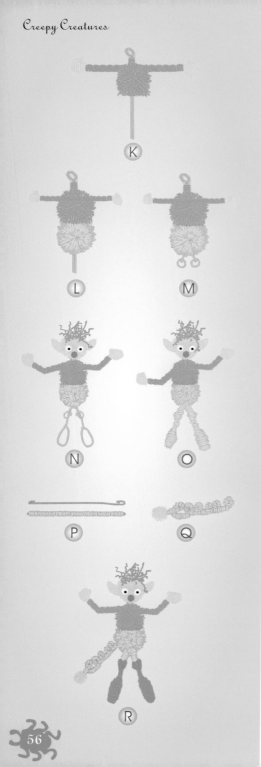

Arms and chest

8   Connect the orange arm bar across the back of the neck and into the shoulders. Connect the arm bar with the spine and add woven thread to blend neck and shoulder bars with upper chest. Trim stray threads and smooth shoulder section. K

Body

9   Insert the lower half of the spine into the flat centre of the bottom pompom. Connect the waistlines, then pull the spine completely through the bottom pompom. L Loop and shape both ends of the spine to make knee loops. M Connect the head to the neck loop with mint yarn.

Legs and feet

10   Curve a pipe-cleaner in half and thread the curved leg bar through the knee loops. Make a 3½in (89mm) foot loop at each end. Push the curved leg bar against the bottom of the grey pompom. Connect the leg bar in place with grey metallic yarn.

Weave additional yarn and trim away stray threads to smooth the bottom area. N Wrap the knee loops and leg bar with grey yarn to completely cover legs and feet and secure both pieces together.

Boots

11   Bend the foot loops at right angles. Wrap the feet with turquoise yarn. Weave additional yarn to the toes and heels on both sides of the foot. Wrap turquoise yarn around the knee loops and stitch vertical strips of yarn over each knee. O

Tail

12   Shape the end of a pipe-cleaner around a pencil to make a loop. Wrap the loop with grey yarn. Cover the tail with four layers of grey yarn. P Wrap the mint green yarn around the small card platform 20 times. Trim the pompom into a round shape. Sew it to the end of the tail with mint yarn. Coil the tail around a pencil. Q Sew the looped end of the tail to the back of the bottom pompom with grey yarn. R

The thing about space travel is that it gives you very different ideas about things.

57

Meet Flippy Floppy — the softest, squidgiest snake in space.

Flippy Floppy

What you need:

Materials

* 4oz (100g) ball of chunky beige yarn
* 4oz (100g) ball of green multicoloured yarn
* Yellow and black yarn strands
* ⅜in (10mm) yellow ready-made pompoms x 2
* 6in (152mm) white pipe-cleaner
* 6in (152mm) pink pipe-cleaner
* ¾ x 4in (19 x 101cm) beige felt

* Sequins
* Green sewing thread
* White sewing thread

Tools

* Craft scissors
* Craft/sewing needle
* Small cardboard platform **(see page 128)**
* Pencil

Body

1 Make 19 two-coloured pompoms by wrapping the chunky yarn around the small cardboard platform 20 times. Wrap the green yarn over the beige yarn 35 times. **A**

2 Place 18 of the pompoms in a line, positioning colours together to create a band of beige at the bottom of the snake and a green band at the top. Sew the beige pompom section together with beige yarn. **B** Use green yarn to connect the top section of the snake body. Trim excess strands from the long tube. Add multicoloured yarn to fill any patchy areas, keeping the beige and multicoloured bands separate.

3 Sew sequin scales to the top of the snake with green sewing thread. Cover the underside of the body with beige chunky yarn. Apply these strands evenly and close together by sewing through the middle of the body pompoms.

4 Position a two-coloured pompom at an angle to one end of the snake. Sew in place with beige yarn. **C**

Head

5 Make one pompom by wrapping the chunky beige yarn around the small cardboard platform 35 times. Trim the yarn on one side to flatten the tongue platform. Attach the pompom to the beige area at the front of the snake with beige yarn. Add more yarn to fill out the head and trim into shape once connected to the neck. **D**

6 Make a pompom by wrapping the multicoloured yarn around the small cardboard platform 55 times. Flatten one section of the pompom to create half of the inside of the mouth. Attach this pompom to the green area of the neck. Add green thread to fill out the head and trim the shape to taper the head at the front. Weave green loops onto the surface of the head to create a scaly appearance and define profile **(see page 139).**

7 Sew yellow pompoms to the sides of the head with white thread. Weave green loops to blend the eyeballs with the face. **E** Sew vertical strands of yellow and black yarn onto the eyeballs to create snake eyes.

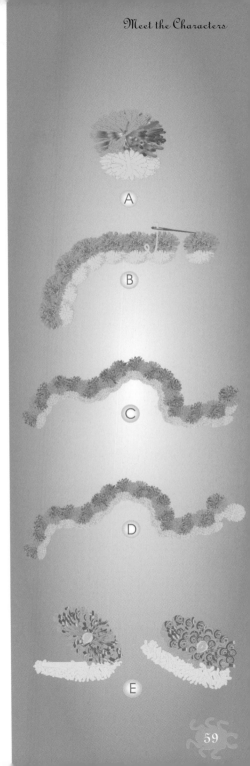

59

Fangs

⭐ 8 Using the white pipe-cleaner, make a bend measuring ½in (13mm) from the end. Make another bend next to this using ¾in (19mm) of material to make a spike. Curve into a fang shape. Bend ½in (13mm) at the other end of the shape. Fold ¾in (19mm) of pipe-cleaner over and curve it into a second fang. Curve the space between the fangs to make a horseshoe shape. Ⓕ Attach the fangs to the upper green half of the face using white sewing thread.

⭐ 9 Cut a mouth from the beige felt fabric **(see page 152)** to cover the pipe-cleaner outline and sew into the top and bottom of the mouth with white sewing thread. Trim the edges into the mouth. Ⓖ

Tongue

⭐ 10 Using a pink pipe-cleaner, make two ¾in (19mm) bends at one end. Fold one bend over the other. Make another bend to form a zigzag. Fold together to make a V shape. Loop the remaining section over the middle of the V-shape, then curl the rest around a pencil to coil the tongue. Make a loop at the end of the coil and attach the loop at the back of the mouth with white sewing thread. Ⓗ

⭐ 11 Finally, trim any stray threads and Flippy Floppy is ready to slither away. Ⓘ

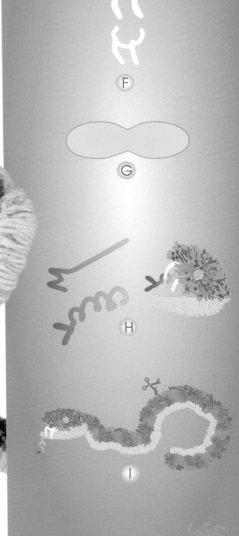

Ⓕ

Ⓖ

Ⓗ

Ⓘ

61

Some days, when he feels more green than blue,
Blue Greenie curls up and naps in the bonsai tree house.

Blue Greenie

What you need:

Materials

* 2oz (50g) ball of turquoise yarn
* 2oz (50g) ball of blue yarn
* 1oz (25g) ball of bright green yarn
* 40in (1m) length of fluffy blue fashion yarn
* 40in (1m) length of fluffy turquoise fashion yarn
* $\frac{3}{8}$in (10mm) white ready-made pompoms x 2
* $\frac{1}{8}$in (3mm) purple ready-made pompoms x 2

* 12in (304mm) yellow pipe-cleaners x 2
* 9in (228mm) yellow pipe-cleaner
* 8in (203mm) yellow pipe-cleaner
* White sewing thread

Tools

* Tools
* Craft scissors
* Craft/sewing needle
* Nail clippers

* Small cardboard platform **(see page 128)**

Head

⭐ Make a pompom by wrapping the blue yarn around the small cardboard platform 90 times. Then wrap the turquoise yarn on top of the blue yarn 100 times, to make a two-coloured pompom **(see page 145)**. Trim away any stray threads and make a round head shape. Ⓐ

⭐ Sew two white pompoms onto the face on the turquoise band. Then position a purple pompom onto each eyeball and attach with white sewing thread. Ⓑ

Body

⭐ Wrap the blue yarn around the small cardboard platform 70 times. Wrap the turquoise yarn on top of the blue yarn 70 times, and 40 layers of green yarn on top, making a three-coloured pompom. Trim stray threads and make a round body shape. Ⓒ

⭐ Fold a 12in (304mm) pipe-cleaner in half and insert both ends into the body pompom, at the green part, to make a spine. Ⓓ Continue to push the pipe-cleaner ends through the bottom of the head pompom.

Pull 1½in (38mm) of each end through the top of the head to form the antennae.

Long arms

⭐ Use a 9in (228mm) yellow pipe-cleaner to make the pod arms **(see page 147)**. Wrap the arms and hands with blue yarn. Wrap one layer of yarn around the elbows, and three layers of yarn to the arms. Add blue bobbled loops to the tops of both hands **(see page 139)**. Wrap each arm with three green bands to decorate the sleeves. Ⓔ

⭐ Separate the body and head pompoms by 1½in (38mm). Connect the arm pods to the spine between the body and head. Wrap blue yarn around this middle section, covering the arms, spine, chest and shoulders. Wrap green yarn around the neck for a green band under the head pompom and add a ½in (13mm) green waistband above the body pompom. Add bobbled loops of blue yarn between the waistband and neck **(see page 139)**. Ⓕ-Ⓖ Wrap the antennae with fluffy turquoise yarn.

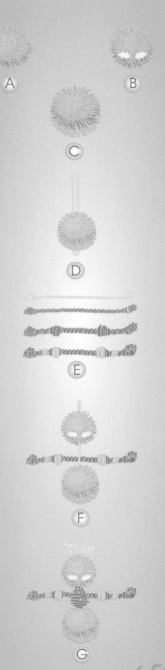

Short arms

7 Make the short arms with the 8in (203mm) pipe-cleaner (**see page 147**). Wrap the hands with blue yarn. They should be smaller than the top hands, so use fewer layers of yarn. Cover the arms with three layers of blue yarn. Add blue bobbled loops to one side of each hand (**see page 139**). H

8 Wrap each arm with two bands of bright green yarn to decorate the sleeves. Insert the middle of the short arms into the lower half of the body pompom and attach with blue thread. I

Legs

9 Make the legs with a 12in (304mm) pipe-cleaner (**see page 147**). Make a 2in (50mm) loop at one end. Make the stick legs and then make another 2in (50mm) loop at the other end. Cover the feet with blue yarn. Apply a stitch of yarn to the heel on each foot, then blend with the layers. J

10 Wrap the legs with two layers of blue yarn. Wrap a two-layer band of green yarn over the knees to make a knee shape and another ¼in (6mm) band above the ankles. Wrap the tops of the legs with blue fluffy yarn. Sew the middle of the stick legs to the centre of the body pompom with green yarn. K

Tail

11 Make a pompom by wrapping the green yarn around the small cardboard platform 35 times. Trim away any stray threads and make a round shape. Position the tail under the stick legs and sew in place with green yarn. L

Only three more Zim bars until lunch. Ooh, I really can't wait.

65

Always on the lookout for a bit of fun,
Tag is a great mate to hang around with.

Tag the Bat

What you need:

Materials

✳ 2oz (50g) ball of blue fluffy fashion
   yarn
✳ ⅜in (10mm) blue ready-made
   pompoms x 2
✳ 12in (304mm) blue pipe-cleaners
   x 2
✳ 4½in (114mm) black pipe-cleaners
   x 2
✳ 2 x 4in (50 x 101mm) blue felt
✳ 3½ x 7in (88 x 177mm) blue felt x 2
✳ Blue sewing thread

Tools

✳ Craft scissors
✳ Craft/sewing needle
✳ Small cardboard platform
   (see page 128)

Body

⭐ 3 Make a pompom by wrapping the blue fluffy yarn around the small card platform 90 times. Trim into a rounded shape.

Head

⭐ 1 Make a pompom by wrapping the blue fluffy yarn around the small cardboard platform 55 times. Cut a pair of bat ears from the 2 x 4in (50 x 101mm) rectangle of blue felt using the ear template on **page 152**. A–B

⭐ 2 Trim the head pompom into a rounded shape. Attach the blue ready-made pompoms into the centre of the head pompom for the eyes. Attach the ears at the top of the head pompom on either side. C

Tail

⭐ 4 Make a tail pompom by wrapping the blue fluffy yarn around the small card platform 25 times. Trim the stray threads into a round shape. Connect the tail to the body with blue yarn. Set the head on top and thread yarn through all body sections to secure the bat into a solid piece. D

A

B

C

D

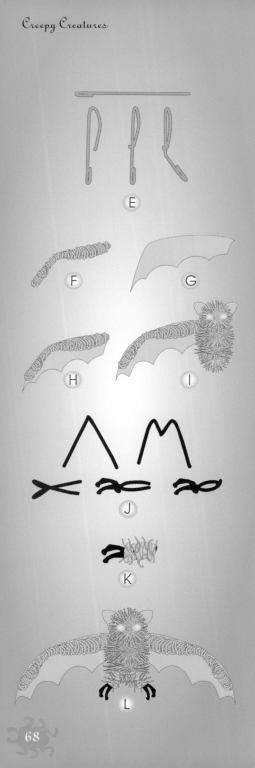

Wings

⭐5 Take a 12in (304mm) pipe-cleaner and fold it over by 1in (25mm) at one end.

⭐6 Make a 3½in (89mm) loop at the other end.

⭐7 Attach the end of the loop back onto the pipe-cleaner 3in (76mm) from the bottom. Bend the pipe-cleaner at an angle just below the join. Make another wing bar in the same way. E

⭐8 Wrap and cover the wing bars with two layers of blue fluffy yarn. Build up three layers of yarn around the upper arm and taper slightly towards the looped end section. F

⭐9 Using the template on **page 152**, cut two bat wings out of the 3½ x 7in (88 x 177mm) rectangles of blue felt. G

⭐10 Attach the wrapped pipe-cleaners onto the outline of the felt wings using blue sewing thread. H Connect the wings into the body by threading blue yarn through the loop at the end of the arm and the side of the shoulder. I

Feet and claws

⭐11 Take a black pipe-cleaner and bend into a V shape. Fold the pipe-cleaner by ½in (13mm) on either side of the bend, to make a W shape.

⭐12 Twist over either side to gather the claws.

⭐13 Curve both claws to shape the feet. Connect the top ends of the legs into a loop. J

⭐14 Wrap the legs with two or three layers of yarn, from the claws up. Connect each leg to the side of the bat with the blue yarn and sew the end loop of the leg in between the tail and body. K–L

Tag the Bat is ready to fly.

It's a complicated arrangement, but it works for us.

He may be lumpy but he's active. Phlump competes in the Lunar Cycle Championships every year.

Phlump

What you need:

Materials

* 4oz (100g) ball of blue yarn
* 2oz (50g) ball of blue fluffy fashion yarn
* 2oz (50g) ball of multicoloured yarn
* 12in (304mm) pipe-cleaners x 6
* ⅜in (10mm) fluorescent green pompoms x 2
* ⅛in (3mm) green pompoms x 2
* Green sewing thread

Tools

* Craft scissors
* Craft/sewing needle
* Medium cardboard platform **(see page 128)**
* Small cardboard platform
* Pencil

Head

⭐ Make a spotted head pompom by wrapping the blue yarn 40 times around the medium cardboard platform. Then wrap 15 layers of fluffy blue fashion yarn over the top. Wrap another band of blue yarn 40 times on top, then 15 layers of the fluffy blue yarn. Repeat this process once more, and finish with 40 layers of the blue yarn. You should have wrapped 205 revolutions in total. Ⓐ

Nose and eyes

⭐ Wrap the blue yarn around the small cardboard platform 20 times to make a pompom. Trim it into a nose shape. Ⓑ Attach the nose to the middle of the head pompom with blue yarn. Weave bobbles onto the surface of the nose pompom to create a lumpy texture **(see page 139)**. Attach the fluorescent green pompoms directly above the nose, spacing them ⅛in (3mm) apart. Sew in place with sewing thread and attach a green pompom onto each eyeball for pupils. Weave six strands of multicoloured thread above each eye to make lashes. Ⓒ

Hairy antennae

⭐ Wrap a pipe-cleaner with blue fluffy fashion yarn. Wrap a layer of the multicoloured yarn over the fluffy yarn, 2in (50mm) at one end – but not the very tip so that this stays fluffy. Wrap the pipe-cleaner around a pencil to coil the antenna. Make a loop at the bottom fluffy end. Make another antenna in the same way and attach the looped ends to the middle of the top of the head. Ⓓ

Body

⭐ Make a spotted body pompom by wrapping the blue yarn 40 times around the medium cardboard platform. Then wrap 15 layers of fluffy blue fashion yarn over the top. Wrap another band of blue yarn 40 times on top, then 15 layers of the fluffy blue yarn. Repeat this process twice more, and finish with 40 layers of the blue yarn. You should have wrapped 260 revolutions in total. Ⓔ

⭐ Connect the head to the body, positioning the head slightly forward. Using the blue yarn, pass the thread completely through body and head pompoms to secure together. Ⓕ

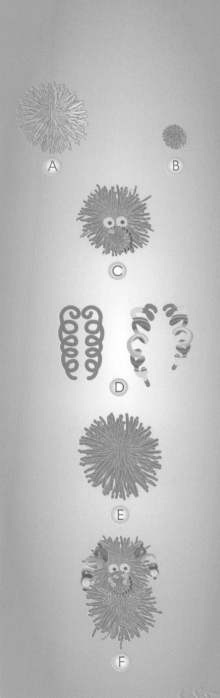

71

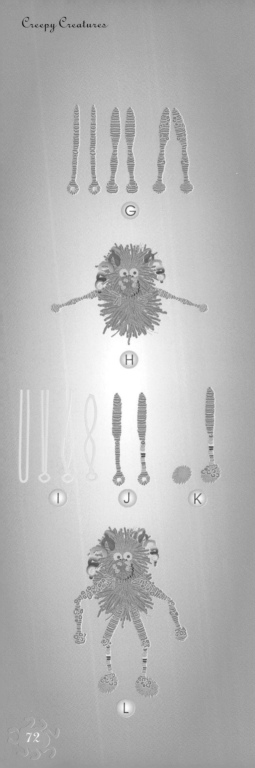

Arms

⭐ 6 Using a blue pipe-cleaner, make a twisted arm pod **(see page 147)**. Cover the arm loop and wrap the hand pod and arm with blue yarn. Wrap additional yarn layers to build up the muscles on forearms and biceps. Add more yarn to the hand pods to make them bigger. Decorate the top of the hand with blue woven loops **(see page 139)**. Add more bobbles up the arm to create texture. Make another arm in the same way. G

⭐ 7 Attach the ends of the upper arm loops to each side of the body with blue yarn. Pass thread through both arm loops and the body to secure in place. H

Feet

⭐ 8 Wrap the blue yarn 25 times around the small cardboard platform to make a foot pompom. Trim a flat area for the bottom of the foot. Trim it to round the shape of the foot pompom. Then weave blue fluffy yarn through the toes to decorate the front of the foot. Make another foot in the same way.

Legs

⭐ 9 Use a 12in (304mm) pipe-cleaner to make a pod leg **(see page 147)**. I Cover the foot loops with a layer of blue yarn. Wrap the leg bars together with two layers of blue yarn. Then wrap the thigh with blue yarn and add more layers to build up the thigh muscles. Make another leg in the same way. Give Phlump some stripy socks by wrapping a layer of multicoloured yarn around the legs from the knees to the feet. J

⭐ 10 Slip a wrapped foot loop into each foot pompom and sew together with blue yarn. K Stitch blue yarn bobbles onto the knees **(see page 139)**. Sew the top of the leg loops into the bottom of the body pompom with blue yarn. L

I simply cannot recommend it enough. Riding your bike in space is completely great, wild and free.

He's bike crazy; he never stops. And as if that wasn't enough, there's even more on page 108.

Despite the teeth, Snork is definitely a space softie.

Snork the Dragon

What you need:

Materials

* 4oz (100g) ball of purple yarn
* 4oz (100g) ball of beige chunky yarn
* 2oz (50g) ball of purple fluffy fashion yarn
* 1oz (25g) ball of white yarn
* 12in (304mm) purple/white pipe-cleaners x 7
* 12in (304mm) gold sparkly pipe-cleaner

* $\frac{3}{8}$in (10mm) purple pompoms x 5
* $\frac{3}{8}$in (10mm) white pompoms x 2
* $\frac{1}{8}$in (3mm) green pompoms x 2
* $\frac{1}{8}$in (3mm) orange pompoms x 2
* 1$\frac{1}{4}$ x 1$\frac{1}{2}$in (31 x 38mm) beige felt
* 1$\frac{1}{4}$ x 1$\frac{1}{2}$in (31 x 38mm) pink felt

* 2 x 4$\frac{1}{2}$in (50 x 114mm) purple felt
* White sewing thread

Tools

* Craft scissors
* Craft/sewing needle
* Medium cardboard platform **(see page 128)**
* Small cardboard platform
* Knitting needle

74

Head

⭐ Make a pompom by wrapping the purple yarn around the small cardboard platform 110 times. Make two pompoms by wrapping the purple yarn around the small platform 100 times. Make a nose pompom with 50 layers of purple yarn. Make a jaw pompom with 25 layers of beige chunky yarn.

Body and Tail

⭐ Blend one strand of fluffy purple fashion yarn and one strand of purple yarn and wrap 100 times around the medium cardboard platform.

⭐ Make a chest pompom with the chunky beige yarn, wrapping it 100 times around the small platform. Make a stomach pompom, wrapping 70 layers of chunky beige yarn around the small platform. Make the bottom of Snork's lower half with 50 layers of chunky beige yarn and two beige pompoms with 25 layers of yarn on the small card platform.

⭐ Make five purple pompoms, wrapping the yarn around the small platform 25 times for each and a larger tail pompom with 100 layers of purple yarn. Connect the four small pompoms in a line and attach to the larger tail pompom with purple yarn. (A) Fold a pipe-cleaner in half and wrap with one layer of beige yarn. (B) Sew the line of tail pompoms onto the wrapped bar with purple yarn. (C)

Face and mouth

⭐ Connect the big purple body pompom to the wide end of the tail with purple yarn. Connect the top of the head pompom next in line. (D) Place one of the 100 revolution pompoms in front on top. (E) Attach the nose to the front of face. (F)

⭐ Attach one small beige pompom under the wide end of the tail, then the smaller and middle beige stomach pompoms together with purple yarn. Next attach the large beige chest pompom below the purple chest pompoms. Attach a small beige pompom in front for the neck with purple yarn and sew all pieces together. (G)

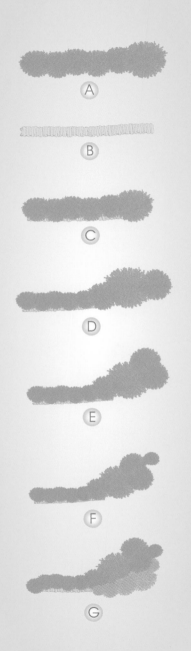

A

B

C

D

E

F

G

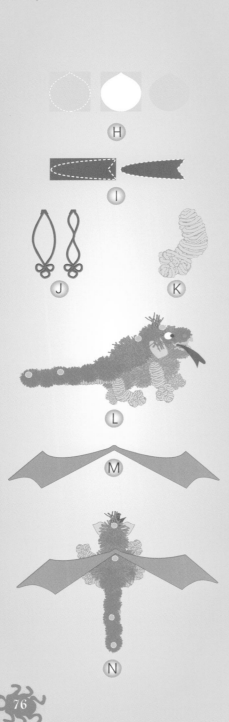

7 Cut a pair of ears from the beige felt **(see page 152)**. (H) Sew an ear to each side of the head, 1in (25mm) behind the eyes.

8 Cut the gold pipe-cleaner in half and curve both pieces. Make six small zigzag bends at the front of one of the curves for the bottom set of teeth. Make four bigger zigzag bends on the other half for the top teeth. Leave a ½in (13mm) straight section at either end of both sets. Sew the bottom set to the top of the lower jaw and the top set to the bottom of the nose with thread.

9 Cut a tongue from the pink felt **(see page 152)**. Sew it through the join at the back of the mouth with white thread. (I)

Legs

10 Use a 12in (304mm) pipe-cleaner to make a three-loop appendage **(see page 150)**. (J) Wrap the toes and foot with chunky beige yarn. Cover the ankles, pulling the yarn taut. Wrap the leg with two layers of thread, adding another layer in the middle for a knee. (K) Add a few stitches of white yarn over the middle toe to make a claw. Then make three more legs in the same way.

11 Sew one pair of legs to the back of the dragon with chunky beige yarn. Sew the front legs into the top of the chest pompom with chunky yarn, sewing through the under body and through the tops of each of the front legs. Bend the knees to pose the dragon. (L)

Wings

12 Cut a set of wings from the purple felt **(see page 152)**. (M) Wrap a 12in (304mm) pipe-cleaner with one layer of purple yarn. Shape the pipe-cleaner around the top of the wings and sew in place with white thread. Sew the wings between the back of the head and the upper body with sewing thread. (N)

Astro Plasto is my favourite ice-cream. It's out of this world!

Accessories

You can't cope without proper pod shoes on a hot planet!

Pod Shoes

What you need:

Materials
* 1½ x 2in (38 x 50mm) magenta felt x 2
* 1½ x 1¾in (38 x 44mm) magenta felt x 2
* ½ x 1in (13 x 25mm) magenta felt x 2
* Sewing thread

Tools
* Craft/sewing needle
* Craft scissors

⭐ 1 Using the templates on **page 153**, cut out the shoe patterns for two shoes. Ⓐ

⭐ 2 Place the heel on the bottom of the sole pattern under the bar and sew in place. Turn the pattern over. Ⓑ

⭐ 3 Place the top of the shoe over the sole, with the curved edges together. Stitch the edges together using sewing thread. Ⓒ

⭐ 4 Tuck the ends of the square flap to the inside of the shoe on each side. Sew in place with a few stitches of thread. Ⓓ

⭐ 5 Repeat the process to make the second pod shoe. Now slip the creature's pod foot through the opening at the back of the shoe.

It is widely acknowledged now that pod shoes will change your life.

Ⓐ

Ⓑ

Ⓒ

Ⓓ

Easy to make, easy to wear: these glasses are highly sought after.

Glasses

What you need:

Materials

✳ 12in (304mm) pipe-cleaner

Tools

✳ Nail clippers
✳ Marker pen

I can see for miles and miles... and I can see all your spots as well!

Frame

⭐ 1 Cut the pipe-cleaner in half. Using one half, make two bends at 2in (50mm) intervals to make a U shape. Ⓐ

⭐ 2 Take the other half and make a ¼in (6mm) fold at one end. Fold this over one corner of the U shape. Wrap the first lens frame around a marker pen to shape.

⭐ 3 Wrap the middle of the pipe-cleaner over the bridge twice, to secure the connection. Ⓑ Then wrap the second lens frame around a marker pen as before.

⭐ 4 Make sure both lenses are equal in size, and then wrap the edge of the top of the lens around the opposite corner of the U shape. Ⓒ Clip away any excess pipe-cleaner from the bottom of the corner connection. This will be about 1½in (38mm) of pipe-cleaner.

⭐ 5 Curve the ends around a marker pen or finger and thumb to shape the back of the glasses. Ⓓ

⭐ 6 Curve the front frame of the glasses to contour with the character's features.

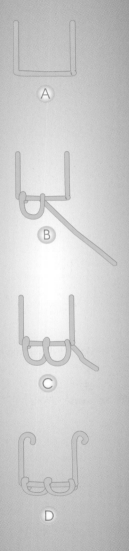

Large or small, this looks good in any universe.
The top hat stands up for all occasions.

Top Hat

What you need:

Materials
* 2¾ x 3¾in (70 x 95mm) green felt
* 5in (127mm) square green felt
* 3½in (88mm) square green felt
* Green sewing thread

Tools
* Craft/sewing needle
* Craft scissors

It's not only impossible to travel faster than the speed of light, it's not right either — your hat would blow off.

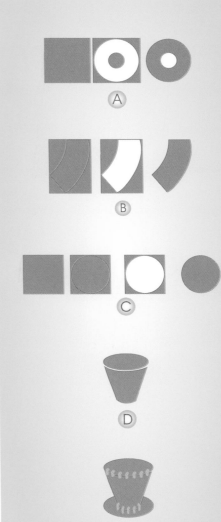

1. Cut the top hat patterns using the template on **page 153**. Cut one of each shape. (A)–(C)

2. Place the straight edges of the hat sides together to make a tube. Sew together with green sewing thread. Connect the little circle onto the wide end of the tube and sew the edges together. (D)

3. Slip the doughnut-shape piece onto the bottom of the hat. Sew the edges of the inner circle and the bottom edge of the hat together with sewing thread. (E)

Beautiful and sharp, these are a gallant creature's best accessories.

Sword and Armour

What you need:

Materials
* 12in (304mm) gold metallic pipe-cleaners x 5

Tools
* Nail clippers
* Pencil

Sword

1 Fold a pipe-cleaner in half. Then bend in half again, 3in (76mm) from the folded point. Ⓐ

2 Curve the tips of each bended half. Pull the curves through the middle of the pointed fold to make the blade of the sword. Ⓑ

3 Cut a pipe-cleaner in half and insert it through the middle of the top of the fold. Place it in the middle, between the blades, then loop the tips of the curves around the bar to secure the shape. Ⓒ

4 Twist the middle bar around the tip of the folded point and then twist them together. Make a loop with the remaining section of pipe-cleaner, and close the shape by folding the tips together. Ⓓ

Armour

5 Fold a pipe-cleaner in half, make a loop around a pencil, and twist together. Fold the other ends to complete the loop strap. Make two more in this way. Ⓔ

6 Make a belt by curving the parallel bars of the loop strap. Fold the end of the strap around the ring to close the shape. Ⓕ

7 To make shoulder straps, curve two loop straps, then thread the belt through the rings and cross either strap over the shoulders of the creature. Weave the ends of the shoulder straps through the bars of the belt. Ⓖ–Ⓗ Then latch the belt ring around the creature's waistline.

Spacey and dreamy and just a few stitches away...ahhh.

Leaf Sleeping Bag

What you need:

Materials
* 12in (304mm) square of green felt
* Green yarn

Tools
* Craft scissors
* Craft/sewing needle

⭐ 1   Cut two leaf shapes and one stalk from the templates on **page 153**. Ⓐ–Ⓑ

⭐ 2   Lay the stalk patch over to one side of the leaf matching the outline of the leaf with the stalk. Sew it in place with the green yarn. Ⓒ

⭐ 3   Attach the two catalpa leaf shapes together and stitch around the edges of both leaves to connect together. Ⓓ

⭐ 4   Leave an area unstitched at the top of the top leaf so that the creature can get in. Ⓔ

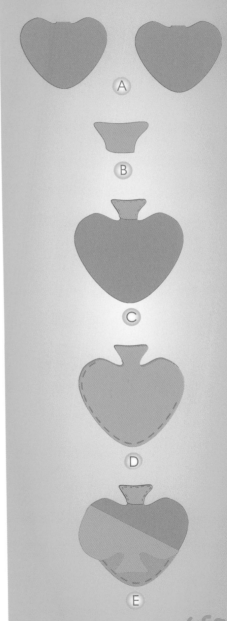

Homes
and Hideaways

Recline and relax in this fashionable resting pod.

Tri Pod Chair

What you need:

Materials
- ✳ ⅝in (15mm) glittery green pompom
- ✳ ⅜in (10mm) glittery green pompoms x 5
- ✳ 12in (304mm) green pipe-cleaners x 3
- ✳ Green sewing thread

Tools
- ✳ Craft/sewing needle
- ✳ Craft scissors

1 Make a 3in (76mm) fold at one end of a pipe-cleaner. Make another 3in (76mm) fold at the other end. Connect the ends by looping them around the middle of the pipe-cleaner. Make two more bars in the same way. (A)

2 Position the bars in a line on a flat surface. Gather in the middle and connect together with green sewing thread. (B)

3 Curve and splay the ends of three bars into tripod legs. (C)

4 Attach a ³⁄₈in (10mm) glittery green pompom into the centre of the curved bars and connect to the centre of the chair frame by sewing together with green thread. (D)

5 Curve the opposite bars in the reverse direction to create the back of the chair and two armrests. (E) Attach the ⁵⁄₈in (15mm) glittery green pompom into the centre of the seat of the chair on the opposite side to the first pompom. (F)

6 Insert two ³⁄₈in (10mm) glittery green pompoms in between the curves of the chair back and connect to the bars with green sewing thread. Add the last two pompoms to the sides between the armrests and the seat of the chair. Connect to the frame with green sewing thread. (G)

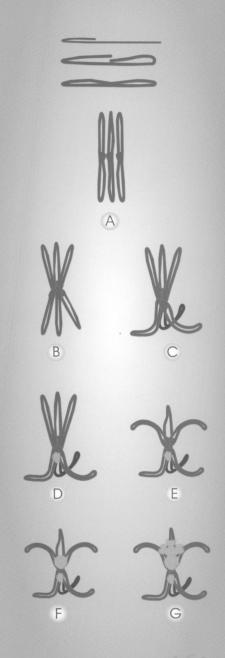

A

B   C

D   E

F   G

This soft, springy lounger is ideal for napping across the Milky Way.

Designer Pod Lounger

What you need:

Materials

* ⅝in (15mm) glittery green pompoms x 3
* 12in (304mm) green pipe-cleaners x 7
* Green sewing thread

Tools

* Craft/sewing needle
* Craft scissors

We celebrate lounging in space and comfort.

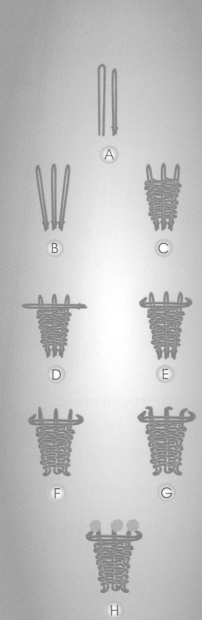

1 Fold a pipe-cleaner in half. Loop the pointed ends together to make a bar. Make three more this way. Arrange the folded bars into a fan shape. Start weaving a pipe-cleaner between the six vertical bars, 1in (25mm) from the bottom. A–C

2 Weave two more pipe-cleaners up the vertical bars. Place the fourth folded bar horizontally across the top, about 1in (25mm) from the end. D Curve the ends of the horizontal bar under the bottom of the lounger platform to form bedposts. E

3 Curl the ends of the vertical bars into bedposts at the narrow end of the lounger. Curve the middle bar in the opposite direction. Curve the the three bars at the widest end of the bed. F–G

4 Attach a glittery green pompom to the top of each bed curve. Sew in place with green sewing thread to finish the lounger. H

95

Terribly useful for posing on, this avant-garde chair
is every creature's sit-down fantasy.

Lawn Chair

What you need:

Materials

- ✳ 2oz (50g) ball of spring green yarn
- ✳ 12in (304mm) yellow pipe-cleaners x 23
- ✳ Green sewing thread

Tools

- ✳ Craft scissors
- ✳ Craft/sewing needle
- ✳ Bodkin
- ✳ Medium cardboard platform **(see page 128)**

★ 1 Make a pompom by wrapping the spring green yarn around the medium cardboard platform 120 times. Make another three pompoms in the same way.

★ 2 Curve two pipe-cleaners and twist together into an arc to form the back of the chair. (A)

★ 3 Cut a 4½in (114mm) length of pipe-cleaner. Position it horizontally across the chair frame, 1½in (38mm) from the top of the arc and loop it around the edges. (B)

★ 4 Use 4in (101mm) of pipe-cleaner to make a V shape. Loop it around the strap bar and the top centre of the arc. (C)

★ 5 Curve a pipe-cleaner and wrap it through the centre of the crossbar. Weave each side into the sides of the chair back. (D)

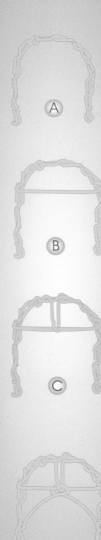

A

B

C

D

6 Fold a pipe-cleaner in half. Wrap the centre of the fold around a pencil to make a rounded chair leg foot. Bend the rounded loop forward to make a foot. Make another leg and foot in the same way. Overlap the legs and rounded feet to make one leg. Make three more legs in the same way. (E)

7 Make a square frame by bending a pipe-cleaner at 3½in (88mm) intervals. Make another this way. Overlap the ends on a flat surface and loop them together. (F)

8 Attach the four chair legs onto the corners of the square frame, wrapping the ends onto the angles of the frame. Make each leg 2in (50mm) in height from the bottom of each chair foot. Cut a pipe-cleaner in half. Place in a cross shape across the centre of the seat frame and loop to the sides. (G)

9 Wrap the ends of the chair back into two corners of the seat frame. The top of the arc should sit 4in (101mm) from the seat frame. (H) Wrap the remaining pipe-cleaners around the seat frame to reinforce the back and leg joints. (I)

10 Place a pompom into each of the seat quarters and attach to the chair frame with green yarn. Weave additional green yarn into patchy areas. Trim the surface of the pompoms to remove unwanted threads and shape the upholstery into a plump cushion. (J)–(K)

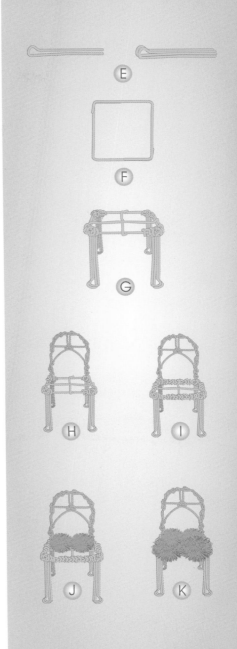

*Some hide special things in trunks
and some try to hide in trunks.*

Trunk

What you need:

Materials
✳ 2oz (50g) balls of beige
 yarn x 3
✳ 12in (304mm) beige
 pipe-cleaners x 22

Tools
✳ Craft scissors
✳ Craft/sewing needle
✳ Nail clippers
✳ Pencil

1   Bend a pipe-cleaner 1in (25mm) from the end. Make another right-angle bend 6in (152mm) from the first, to form half a rectangle. Make another piece in the same way. Connect the bars into a rectangular shape on a flat surface. Then twist the ends together to form the rectangle. Make three more rectangles in the same way. (A)

2   Cut two pipe-cleaners in half, and then curve all four pieces into arches. Position all four arches onto one of the rectangle frames, one at either end and two in the middle. Make sure they are equally spaced and loop the ends to secure in place. (B)–(C)

3   Weave a pipe-cleaner through the top of the arches in the middle. Bend down both sides and twist the remaining strip over the side bars of the rectangle. Apply two more straps across the top of the lid in the same way, spacing them equally apart. (D)

4   Wrap the bars and weave over all the open areas with beige yarn to cover the surface of the lid. (E)

5   To make the base of the trunk, bend a pipe-cleaner into three equal sections. Measure 4in (101mm) from each bend. Make four more sections in this way. (F)

6   Attach one of these square shapes onto one end of the rectangle, twisting the ends over the rectangle edge. Make the side 3½in (89mm) in height. Repeat the same for the other end of the trunk. (G)

7   Take a rectangle bar and unfasten the connections. Carefully weave it through the sides of the trunk to form a rectangular base. Connect the ends of the bars to close the rectangle. Repeat the process, setting another horizontal rectangle through the centre of the trunk. (H)–(I)

8   Place one of the square shapes around the sides and bottom of the trunk, then twist the ends onto the top bar of the trunk to secure in place. Attach two more in the same way, spacing them equally between the middle and outside bars. (J)–(K)

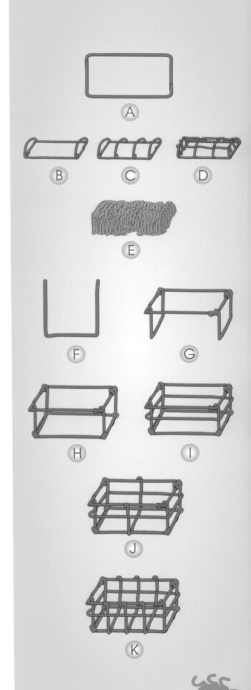

L

M

N

O

P

9 Weave a pipe-cleaner through the centre of the bottom of the trunk and secure the ends onto the middle bars. L

10 Cut a pipe-cleaner in half and place in a cross shape on the bottom. Twist and connect the ends onto the bars of the box to reinforce the trunk shape. Cut another pipe-cleaner in half and attach each piece diagonally across each side of the trunk. M

11 To make a latch, curve a 6in (152mm) length of pipe-cleaner. Make a 2in (50mm) loop in the middle. Bend the remaining ends into looped coils. Wrap the coils and latch with yarn. N Insert the coils into the centre of the rim of the trunk lid and connect the latch to the trunk lid. Fold the latch over a pencil to bend it into shape against the side of the trunk.

12 Weave the yarn through the lid grid and cover the entire surface. Weave yarn through the grid bars of the trunk, completely covering the surface. O Sew the trunk lid rim onto one of the trunk's top edges by matching the rectangle shapes. P

The angular shape will soften if the pipe-cleaner bars are pulled too vigorously when applying yarn to the grid. Adding further grid bars to the frame of the trunk will tighten the weave texture of the surface.

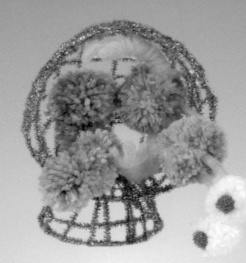

A circle is not just a circle, and the creatures will agree that this web chair is the most chic of seats.

Designer Web Chair

What you need:

Materials
✳ 12in (304mm) gold metallic
   pipe-cleaners x 28

Tools
✳ Nail clippers

The space inside the chair becomes the reality.

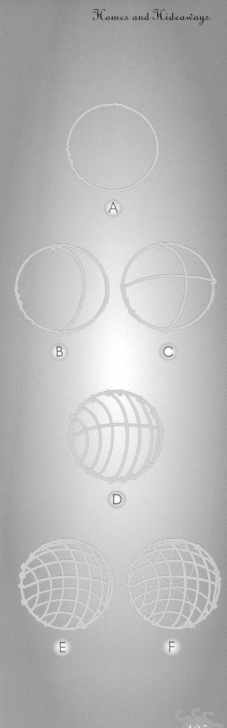

⭐ Curve three pipe-cleaners. Overlap the ends and twist together to make a 16in (406mm) circle for the front of the chair. Ⓐ

⭐ Cut a 10in (254mm) piece of pipe-cleaner and curve into a semi-circle. Position the curve over the middle of the big circle and loop the ends to attach in place. This will form the back spine of the chair dome. Ⓑ Curve another 10in (254mm) length of pipe-cleaner and attach it to the big circle, this time horizontally. Ⓒ

⭐ Curve twelve pipe-cleaners and loop all the ends. Connect six of the curved pieces to the back of the chair, starting next to the vertical spine. Set them 1in (25mm) apart, looping them onto the rim to make the vertical lines of the web. Ⓓ

⭐ Connect and loop the other six curved bars, starting next to the horizontal centre bar. Set them 1in (25mm) apart and loop them onto the rim to make the horizontal lines of the web. Ⓔ

⭐ Curve a pipe-cleaner into a circle shape. Weave it through the top half of chair, in the middle, to create a ring design. Add another ring to the bottom of the chair. Ⓕ

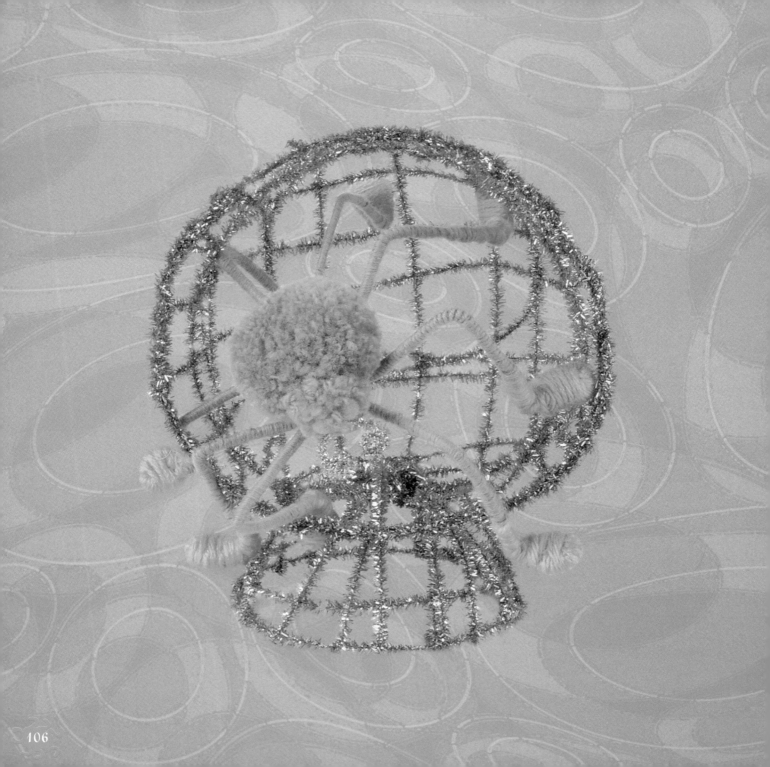

6 Cut two pipe-cleaners into halves and curve into four semi-circles. Weave the semi-circles into the web, placing them equally around the dome at the top, bottom and sides. G To complete the chair, push against the grid surrounding the rim to make a curved lip around the edge of the chair.

7 To make the base, curve a pipe-cleaner into a circle and loop the ends together. Curve four more pipe-cleaners and cut in half to make eight semi-circles. Place the full circle on a flat surface and connect one semi-circle horizontally across the ring. Connect another semi-circle vertically to make a cross. Attach three more vertical and three more horizontal semi-circles in the same way, to form a grid dome base. H

8 Curve two pipe-cleaners. Wrap a circle around the bottom section of the base, weaving through the curved spokes. Cut the second curved pipe-cleaner in half and make two semi-circles. Place the dome chair on top of the pod base and weave the semi-circles through the top of the base and the bottom of the chair to secure together. I

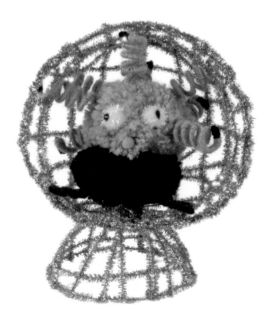

G

H

I

107

The bicycle is the perfect size for long-legged creatures.
The wheels roll round whatever the weather.

Bicycle

What you need:

Materials

* 1oz (25g) ball of turquoise yarn
* 1oz (25g) ball of grey yarn
* 12in (304mm) grey pipe-cleaners x 21
* White sewing thread

Tools

* Craft scissors
* Craft/sewing needle
* Small cardboard platform **(see page 128)**
* Nail clippers
* Pencil

1 Curve one
pipe-cleaner into
a perfect circle by looping the ends
together. Make another circle exactly
the same shape and size.
Cut two pipe-cleaners in half and fold
the ends of each piece to make the
spokes. Connect two spokes to each
circle by looping the ends around the
wheel and make a perfect cross in
the middle. Place two circles together
to make an eight-spoke wheel. (A)
Bind the edges together with a layer
of grey yarn. Make another wheel
exactly the same way.

2 Cut a pipe-cleaner into
quarters. Bend one quarter in half
and insert it through the middle of
the spokes in one wheel. Repeat for
the second wheel. Tie both bars into
the middle of the spokes with grey
yarn. Cut another pipe-cleaner into
quarters and use them to wrap the
ends of the support bars. (B)

3 Bend a full-length pipe-cleaner
into a triangle, making one side 3¼in
(82mm) in length. Loop the ends to
close the shape. Make another
triangle in this way. (C)

4 Connect the looped end of
each triangle onto either side of
the wheel support bar. Wrap a ¼in
(6mm) pipe-cleaner strip around the
bar and triangle point to connect
the wheel to the back of the frame.
Repeat the same on the other side of
the frame. Wrap another pipe-cleaner
to secure the shape. (D)

5 Bend a pipe-cleaner 4¼in
(108mm) from one end. Make
another bend 1in (25mm) from the
first bend. Make a third bend 3in
(76mm) from the second bend. Bend
a second pipe-cleaner in this way.
Loop the ends of both pieces by ¼in
(6mm) and connect together. (E)

6 Fold a pipe-cleaner in half. Fold
the ends by ¼in (6mm) and loop
together. Bend the pipe-cleaner at a
right angle 1in (25mm) from the fold
to make a saddle post. Bend the front
loop at the same angle for the
handle bar post. (F) Align the saddle
bar on top of the middle frame. Push
the saddle post back ¼in (6mm). Tie
the middle frame onto the back
wheel frame and bind with grey yarn.
(G) Bind the middle bar and saddle
post with a wrapped pipe-cleaner.

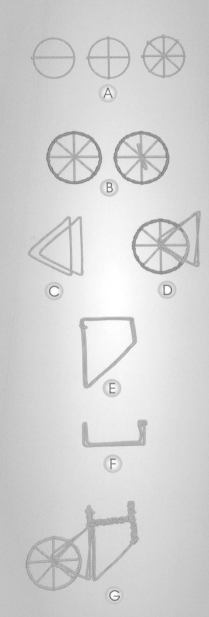

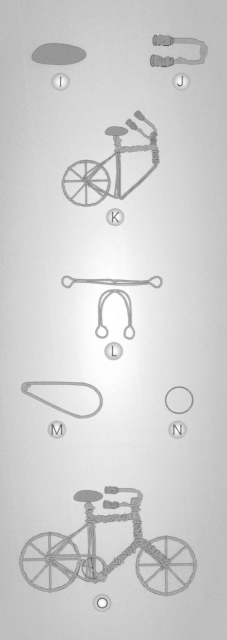

7 Make a turquoise pompom by wrapping the yarn around the small cardboard platform 40 times. Trim into a rounded shape and flatten the top and bottom. Trim the front into a soft point. (I) Sew to the top of the saddle post with turquoise yarn.

8 Twist two pipe-cleaners together. Make a ¾in (19mm) fold at each end and wrap the handle bars with three layers of grey yarn. Wrap the ends with a ¾in (19mm) strip of turquoise yarn. Curve the bars ¾in (19mm) from the handles. (J)

9 Loop the end of the seat crossbar around the middle of the handle bars. Wrap a pipe-cleaner around the connection and down the front post of the bicycle. (K)

10 Fold a pipe-cleaner in half and make ¼in (6mm) loops at the ends. (L) Curve the bar around a pencil. Thread the ends through the wheel frame and bend down each side of the bicycle to make front wheel supports. Place the loops on the wheel support bar.

11 Wrap and bind the end of the wheel support bar with a ¼in (6mm) piece of pipe-cleaner. Wrap the wheel supports with a pipe-cleaner and around the lower frame.

12 Cut 2in (50mm) from a pipe-cleaner and loop into a circle. Bend the loop to form a point. (M) Place onto the back wheel support bar over the triangle bar, looping the ends to secure. Wrap 1in (25mm) of pipe-cleaner around the ends to secure the chain on support bar.

13 Curve a 6in (152mm) piece of pipe-cleaner into a circle and loop the ends together. (N) Place a ¼in (6mm) length of pipe-cleaner across the middle of the circle, looping the ends to secure. Position on the rounded end of the bicycle chain. Sew the circles together with white sewing thread. Insert 3in (76mm) of pipe-cleaner through the chain circle and wrap around the cross bar and the bicycle frame to secure. Wrap the ends of the pedals with ¼in (6mm) of pipe cleaner. (O)

Sharing bicycles in any universe is a grand gesture. Now all we need to do is convince Phlump about this.

The cave is an easy and cosy project to make.
It also doubles as an alien party hat.

Cave

What you need:

Materials

* 4oz (100g) ball of brown chunky fashion yarn
* ⅜in (10mm) orange ready-made pompoms x 2
* ⅜in (10mm) red ready-made pompoms x 2
* 12in (304mm) yellow pipe-cleaners x 8
* 12in (304mm) brown pipe-cleaners x 2
* 12in (304mm) green pipe-cleaners x 2
* 1⅜in (35mm) square green felt x 4
* 1⅜in (35mm) square orange felt x 2
* 1⅜in (35mm) square magenta felt x 2
* Red, green and orange sewing thread

Tools

* Craft scissors
* Craft/sewing needle
* Nail clippers

Cave frame

★ Curve six of the yellow pipe-cleaners. Fold the ends together to make six circles. Place one of the circles onto a flat surface, then set the remaining circles around it to make a flower shape. (A)–(B) Cut two brown pipe-cleaners into quarters. Use these pieces to connect the circles into a dome shape. (C)–(D)

★ Cut a yellow pipe-cleaner in half. Loop the ends of one half and lay it across the middle ring to make a bar at the top of the dome. (E)

★ Connect the second half of the pipe-cleaner with a full-length pipe-cleaner and loop together to make a long strip. Wrap the strip around the dome and attach to the circles. Leave one entire circle open for the front entrance of the cave. (F)

★ Weave thick chunky yarn across the bars and cover all the sections, wrapping the yarn with your fingers. The chunky yarn will cover big sections of the cave and can be overlapped in places to make natural contours. Fill all empty spaces with chunky yarn, covering the yellow pipe-cleaners. Add patches of yarn to spot areas to enhance the shape of the cave as desired. (G)

The cave is always a perfect temperature.

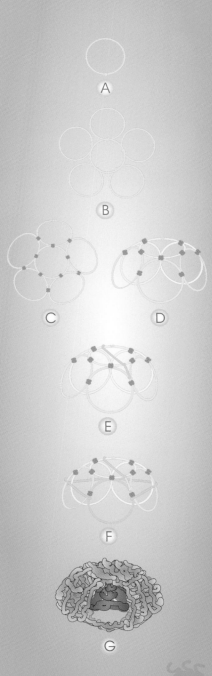

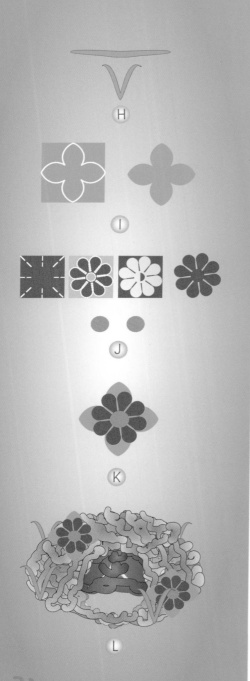

Leaves and flowers

⭐ Cut two green pipe cleaners in half. Clip the ends of both pieces into a point with the craft scissors. Curve the pointed tips and fold each section in the middle. Place around the edge of the cave to decorate. Ⓗ

⭐ Cut four leaves from each green square of felt using template. Ⓘ

⭐ Using template Ⓙ cut two pink flower shapes and two orange flowers.

⭐ Sew the flowers and leaves together using matching thread. Ⓚ Trim the pompoms to make one flat side and sew the flat bit to the middle of each flower. Place around the entrance of the cave and attach with sewing thread. Ⓛ

The stringy swamp hut is a cool resting spot on hot solar system days.

Swamp Hut

What you need:

Materials

✳ 2oz (50g) ball of stringy green fashion yarn

✳ 12in (304mm) pipe-cleaners (green or grey) x 23

Tools

✳ Craft scissors

✳ Craft/sewing needle

1　Start by curving two pipe-cleaners and loop the ends of both curves to make a large circle. Cut a pipe-cleaner in half, place the bars on either side of the large circle and loop onto the edge. (A)–(B)

2　Curve two pipe-cleaners and connect between the straight cross bars, making an eye shape in the middle of the circle. (C) Curve two more pipe-cleaners and set the second pair next to the first pair, weaving them through the first pair to reinforce the shape. (D)

3　Curve a pipe-cleaner, then gently bend it in half. Bend another one in this way. Weave them through the centre of the design to secure the semi-circles. Attach the ends onto the outside edge of the base. (E)

4　Reinforce the base by weaving two curved pipe-cleaners through the bars around the edge. Attach the ends onto the large outer ring. (F)

5　To make the roof, curve three pipe-cleaners. Make a door frame by placing one of the curves onto the ring, spacing the ends 1in (25mm) from the design in the centre. Loop both ends onto the edge of the large circle. Connect another curved pipe-cleaner onto the top of the door frame, looping the ends to secure. (G)

6　Place the third curve on the opposite side to the door frame and loop through the second top curve. Place the ends 1in (25mm) from the design in the centre and loop onto the edge of the outside ring. (H)

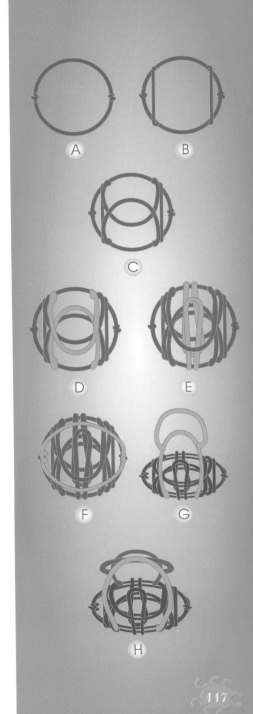

117

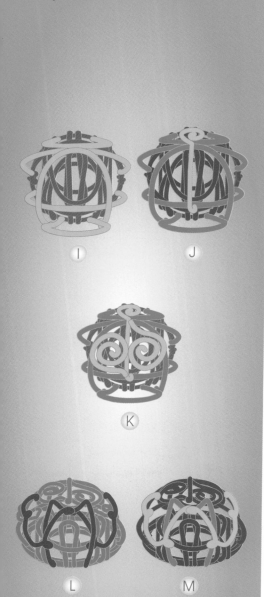

I

J

K

L

M

7. To make the sides of the swamp hut, curve two pipe-cleaners. Place both curves under the roof frame and attach to the outside ring by looping the ends onto the edge. I

8. Wrap three full-length pipe-cleaners with stringy fashion yarn and shape them into curves. Connect one wrapped pipe-cleaner across the top centre of the roof and wrap around the back curve. Take the remaining section of the pipe-cleaner and shape into a flat swirl to fill the area at the back arched panel. J

9. Make flat swirls with the other two wrapped pipe-cleaners. Place the swirls on top of the roof. Connect to the frame and blend the shapes into the roof with stringy yarn. K

10. Wrap and completely cover four pipe-cleaners with stringy fashion yarn. Weave them in a criss-cross pattern across the back and sides of the hut, wrapping diagonally through the bars. L–M

This tree is a nice place to hang out, and an ideal home for creatures from any world.

Bonsai Tree House

What you need:

Materials

* 9in (228mm) brown or black pipe-cleaners x 130
* 4oz (100g) ball of brown yarn x 3
* 4oz (100g) ball of brown chunky yarn x 2
* 12in (304mm) square orange felt
* 12in (304mm) square brown felt

Tools

* Craft scissors
* Craft needle
* Bodkin

Platforms

⭐ For the base of the tree, curve two pipe-cleaners and overlap the ends by ½in (13mm). Loop the ends to make a circle. Ⓐ Cut another pipe-cleaner in half and curve into a small circle. Overlap the ends by ¼in (6mm) and connect together. Position in the centre of the larger circle on a flat surface.

⭐ Cut two pipe-cleaners into quarters. Build a grid by connecting the quarters to the inner and outer rings. Ⓑ Wrap the rim of the large circle with more pipe-cleaners to reinforce its edge. Ⓒ Make another platform in the same way.

⭐ For the top platform, curve three pipe-cleaners and overlap the ends by 1in (25mm) to make a circle. Make another circle with two pipe-cleaners and a centre circle with one pipe-cleaner. Ⓓ Cut four pipe-cleaners in half and loop the ends onto the outside ring. Space evenly and secure the ends onto the central ring. Ⓔ Cut two pipe-cleaners in quarters and connect the outer rings in the same way. Ⓕ Reinforce the outer ring with pipe-cleaners. Ⓖ

Trunk and Branches

⭐ Connect 13 pipe-cleaners to the outside ring of the base platform. Leave an opening at the front of the tree. Loop the vertical bars onto the outside ring of the middle platform. Ⓗ–Ⓘ

⭐ Weave pipe-cleaners between all the vertical bars, spacing them 1in (25mm) apart. Connect a curved pipe-cleaner through the sides of the door frame for the entrance. Ⓙ

⭐ Use 13 pipe-cleaners to connect the top platform to the middle platform, looping the ends onto the outer rings. Weave pipe-cleaners through the vertical bars 1in (25mm) apart and make an arched entrance as before. Ⓚ

⭐ Bend three pipe-cleaners into lumpy shapes. Twist them into one piece. Wrap a pipe-cleaner around the sharp ends, then loop it between the bars. Weave three or more pipe-cleaners in this way. Make eight branches in various lengths and thicknesses. Wrap each one with three layers of brown yarn. Ⓛ

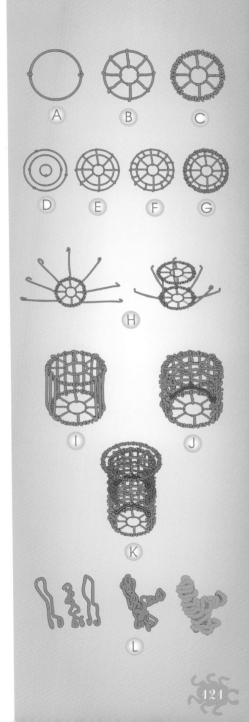

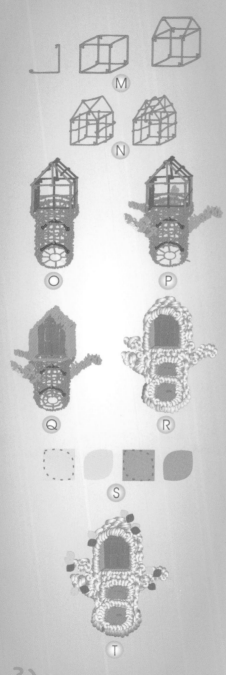

8 To make the roof hut, bend eight pipe-cleaners in half. Use six to make a four-sided box. Loop the connections securely. Add the other two pipe-cleaners to make a triangle at each end of the box. Attach half a pipe-cleaner across the roof to connect the triangles. (M)

9 Cut seven pipe-cleaners in half. Connect one to three sides of the box, then two to each half of the roof to make a grid. (N)

10 Attach the roof to the centre of the top platform. Secure in place by weaving across both structures with brown yarn. (O)

11 Attach branches to the trunk, weaving pipe-cleaners through the grid and branches like a needle and thread. Secure the connections with brown yarn. (P)

12 Apply layers of brown yarn to the roof, weaving it through the grid and wrapping over the bars. Weave yarn over three sides of the hut, leaving the front panel open. (Q)

13 Cover the sides and the platform with one layer of brown yarn. The shape of the tree trunk will shift as layers of thread cover spaces and pull at the grid bars.

14 Cover the entire tree with two layers of brown yarn. Wrap a layer of the thick chunky yarn on top to build up a lumpy bark texture. Don't coat the inside with chunky yarn. The tree will stiffen as the layers build up. (R)

15 The tree base may need extending as the layers of yarn affect the balance. Add a grid extension by looping a curved pipe-cleaner onto the front of the base platform. Apply grid bars to reinforce the shapes. Weave brown yarn to blend the surfaces. Wrap all the entrances and edges with chunky yarn.

16 Cut 60 leaves from the brown and orange felt using the template in (S). Sew the leaves in random clusters on the branches and the trunk using brown yarn. (T)

Gus, do you think we can all hold on to this tree in the comet trail?

123

Creating your Creepy World

You really don't need much in space.

What You Need

Yarn

Natural, synthetic, blended and fashion thread 4-ply yarns have been used in this book.

Yarn wrapped onto fingers or cards can be made into pompoms that can be elaborated with spots and bands. Yarn-wrapped pipe-cleaners create solid structures that can be formed into any shape. It can also be sewn through pompoms and around pipe-cleaners to bind and reinforce structures.

A Pipe-cleaners

Pipe-cleaners come in various sizes, colours and textures and are made with a wire core that is upholstered with twisted fibres made from cotton or synthetic chenille fibres. Pipe-cleaners are widely available and either come as single stems or in multiple packs of 25.

Pipe-cleaners are ideal for manipulating into frames, grids and shapes by bending, coiling, curving, zigzagging, looping and twisting.

They are available in vivid colours and textures including chunky, bumpy, fluorescent, metallic, flecked, striped, glittery and plain.

Chenille-covered pipe-cleaners (chenille stems) generally come in 12in (304mm) lengths. Normal pipe-cleaners are generally available in 9in (228mm) lengths. The projects can combine both, but I prefer chenille stems because the fibres are easier to trim and carve.

Hint: When making eyes and components, keep measurements and shapes consistent for each set.

Cardboard platforms for wrapping pompoms

The pompoms in this book are made by wrapping yarn around cardboard platforms (for how to do it, **see page 142**). The projects use the small or medium-sized cards.

How to make cardboard platforms

To make a small cardboard platform, cut three strips of corrugated card (recycle an old box) measuring 3 x 1¼in (76 x 31mm). Stack all three pieces together and tape them into a block shape. Cover with sticky tape to secure together. The surface should be slippery so that the yarn slips off the card. For a medium-sized platform cut a cardboard strip measuring 10 x 2in (254 x 50mm) and fold it twice equidistantly (fold it in half, and half again) to make one

card. Tape the folds together and cover the entire platform with tape to make it slippery. (B) ★

Hands and fingers

The yarn is wrapped onto the card platform to make a pompom. (B) 2 But you can also make pompoms by wrapping yarn around your fingers.

Ready-made pompoms

As well as making wrapped pompoms, (C) you will also need commercially manufactured pompoms. These pompoms are sold by their diameter in multi-packs, and come in a range of sizes and intense colours, including metallic, sparkly and plain. Most of the projects using these pompoms

will require a range of ⅛in (3mm), ³⁄₁₆in (5mm), ⅜in (10mm) and ⅝in (15mm) for making pupils, eyeballs and noses, heads and body shapes. Buy a few more than you need so you don't have to hunt around for items later, that you may not be able to match precisely. (D)

The centres of commercially manufactured pompoms are usually bound with tiny metal rings or strong thread. They can be trimmed and carved, but be careful not to break the centre string when clipping and shaping with scissors. The pompoms have fine synthetic fibres, and can be sewn with sewing thread but cannot easily be sewn into with yarn.

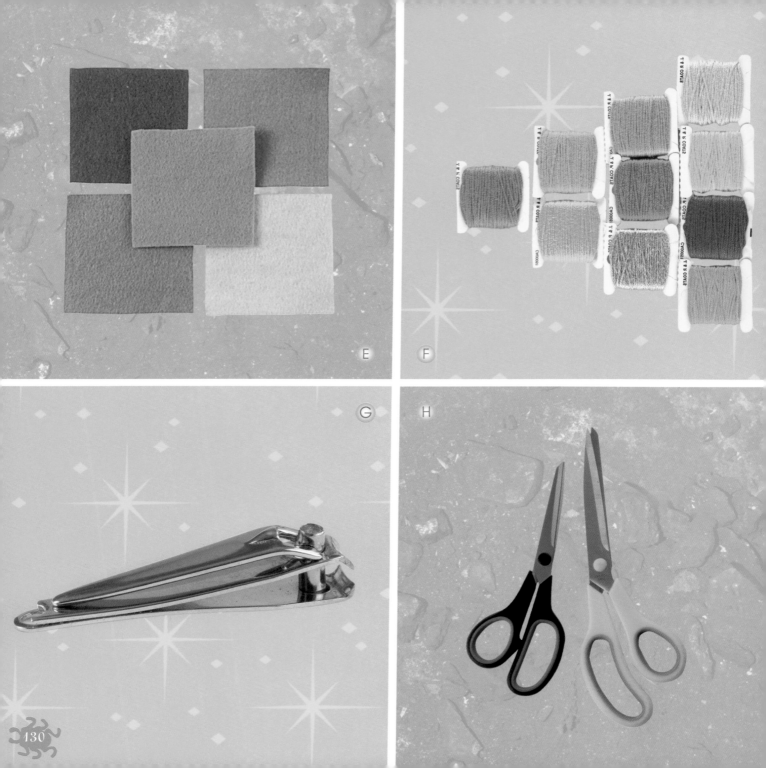

E

F

G

H

130

Hint: Always purchase pipe-cleaners that are perfectly straight.

A pipe-cleaner wire has a memory, so a bend will be awkward to straighten out later.

Ⓔ Felt

Felt is a luxurious material and is ideal for craftwork. The material does not require hemming because the edges do not fray. The fabric cuts precisely and easily using sharp scissors. Embroidery and sewing thread pass through felt with ease. Hand-made felt is the best quality and comes in subtle, natural and vibrant colours. Buy a little more material than you think you need, which will give you room for making errors and expanding your projects if you need to.

Ⓕ Embroidery thread

Embroidery thread is a multi-strand thread made mostly from cotton, available in many colours, including glittery and metallic shades. It can be used for embroidering details and bobbles and also works well as a sewing thread. Buy it in colourful multi-packs, when a range of yarn colours is needed for a project. Embroidery thread can be adapted to various thicknesses, and can also be separated to a single sewing thread strand, making it more economical than individual spools of sewing thread.

Ⓖ Clippers

Nail clippers are ideal for cutting pipe-cleaner wire. The leveraged wedge makes it easy to cut the wire exactly. Make sure you buy a set that you use specifically for pipe-cleaners only, making it easier to keep the material on the surface of the pipe-cleaner neat and clean. Big nail clippers are easiest to use.

Ⓗ Craft or sewing scissors

Sewing scissors are useful for cutting felt patterns, clipping yarn and sewing thread, carving designs into pompom shapes and contouring pipe-cleaner fibres. Scissors with pointed tips, sharp blades and flexible handles are better than rounded-tip scissors. Flexible handles work well when cutting small shapes, curves and angles. Separate these scissors and use only for cutting fibres and fabric.

Scissor sharpeners

Scissor sharpeners are used to sharpen scissor blades when they become blunt.

Scissor care

Designate scissors for a single purpose; do not use them for anything other than cutting thread and fabric. When using scissors to shape the pile on a pipe-cleaner, make sure to keep blades clear of the wire in the centre. This will preserve blade sharpness and precision fabric cutting. Use separate scissors for cutting cardboard and nail clippers for cutting pipe-cleaner wire.

Dum de de dum,
sequins and thread,
de de dum dum dum…

Sewing needles are used when sewing ⅛in (3mm) eyeball pompoms and felt. Commercially made pompoms have fine fibres and so a finer-gauge sewing needle is best.

K Sequins

Sequins are used to add texture and a reflective quality to the surface of the models. Use thread colour that matches the colour of the sequin.

Glue

Glue is not required and should not be used. It permanently damages the structure of fibres, which is why we use thread to bond, stick, attach and bind project components. Threads can be pulled out or severed so that material can be adapted, reshaped and recycled into new pieces.

I Needle threader

A needle threader is recommended for threading fashion yarn into needles to save time and patience. They are also helpful for younger children.

J Sewing thread

Sewing thread (and embroidery thread) is used for binding and connecting commercially made pompoms and felt patterns. To make stitches less noticeable, choose a colour that closely matches the fabric or yarn. The most useful thread to have for connecting lighter colours is white and for dark colours, brown, grey, blue or black. Embroidery thread can be used in place of sewing thread, but divide strips into single strands before threading the sewing needle.

Sewing needles

Select yarn or darning needles in various lengths and eye widths, equivalent to assorted yarn gauges.

L Bodkins

Bodkins are useful for threading thicker-gauged yarn, ribbons and elastic. They usually come in different forms – either round or flat.

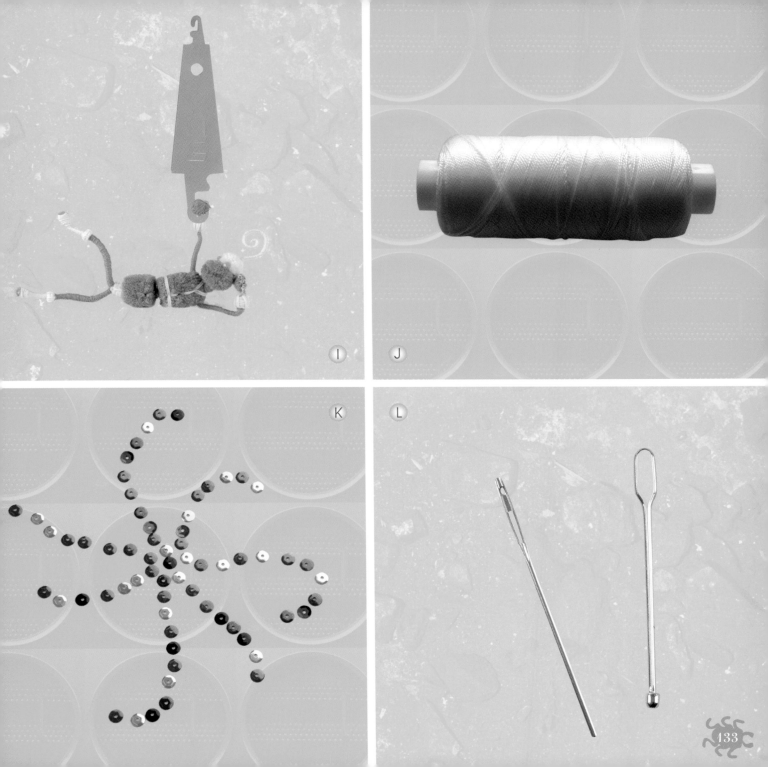

I

J

K

L

433

Flexibility is the key.

Working with Pipe-cleaners

Pipe-cleaners are wonderful to work with. They have a colourful fabric crust which can be trimmed with scissors to create features such as wrists and ankles. Because they are so bendy they can be manipulated into any imaginable shape, and they can also be wrapped with yarn.

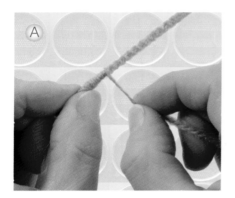

Wrapping pipe-cleaners

Pipe-cleaners are wrapped with yarn to strengthen them, to blend colours and create details, shapes and muscle bands and for weaving appendages together. Wrap a pipe-cleaner by knotting yarn at the end of a strip. Wrap yarn over the knot to blend and secure thread onto the pipe-cleaner. Apply thread evenly along the pipe-cleaner, trying not to overlap the strands. Make a wrapped pipe-cleaner even thicker by wrapping more layers of thread. Make sure that coverage starts at one end and finishes at the other so that the thread covers the entire shape evenly. Follow with another layer to build up again. (A)

Zigzags

Folding pipe-cleaners abruptly in evenly measured intervals will produce a zigzag pattern.

Coiling pipe-cleaners

Take a length of pipe-cleaner and hold one end against a tube, pencil or pen with your thumb. Use the other hand to roll the pipe-cleaner around the tube. Pull the pipe-cleaner taut against the tube and wrap closely to form a tight springy coil. Slip the coil off the end of the tube. Adjust the coil by pulling the spring apart. (B)–(F)

Looping pipe-cleaners

Pipe-cleaners can be looped to make long bars, grids and crosses. To loop pipe-cleaners, bend ¼in (6mm) of the end at a right angle. Push the angle towards the bar of the pipe-cleaner to protect hands. Repeat the same process on another pipe-cleaner. Link the angled tips together and press the tips to close the connection between the pipe-cleaners. (G)–(I)

Curving

Use your finger and thumb to pinch the end of a pipe-cleaner. Keeping a grasp on the pipe-cleaner with finger and thumb together, pull against the entire length with an arching tension. This will give the pipe-cleaner a curved shape and is instrumental for making circles, arches and oval shapes. (J)

Carving pipe-cleaners

Embroidery or sharp craft scissors can be used to carve sections of pile from pipe-cleaners. Chenille-covered pipe-cleaners are more suitable for this, as those covered in cotton are slightly resistant to the process.

Take a pipe-cleaner and shape it as desired. Fine-tune the details by clipping away pile from the surface of the pipe-cleaner. Work in stages and apply the same process to duplicate pieces, for example shape ankles, wrists or elbows at the same time so that they match. Antennae, legs and arms involve the clipping process.

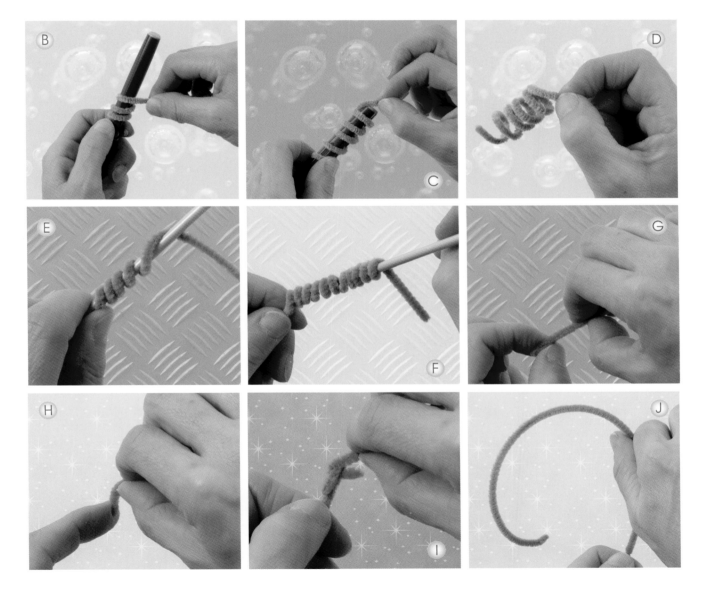

Invisible seams

When wrapping pipe-cleaners, colour bands can be added by changing yarn along the way. To keep colour seams invisible, overlap a small length of differently coloured thread, then continue wrapping as before. (A)

Adding muscular contours and lumps

Wrap a pipe-cleaner with an even layer of yarn. Build specific areas by overlapping additional layers of thread to specific areas. Embroidery stitches will build little lumps for thumbs, elbows, knees and toes. Apply a stitch to the surface of the fabric and layer another on top of this to build up the mass. Repeat the process to make the lump the desired size and shape. (B)-(E)

Adding bobbles

Wrap an object with layers of yarn. Thread a yarn needle and pass into the layered surface. Pull the needle up through a small section of the material. Leave a small loop of yarn on the surface to make a bobble. Reinsert the needle, follow the same process, and cover the desired area

with small loops. Keep the length of material consistent to keep the bobbles even. (F)

Weaving pipe-cleaners

Pipe-cleaners can be woven into grids. These in turn can be woven with thread to make up structures and panels.

Hint: The metal tips at the ends of pipe-cleaners are sharp. It is best to fold them over (using fingers or pliers) or wrap them with yarn.

Weaving a panel

To weave across a pipe-cleaner grid, thread the yarn through an appropriately sized needle, and tie the ends of the thread around one of the pipe-cleaner bars. Weave across the grid, passing the thread over and under the bars alternately. (G)-(I)

Double weaving skins

Once a grid is covered with a layer of yarn, another layer can be woven over the top of the first layer. This works especially well with chunky knit yarns. A chunky texture fills in cavities and thickens the walls, adding weight and substance to the model. The first skin acts to bind the grid and component pieces into one solid model. The second layer creates a skin on the surface and a different texture or colour to the inside; it also reinforces the structure.

Making Pompoms

Making pompoms with discs

Although discs are readily available I do not recommend them, which is why they are not mentioned in **'What You Need'.** Pompom discs limit you to making pompoms in the sizes of the discs available, and although the projects can be made with the commercially available small and medium plastic discs, they have actually been created with the finger- or card-wrapping technique. If you prefer to use them, though, instructions are given here.

 Thread a large-eyed darning needle with a long length of yarn. Take two discs and, holding them together, wrap the yarn around both of them through the hole in the discs. Wrap until you have covered the entire circumference of the discs – the thicker the layer of yarn the more dense the pompom.

Cut around the circumference between the two discs and, with the discs still in place, insert a length of yarn between them. Secure with a firm knot. Remove the discs and trim the pompom as required.

Making pompoms with fingers or cardboard platforms

Making pompoms by wrapping yarn around your fingers or a cardboard platform is more versatile and faster than disc wrapping. It is possible to blend yarns together such as fashion yarn with plain or textured yarn, and make pompoms in lots of different sizes.

⭐ Secure a length of yarn against your first finger and wrap the yarn around your first and middle fingers Ⓐ or alternatively around your cardboard platform. Ⓑ Continue wrapping, counting each full revolution as you do so. Ⓒ

⭐ Cut the yarn and remove it by gently pushing the thread off the cardboard or down to the end of your fingers and onto a surface.

⭐ Take a piece of thread, approximately 12in (304mm) and double it over then place it under the mass of thread, being careful not to separate the loops. Ⓓ Tie the doubled-over thread tightly around the mass of loops, then tie it again on the opposite side. Ⓔ

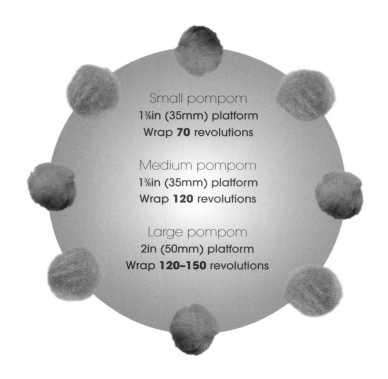

Small pompom
1⅜in (35mm) platform
Wrap **70** revolutions

Medium pompom
1⅜in (35mm) platform
Wrap **120** revolutions

Large pompom
2in (50mm) platform
Wrap **120–150** revolutions

⭐ Cut through the loops on either side of the tied thread, Ⓕ then separate the strands and trim the pompom to shape. Ⓖ–Ⓗ

Size of pompom

The number of times you wrap your yarn determines the density, and the width of the platform or size of your fingers determines the final size. The projects mostly incorporate two sizes of pompom: small and medium.

There are slight variations in wrapping formulas to create subtle differences in body shapes and parts. Note that 2-ply yarn may require more wraps than 4-ply. Doubling up on yarn will reduce the number of revolutions. For example, a medium pompom takes 70 revolutions, but by using two strings of yarn, only 35 revolutions are necessary.

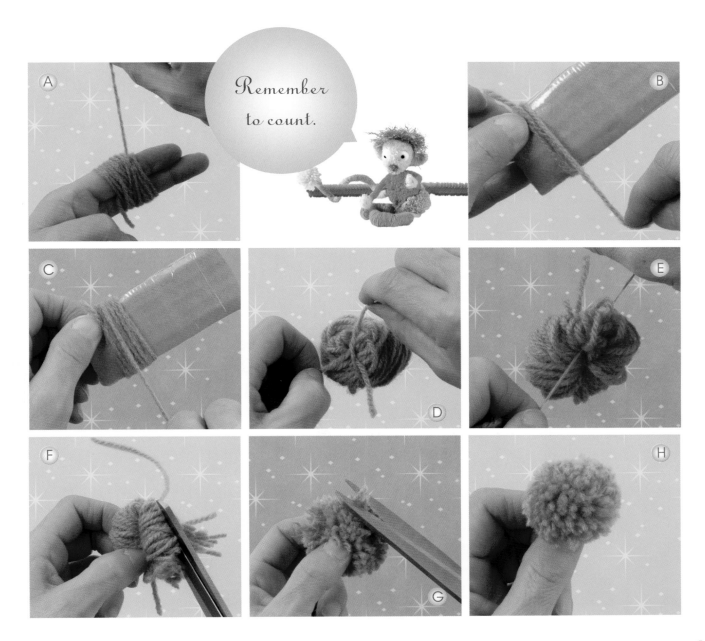

Remember to count.

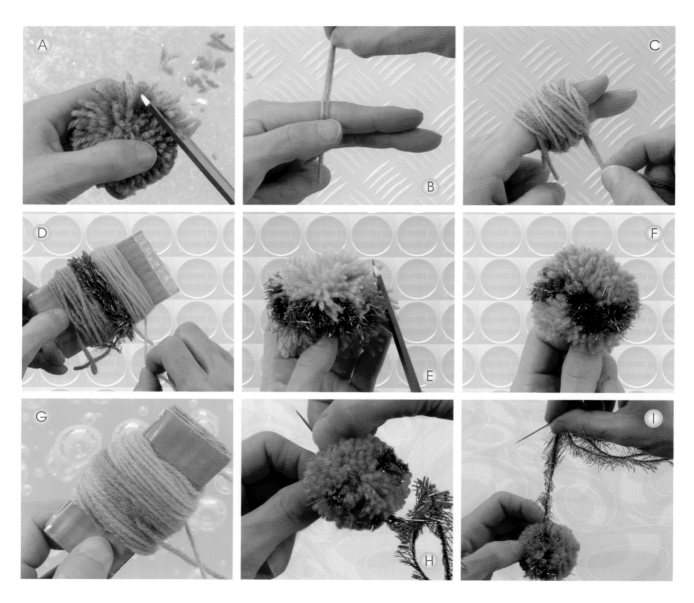

Shaping pompoms

For some projects, shaping and rounding out pompoms is not necessary. Ragged threads and soft strands can enhance the overall appearance of characters like Squidge and Phlump. For most projects though, the wrapped pompoms will need shaping once the strands have been tied together into a round shape. Ⓐ

Usually a hand or card-wrapped pompom is slightly oval in shape. To make a pompom into a round ball, turn the pompom and find the longest threads. Turn again to find the other ends of the threads, which are usually on the opposite side. Cut away the longest bits to match with shorter threads and follow the curve of the pompom. Repeat on the opposite side.

Variegated pompoms

Take two balls of yarn in different colours. Place both strings together then begin to wrap over fingers or platform with an even tension. Ⓑ Try not to cross yarn colours over. Apply the yarn evenly from side to side, covering about 1in (25mm) in width. Ⓒ

Two-colour pompoms

Colours wrapped together in blocks create pompoms with distinct colour bands. For two-colour pompoms, divide in half the number of times you will wrap the finished pompom. If the total pompom size is 60 revolutions, apply 30 revolutions of the first colour, then place the remaining 30 revolutions of the second colour next to the first band. Wrap the yarn tightly, keeping the colour bands separate. Overlapping

thread will create blotches of colour in adjacent colour bands on the finished pompom. Ⓓ–Ⓕ

Spot-colour pompoms

⭐ To make a pattern of spots, wrap the cardboard platform or fingers with a 1in (25mm) band of 30–50 layers of yarn. Then apply another yarn colour, wrapping in the centre of the first layer. For small spots wrap 10–15 revolutions of yarn.

⭐ Keep the threads together in the middle, in a section about ½in (13mm). Ⓖ Now wrap the other thread over the small band and completely cover it. Wrap about 30 to 50 revolutions of the first layer colour to cover the 'spotty' section. Repeat the process to build up multiple spots.

Building up areas

Building up specific areas of the pompom follows the same process as the spot-colour pompom technique. Apply additional thread to patchy areas by weaving a needle through the bare area, then cut the added thread down so it is level with the pompom. Ⓗ–Ⓘ

Limbs are very important.

Appendages

Jointed pod arms and legs

⭐ 1 Take a full-length pipe-cleaner and fold in half, shaping the centre around a tube, finger or thick pencil. Twist the bars to make a ring shape. Ⓐ–Ⓑ

⭐ 2 Twist the parallel bars together to make a joint in the middle. Fold the ends of the pipe-cleaners over and make a loop at the top to close the shape of the arm. Ⓒ

⭐ 3 Wrap the pod ring with yarn, then cover the middle section with an even layer of material. Pull the thread taut around the twisted wrist/ankle joint above the pod ring to strengthen the join. Continue to wrap around the bars, covering both sides with yarn. Ⓓ–Ⓔ

⭐ 4 Wrap the entire shape with a layer of yarn. Wrap additional layers to any muscle areas to make muscle contours. Wrap yarn over the lumps to blend with the contours of the appendage. Ⓕ

Hint: Apply yarn with double strands of thread and make sure the strands do not overlap each other.

Stick pods

⭐ Fold a full-length pipe-cleaner in half, shaping the centre around a tube, finger or thick pencil. Twist the bars to form a ring shape. Bend the ends of the bars over and loop them together. Ⓐ–Ⓑ

⭐ Wrap yarn through the middle of the ring and cover the surface with thread. Then add a layer of yarn to completely cover the ring.

⭐ Continue to cover the stick pod, wrapping both parallel bars with even layers of thread. Ⓒ

Double pods

⭐ Using a full-length pipe-cleaner, wrap one end around a tube, finger or thick pencil and twist it back on itself to form a ring shape. Make a ring at the other end in the same way. Ⓐ

⭐ Wrap yarn through the middle of the ring and cover the surface with thread. Then wrap over the entire ring with a layer of yarn. Increase the pod mass with another even layer of yarn. Apply more thread to the centre of the pod to create a hand dome shape. Ⓑ–Ⓒ

⭐ Wrap the length of the pod with a layer of yarn. For foot pods build only the topside of the feet to make the instep of the foot. Ⓓ

⭐ To make thumb buds, wrap the pod following the procedure above and then weave a mound of stitches to the thumb area of each pod. Ⓔ

Wrapping stick arms and legs

⭐ To wrap legs, pinch the parallel bars and wrap yarn around both bars. Pull the yarn taut to bind the bars together and build a tube. Apply three or four layers of materials to the area to form a sturdy tube. Follow the same procedure for a leg with a single bar and foot loop.

⭐ For the arms, wrap yarn across both parallel bars. Pull the yarn taut to bind the bars together and build a tube. Form a sturdy tube by applying two or three layers of materials to the whole area. Follow the same procedure for an arm with a single bar and hand loop.

148

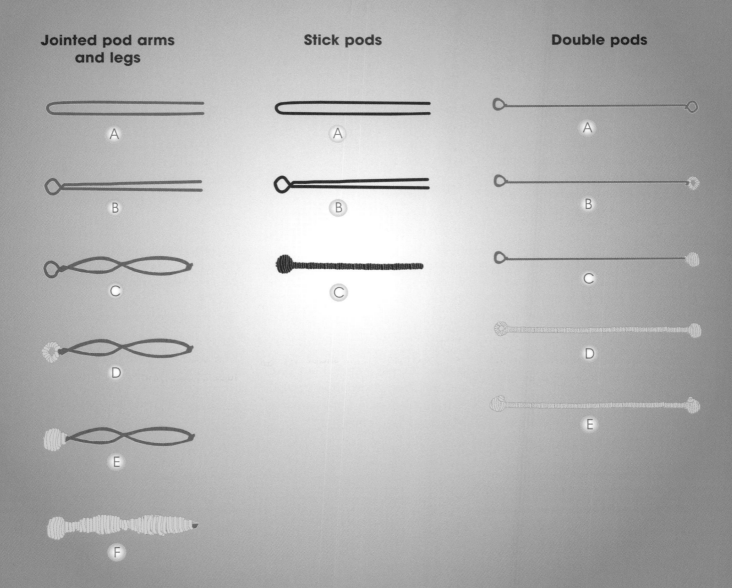

Jointed pod arms and legs

A

B

C

D

E

F

Stick pods

A

B

C

Double pods

A

B

C

D

E

149

Three toe appendage

⭐ Fold a pipe-cleaner in half around a pencil to make a rounded loop, then twist the bars over to make a circle. Ⓐ

⭐ Place the pencil above the circle and twist the left bar around the pencil to make another circle. Twist the right bar around the pencil to make a circle on the other side. Ⓑ-Ⓒ

⭐ Curve the remaining sections of pipe-cleaner. Make a tiny fold at the end of the bars and loop together to connect both sides. Use this piece to make the legs of the Coily Haired Creature. Ⓓ

⭐ Twist the bars in the middle of the curve to make another loop. Use this piece to make Snork the Dragon's legs. Ⓔ

⭐ To wrap the feet and toes, thread yarn through the middle and around all the rings. Wrap a layer of yarn over the toes and legs. Add more layers to build up the knees. Ⓕ-Ⓗ

Three claw appendage

⭐ Bend a pipe-cleaner in half to form a V shape. Make another bend ½in (13mm) from the first bend and curve the section between the bends around your finger to make a curve. Do the same on the other side to make a third claw. Ⓐ-Ⓒ

⭐ Twist the parallel bars together just above the claws. Curve the bars and twist them together in the middle to make a ring above the hand. Fasten the tips of the pipe-cleaner together. Use this shape for Bobbly Nobbly. Ⓓ-Ⓕ

⭐ Wrap around the claw bars with a layer of yarn. Leave the pointed tips of the claws bare. Wrap the hand above the claws. Continue to wrap the outside of the rings to fill all spaces with yarn. Ⓖ

Finger loops

⭐ Fold a pipe-cleaner in half around a pencil. Squeeze the bars on either side to make an open finger loop. Ⓐ

⭐ Make a second loop above the first loop in the same way. Then make a third loop on the other side to complete the hand. Ⓑ-Ⓒ

⭐ Make a tiny fold at the ends of the bars. Loop together to connect. Make a twist in the middle of the shape to make an elbow. Ⓓ-Ⓔ

⭐ To wrap the finger loops, thread yarn through the centre of the hand shape and wrap the bars with two layers of thread. Stitch across the finger loops and fill the spaces between the hand region.

⭐ Wrap a layer of thread around the outside bars. Wrap the lower arm. Wrap around the upper arm with a layer of thread. Build up the muscles with additional layers of thread. Use this claw for Squidge. Ⓕ

Three toe appendage

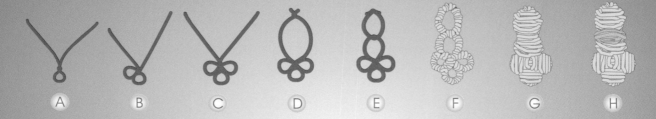

A   B   C   D   E   F   G   H

Three claw appendage

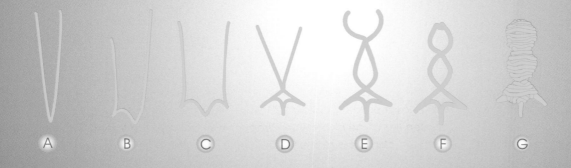

A   B   C   D   E   F   G

Finger loops

A   B   C   D   E   F

Templates

All templates need to be photocopied at 150% unless otherwise stated.

Tag the Bat: wings

Tag the Bat: ear

Flippy Floppy mouth
Photocopy at 100%

Owl wings

Snork the Dragon

wings

tongue

ear

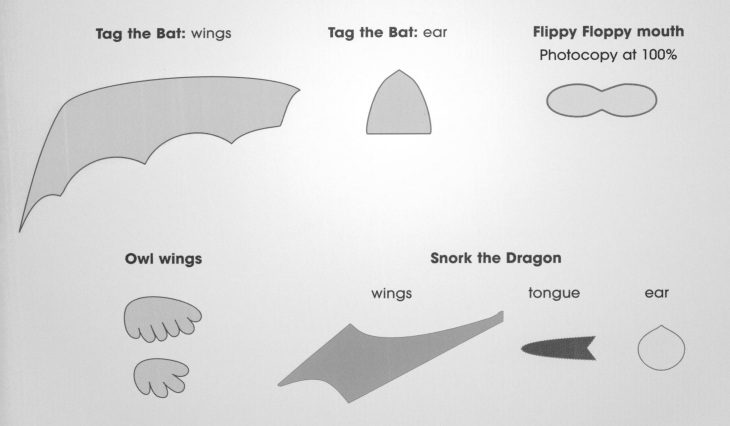

152

Leaf Sleeping Bag

Pod shoes

Top Hat

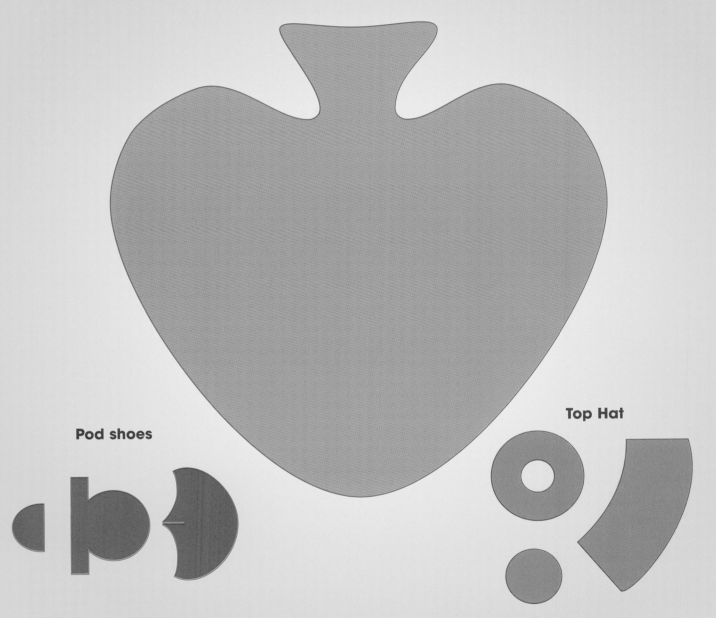

Suppliers

AUSTRALIA

Australian Craft Network
Pty Ltd
PO Box 350
Narellan
NSW 2567
Tel: +61 (02) 4648 5053
www.auscraftnet.com

CANADA

Lewiscraft
www.lewiscraft.ca

USA

CraftAmerica.com
498 Dreyfus Road Berea
KY 40403
Tel: +1 877 306 9178
www.craftamerica.com

UK

Calico Pie
305 Lancaster Road, Morecambe
Lancashire LA4 5TP
Tel/Fax: +44 (0) 845 1662678
www.calicopie.co.uk

English Yarns
19 East Street, Shoreham-by-Sea
West Sussex BN43 5ZE
Tel: +44 (0) 1273 461029
www.englishyarns.co.uk

Fred Aldous
37 Lever Street
Manchester M1 1LU
Tel: +44 (0) 8707 517301
www.fredaldous.co.uk

Hobbicraft
40 Woodhouse Lane
Merrion Centre
Leeds LS2 8LX
www.hobbicraft.co.uk

Hobbycraft
PO Box 5591
BH23 6YU
Tel: +44 (0) 800 272387
www.hobbycraft.co.uk

Peachey Ethknits
6–7 Edwards Walk, Maldon
Essex CM9 5PS
Tel: +44 (0) 1621 857102
www.ethknits.co.uk

Texere Yarns
College Mill, Barkerend Road
Bradford BD1 4AU
Tel: +44 (0) 1274 722191
www.texere.co.uk

154

Index

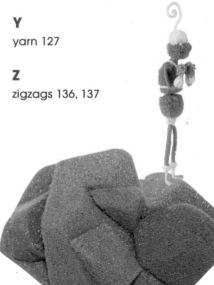